SYSTEMATIZE *your* REAL ESTATE ADMINISTRATIVE PROCESS

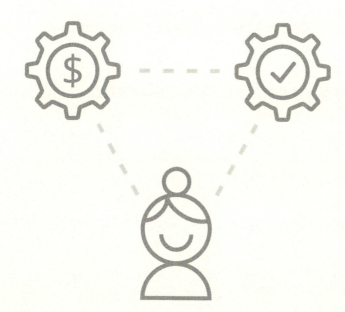

ADMIN: Systematize Your Real Estate Administrative Process

Authored by Brian Icenhower

© 2018 Copyright Icenhower Coaching & Consulting, LLC

ISBN: 9781723816055

TABLE OF CONTENTS

BRIAN ICENHOWER

Brian Icenhower is the CEO and Founder of Icenhower Coaching & Consulting (ICC), which provides customized and structured coaching and training programs for real estate agents and team leaders, and represents many of the top producing agents in North America. ICC also offers broker/owner consulting on agent recruiting, training, and retention. ICC now has over 120 coaching clients and a rapidly growing team of talented coaches. This progressive company is quickly advancing with online classes, podcasts, training materials, speaking events, video modules and real estate books.

Brian is also the creator of TheRealEstateTrainer.com, the world's leading production training website for real estate agents with a subscriber base of over 850,000.

Brian began his career in real estate as a top producing real estate broker in the early 1990s until launching and operating a number of production-focused real estate offices in California and the Midwestern United States. His implementation of extensive real estate productivity coaching, training and recruiting programs propelled these companies to be repeatedly recognized as some of the highest producing and fastest growing offices in North America by a number of major industry media sources.

Throughout his career, Brian has had the privilege of coaching, consulting and training many of the highest producing agents in the country. He has also opened various escrow companies, real estate licensing schools, and property management and commercial real estate divisions affiliated with these real estate brokerages.

Brian is also an attorney, a former instructor in real estate law at the College of the Sequoias, and a frequently published author. Brian served as the President of the Tulare County Association of REALTORS in 2011, and has served as a California Association of REALTORS State Director, a Missouri Association of REALTORS State Director, and a National Association of REALTORS Director.

Icenhower Coaching & Consulting (ICC)

Icenhower Coaching & Consulting (ICC) is a full-service coaching and consulting firm, primarily serving the real estate industry.

We offer coaching and consulting services that include online courses, podcasts, training materials, speaking events, training workshops, video modules, and of course client guidance by weekly calls and strategic planning.

COACHING & CONSULTING

ICC believes that people learn in various ways, including visually, audibly, verbally, physically, and logically with reasoning. As a result, whether it be visually, audibly, verbally, kinetically, or through engaging interaction, ICC's programs are designed to accelerate the learning processes while engaging clients more effectively. ICC's vast resource library is made up of training modules, videos, scripts, tools, job descriptions, budgets, business plans, workflows, systems and other interactive tools to help clients grow their business systematically.

In 2017 we have focused on developing training materials clients can print out and touch, videos they can watch, calls they can listen to, and workbooks that really break down processes. These materials dramatically enhance the coaching process because clients are left with more than a recap email at the end of every coaching call. They are actually able to keep materials in their file library or hand them to their team members as learning tools. They are also able to track their activities, communicate with their coaches and monitor their businesses at the touch of their fingers in between weekly coaching calls. This progressive and innovative approach to coaching has been received exceedingly well by the public. In 2017, ICC has added 8 new coaches to its staff and represents more than 125 individual coaching clients.

ICC coaches are experienced real estate business consultants that offer strategic planning and a full library of training resources to elevate agents' businesses and their careers. Coaching clients are continuously engaged with their coaches through ICC's Online Coaching Platform where agents can communicate with their coach, track their activities, attend training courses, monitor their businesses, and access the ICC training library.

ICC TRAINING MATERIALS

The creation of these video training modules and agent workbooks to supplement the coaching process provided an opportunity to launch online classes at a more affordable price point than one-on-one coaching. Through our training materials, ICC is able to deliver this valuable information to many more people across a user-friendly platform. In 2017, ICC launched several productivity-focused online courses centered around prospecting for new business, geographic farming and growing a sphere of influence referral database. Additionally, ICC developed several new courses devoted to real estate teams, such as hiring sales agents and administrative staff, training administrative staff members and onboarding newly hired sales agents. Finally, ICC produced a series of courses devoted to the recruiting, hiring, training and leading Inside Sales Agents (ISAs).

Brian Icenhower's real estate productivity coaching, training and recruiting programs have propelled a number of real estate companies to be repeatedly recognized as some of the highest producing and fastest growing offices in North America by a number of major industry media sources. ICC's production department now produces video training modules on a wide variety of productivity focused topics. These modules come complete with agent workbooks, instructor's manuals and audio files that can be white-label branded for any real estate company. Additionally, ICC's broker/manager coaches are available to consult with company leadership to ensure proper understanding and implementation of brokerage retention, training, and recruiting systems.

ICC SPEAKING & TRAINING

Brian Icenhower, along with a number of ICC's trainers and coaches, are available to speak and train on a variety of real estate and business topics by request. Event programs can feature any combination of real estate, educational, motivational, business or leadership focused training as well. Brian's interactive training style provides a high level of energy that keeps attendants engaged and receptive to learning throughout the entire event.

Brian has presented for many organizations across a wide number of industries. He has presented at real estate companies, trade conferences, realtor associations, financial institutions, non-profit and service groups, and for a variety of national corporations. Brian has also been a keynote speaker for numerous organizations. Event sessions can be conducted by the hour, half day, full day or over multiple days depending on the topic and audience. Audience sizes have ranged from a group of ten to a room of thousands.

PUBLISHING

ICC also started a publishing division to expand upon our custom training materials and deliver informative real estate training books to the masses in paperback, ebook, and audiobook versions. Our first book entitled FARM—The Ultimate Guide to Geographic Farming is currently available for purchase. ICC's publishing division is already in the final stages of releasing its next four books in the first half of 2018.

OUTREACH

For decades, Brian Icenhower has coached and trained many top performing agents, teams and industry leaders solely based upon word of mouth. In 2017 Brian's true passion for coaching and consulting became his business objective with a new focus on growth. This year, ICC has sponsored and produced The Real Estate Trainer Podcast as well as hundreds of helpful Youtube interviews for real estate agents on a variety of topics. In addition, 850,000 email subscribers rely on useful content and real estate information from the ICC sponsored training website: TheRealEstateTrainer.com. Finally, Brian Icenhower has appeared at more than 20 different speaking and training events across North America in 2017.

As a result of these marketing and outreach efforts, ICC has been able to hire several administrative staff members, a number of new coaches, and a full-time production and editing crew, while also launching a publishing division.

INTRODUCTION

ICENHOWER
COACHING & CONSULTING

WELCOME TO ADMIN

Welcome to Brian Icenhower's *ADMIN: Systematize Your Real Estate Administrative Process*. This book, along with the supplemental materials in the course, will teach you everything you need to know to succeed and excel as the administrator of your real estate company.

Now, chances are you have a different professional title at the company you work for and are not actually referred to as an "Administrator". Many of you, for example, have recently been hired as a Real Estate Administrative Assistant. Congratulations! You are now tasked with the enormous responsibility of being the backbone of your company's entire operation, no matter how big or small, but don't worry—we've got your back.

Congratulations! You are now tasked with the enormous responsibility of being the backbone of your company's entire operation, no matter how big or small, but don't worry—we've got your back.

Meanwhile, many of you are already the backbone of your company's entire operation. In fact, you—and you alone—*are* your entire operation: a solo agent prospecting for new leads, conducting listing appointments and buyer consultations, writing offers and negotiating contracts, while also handling the entire transaction from listing until closing, coordinating home-cleanings and repairs, not to mention your marketing and social media, and making your own coffee (which always seems to go cold before you've had a chance to drink it!).

At the very least you're juggling and, perhaps, you're even struggling. While you wish that you were in a position to hire an assistant to support you with the never-ending stream of administrative tasks, you're not quite ready for that next step but desperately need some help staying organized and efficient. Or, perhaps you're a solo agent who has finally reached their breaking-point and is ready to hire an assistant but isn't quite sure how to structure their position and train them on everything they will be doing for you. Don't worry—we've got your backs, too!

> *This book is for anyone who performs the administrative activities and tasks that are necessary to keep a real estate company operational and functioning in a smooth, systematized, and efficient manner.*

No matter your title, or your other roles and responsibilities, this book is for *anyone* who performs some or all of the administrative activities and tasks that are necessary to keep a real estate company operational and functioning in a smooth, systematized, and efficient manner.

 To keep things simple, throughout the book we will use generic terms such as 'administrator' or 'administrative role' when referring to the person responsible for administrative activities in general. Later in the book, as we explore the

four hats of the administrator role, we will use specific titles such as Administrative Manager, Listing Manager, Transaction Coordinator, and Marketing Director. At larger real estate companies, the administrative role might be heavily divided, and several individuals might perform specific portions of these roles. But it is equally likely that a single person is responsible for all these duties at your company, in which case each of these terms and titles is referring directly to you.

Occasionally, we will cover a topic that pertains specifically to assistant roles and addresses their unique responsibilities and needs. However, solo agents without any administrative support whatsoever will equally benefit from these tips and insights, so please make sure that you don't skip over anything or think it's irrelevant just because it has the word 'assistant' in it.

In fact, we think you should do quite the opposite and view the word 'assistant' as absolutely referring to you. When you think about it, solo agents are actually multiple different people and, as you work through each section of this book, there are times when it might be best if you can momentarily forget that you are an agent and begin to think of yourself as an assistant. That is: you yourself are your very own personal assistant. Let us explain.

Super Sales Heroes & Administrative Alter Egos

One time, we heard a busy agent refer to herself as a human *matryoshka* doll—those wooden figures that open up to reveal a smaller figure nesting inside it which, in turn, opens up to reveal another smaller figure, and so on. The poor agent was wearing so many different hats that she had begun to think of herself as being a dozen different people inside the same single body.

That's a pretty good analogy but, frankly, we like to think of you solo agents less as wooden dolls and more like superheroes with an alter ego! Think Superman and Clark Kent, or Wonder Woman who's an army nurse as well as a warrior princess. You've probably even had some Bruce Banner days where the stress of it all gets to you and you've gone a little bit Hulk on the world!

In short, solo agents are two distinct identities in the same body: the lead-generating salesperson that brings in the business, and the administrator that manages their CRM, prepares their own profit-and-loss statements, and sometimes remembers to put new paper in the photocopier!

The administrator is the superhero—swooping in, saving the day, and coming to your relieved and grateful rescue!

Now you might think that the superhero in you is the salesperson—and it is. That's definitely your primary identity and the thing that you do best to serve the world. To a salesperson, the administrative side of you is definitely your less-exciting alter ego but, in this book, *the administrator is the superhero—* swooping in, saving the day, and coming to your relieved and grateful rescue!

Of course it would be nice, in real life, if someone did swoop in and come to your rescue. But for solo agents, until you are in a position to hire an assistant, the only person who is coming to save you is yourself. You are your own personal assistant, and this book will give you all the tools and strategies you need to come to your own rescue on a daily basis.

This book will teach you how to use your divided-time wisely, handle distractions, develop routines, and establish workflows that will help you move deftly and efficiently between your super sales hero self and your administrative alter ego!

Like any assistant, your administrative alter ego exists for two reasons: (1) to make your life as an agent easier and less stressful, and (2) to create and maintain seamless systems that keep the business running so that the agent can focus exclusively on sales. Administrative assistants must ensure that agent activities are limited to, and held accountable to, listing property, showing property, negotiating contracts and lead-generation.

We completely understand that solo agents cannot focus *exclusively* on sales. To some extent, you will need to compartmentalize. In the moments when you need to sit down and focus on bookkeeping or social media, you're not an agent anymore—you are your administrative assistant alter ego.

However, as your own personal assistant, you are ultimately responsible for creating and maintaining quick and efficient systems that make your life easier, less stressful, and enable you to focus *predominantly* on your key activities. You literally cannot afford to spend half a day on bookkeeping or countless hours on social media.

When we say that you are your own personal assistant, we don't mean that you should spend hours and hours each day in that persona. In order to be the best agent you can be, you must also be the best personal assistant you can be, and the best assistants are extremely organized, highly efficient, and remain calm and composed in stressful situations.

As you read through this book, then, rather than being frustrated or overwhelmed by all the things you have to do by yourself, understand that by taking this course you are taking the time and care to assist, serve, and save yourself. For now, you are your own right hand man, and this book will teach you how to use your divided-time wisely, handle distractions, develop routines, and establish workflows that will help you move deftly and efficiently between your super sales hero self and your administrative alter ego!

Next Steps

Returning to those of you who are truly 'just' assistants for a moment, we hope that you have also been paying attention and not dismissing the unique challenges of solo agents as irrelevant to you. Rather, we hope you have a sense of how enormously difficult it is to manage an entire company by yourself and how much your agent is relying on you to turn chaos into order and whip things into shape.

On any real estate team, no other position is as integral to the agent's success as their administrative assistant(s). Your mission is to be the ship-shape, detail-oriented hero that they've hired you to be!

And, as you'll soon see, there is no such thing as 'just' an assistant. Administrative assistants also wear many hats and hold several different titles, from Listing Manager to Transaction Coordinator and Marketing Director. In the same way that solo agents need to divide their time between their salesperson identity and their administrative alter ego, you will also need to divide your time expertly and efficiently between the many tasks and activities that will make up your busy days and weeks.

> On any real estate team, no other position is as integral to the agent's success as their administrative assistant.

So let's dive in and see exactly what's involved in running the operations side of a real estate company and all the things you'll need to know to be a great administrator for you company—whether you've been hired to support a bigger team or you're a one-man-show struggling and juggling to be a dozen different people all at once.

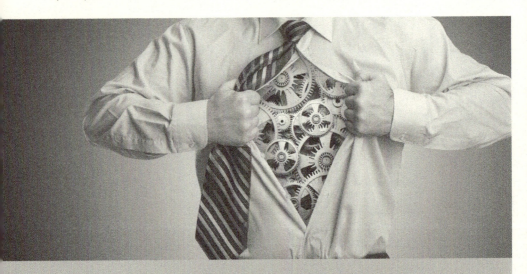

CHAPTER : 1

COMMUNICATION –
PART 1: FOUNDATIONS

ICENHOWER
COACHING & CONSULTING

LEARNING OBJECTIVES

- Recognize ways in which the DISC assessment can improve communication skills
- Distinguish between effective and non-effective communication styles
- Formulate appropriate greetings and responses for office communications
- Organize and categorize materials in a Business Operations Manual

I.   COMMUNICATION PART I: FOUNDATIONS

II. THE DISC BEHAVIOR ASSESSMENT

   A. The Four DISC Behavior Profiles
   1. Dominance
   2. Influence
   3. Steadiness
   4. Compliance
   B. Communicating with DISC Behaviors

III. COMMUNICATION SKILLS

   A. Speaking
   1. In person
   2. On the Phone
   B. Writing
   1. Email Communication
       i.   DISC Behavior & Email
       ii. General Email Guidelines
   2. Documents
   3. Texts
   C. Gesturing & Facial Expressions
   D. Listening
   E. Delivering Bad News
   F. Following Up with the Agent

IV. CREATING YOUR PROCEDURES MANUAL

   A. Format and Layout
   B. Content

V.   APPENDIX

COMMUNICATION PART I: FOUNDATIONS

I f you were to ask someone with a C-behavior to describe the real estate industry, they would tell you that the buying and selling of real estate is a legal and financial transaction. Real estate is heavily regulated at the state and federal level, and in most residential real estate transactions the buyer is obtaining a mortgage from a bank or other financial institution, a process that is also subject to complicated legislation and regulations. This is a fact. As you'll soon see, C-behaviors like to stick to the facts.

On the other hand, if you were to ask an I-behavior to describe the real estate industry, their eyes will light up as they launch into a long and moving story about helping a couple and their young family to find the forever home they've always longed for. An I-behavior will tell you that the buying and selling of homes is about people and their hopes and dreams.

Now, if you were to ask a D-behavior the same question, they may very well tell you to look it up yourself in the Dictionary! D-behaviors can be blunt like that. In times like those, you might need the steady, supportive shoulder of an S-behavior.

If you ask us, the I-behavior is right—the real estate industry is about people.

However, we also know that people who are a C-behavior don't speak the warm and fuzzy language of hopes and dreams, and when you're helping them to buy or sell their home, you need to communicate with them in the language of data and facts. Likewise, if you're helping a D-behavior to buy or sell their home, you better communicate with them quickly and get to the point as soon as possible; but if you're communicating with an S-behavior, they'll appreciate it if you slow down and take your time to support them through the process.

In short, *the real estate business is about different kinds of people who behave and communicate in very different ways*. Whether you're an agent or an assistant, communication is the foundation of your business, and you will need excellent and flexible communication skills when talking to buyers, sellers, other agents, and your various partners in the industry. As you will see, each of them has a different DISC behavior type, and this chapter will help you better understand each behavior's traits and tendencies and the best way to communicate with them.

This chapter has been designed to help you:

- Recognize ways in which the DISC assessment can improve communication skills.

- Distinguish between effective and non-effective communication styles.

- Formulate appropriate greetings and responses for office communications.

- Organize and categorize materials in a Business Operations manual.

THE DISC BEHAVIOR ASSESSMENT

The DISC model is the most widely used assessment tool when it comes to identifying behavior types. When people think of the DISC, they tend to confuse it with personality types but they are two very different things. With the DISC, we don't know how or why somebody became a D-behavior or an I-behavior. We don't know about their childhood or their past, their morals and ethics, or their different character traits. We don't know what they believe or what they are thinking and feeling on the inside.

Rather, the DISC assessment is about behavior, which is more of an activity than a personality. Behavior is something that can be visibly observed and described in a way that personality cannot. We communicate our behavior type in the way that we talk, write, or even in our posture and our hand gestures. Behavior is about what we *do* and how we *act* in our real, everyday lives.

By learning how people act and react to different situations, you'll be better able to communicate with them and support them in meeting their needs. You'll also be able to get your own needs met, too. Understanding how DISC behaviors work means understanding how people think and work together.

Behavior is about what we do and how we act in our real, everyday lives.

Those who learn how to maximize the findings from a DISC evaluation are more productive and more effective in their jobs than those who do not use this assessment tool. We highly recommended that real estate professionals utilize the DISC in every aspect of their business, from hiring and training to communicating and boosting business-generation.

The DISC model identifies how people express their emotions using four innate behavior types:

No behavior is better or worse than another. Each behavior has its strengths as well as potential weaknesses that come out when that person is under pressure or stress. Your DISC profile is not an evaluation or judgment of your character. It is simply a tool that explains behavioral inclinations and how each of us tends to do certain things in certain ways. It's a fantastic way to know and understand yourself, as well as know and understand what motivates the people you're working with.

It's also important to understand that no one person is exclusively one behavior style. There's no such thing as 100% Dominance or 0% Influence. Typically, we see a combination or blend of behaviors, such as DI, SC, CD, or IS, etc. When a DISC assessment is completed, the written report will detail which behavior profile scored above and below a 50% midline and tell you the person's exact behavior profile or behavior blend.

Your DISC behavior blend will reflect your strongest behaviors, priorities, tendencies, and habits. The first letter reflects your most pronounced or unmistakable behaviors and priorities. This is your primary behavior or lead profile. The second letter reflects those behaviors and tendencies that, while less prominent than the primary behavior type, are still very much apparent and more unmistakably 'you' than the other behavior types.

To keep things simple, let's look at each behavior type in isolation, paying particular attention to each behavior's communication style.

DISC PROFILES

DOMINANT (D)

Dominant, leader, quickly frustrated, initiator, stubborn, competitive nature, decision maker, direct, practical, self-reliant

WORK PREFERENCES
- Overcoming challenges and problem solving
- High priority projects and challenges
- Work that yields clear results
- Exemption from day-to-day tasks
- Comfortable in changing environments

PROFILE
WANT: Monetarily driven, appetite for efficiency
SEEK: High output, driven by profit
FEAR: Wasting time, being taken advantage of
COMMUNICATION STYLE: bullet points, closed questions

INFLUENCER (I)

Social, optimistic, flexible, put together, persuasive, friendly, trusting, well-liked, communicative, autonomous, direct, practical, self-reliant

- Compliments, positive reinforcement, and others opinions
- A warm and cordial environment
- Absence of excessive rules and guidelines
- Supportive roles to handle the details

WORK PREFERENCES
- Logical processes in place
- Limited confrontation in the work place
- Absence of limitations allowing for speed
- An open dialogue for ideas
- Collaborative approach in work and play environments

PROFILE
WANT: Enjoy themselves, gloat
SEEK: Acknowledgment, fun
FEAR: Rejection
COMMUNICATION STYLE: playful, don't sweat the small stuff

STEADINESS (S)

Dependable, compliant, easygoing, resistant to change, tactful, practical, passive, good listener, controlling, reserved, calculated, direct

- Recognition
- No abrupt changes
- Tasks with a beginning and end
- Benefits, security

WORK PREFERENCES
- Logical processes
- Stability/uniformity in the day-to-day
- An order of operations
- Limited confrontation in the work place
- Collaborative environment

PROFILE
WANT: Safety and security
SEEK: Approval
FEAR: Change
COMMUNICATION STYLE: ask open-ended questions, consider their opinions and feelings

COMPLIANCE (C)

Calculated, detail oriented, balanced, reliant, risk averse, orderly, traditional, logical, accurate, thoughtful, deliberate, direct, practical, self-reliant

- Measures of quality
- Minimal social activities
- Tasks with a high level of detail
- Systematic organization of information

WORK PREFERENCES
- Tasks with a beginning and end
- Technical work
- Logical processes in place and routines
- Limited confrontation in the work place
- Explanation and evaluation of their work

PROFILE
WANT: Logic, equality, systems in place
SEEK: Accuracy
FEAR: Criticism
COMMUNICATION STYLE: give explanations, process maps, instructions, reasoning

The Four DISC Behavior Profiles

Dominance

 Let's begin with the D-behavior. Their biggest fear in the world is losing—especially when it comes to losing time. You can usually spot a D by the way they speak. They're a fast talker and we mean fast! They do not like to waste time. They're certainly not afraid to talk and, when they do talk, they expect people to listen to them.

On the other hand, they don't like to talk for too long because time and efficiency is always their primary concern. They don't like tangents or what they see as irrelevant details. They're impatient, quickly frustrated, and just want you to hurry up and get to the bottom line.

D-behaviors are motivated by winning and success. They are very results-oriented. They like to overcome a challenge and they are ultra competitive. D-behaviors do not mind taking risks and are comfortable with change. They are the most assertive and dominant of all the behavior profiles. They are extremely driven and are always pushing forward at all costs. Oftentimes, they're the leader of their group or organization.

D-profiles value concrete action and, because they are highly individualistic people, they are motivated by what affects them personally. Therefore, they tend to ask 'What?' questions. What's the bottom line? What's your point? What's in it for me?

D-profiles may appear to lack sensitivity and concern for others. When communicating, they can be extremely blunt, and their impulse to get to the point can express itself as impatience and frustration. D-behaviors may not take the time (or allow others to take the time) to deliberate or think things through before taking decisive action.

A typical D-behavior is: Impatient, Competitive, Demanding, Independent & Strong-Willed.

INFLUENCE

Next up is the I-behavior. I-behaviors are very gregarious and outspoken, and others tend to listen to them. They are extremely positive, effusive people. They're very influential. They like acknowledgement, flattery, and recognition. They like to stand out and enjoy being the center of attention. The I-profile's biggest fear is rejection, disapproval, and loss of social influence.

Like the D-behavior, I-behaviors also talk very quickly and move fast. The difference between a D and an I is that the I-behavior doesn't stop: whereas the D talks quickly in order to get to the point, the I-behavior talks quickly because they are so positive and bubbly.

I-behaviors love life. They enjoy themselves and like to have fun. They like to be around people. When they communicate, they'll have fun with the communication, whereas the D just wants to get to the point. I-behaviors tend to talk more than they listen. On the other hand, their love of people coupled with their warm, enthusiastic attitude makes them good collaborators, as they tend to bring people together.

I-behaviors are motivated by relationships with people so, naturally, they ask a lot of 'Who?' questions. Who'll be at the meeting? Who else is using this lead-generation technique? Who's following me on social media?

I-profiles dislike it when they think they're being ignored, and they may appear overly talkative in the eyes of others. They may also appear to lack focus.

Typically, an I-behavior excels in a sales environment because they enjoy—and are good at—talking. After all, Sales is a game of making contacts, talking, and striking up conversations. I-behaviors are very good at this, as long as we can get them to focus and complete the sale.

A typical I-behavior is: Optimistic, Influential, Social, Effusive, Gregarious & Persuasive.

STEADINESS

As its name implies, someone with an S-profile is a very steady, stable, and dependable person. Their biggest fear is change and loss of stability. Change is extremely difficult for an S because they tend to get in a groove and like to stay there.

S-behaviors are very supportive. Communication-wise, they tend to listen more than they speak. They are very sympathetic, and like to encourage and make others happy. Like the I-behavior, the S is good with people, but they are much more reserved and prefer close, one-on-one relationships or to work in small groups.

Unlike the D and the I-profile, S-behaviors operate at a much slower, steadier pace. They speak slowly and quietly. They like to gather lots of information and input from other people before proceeding with something or making a decision. They spend a long time in preparation before moving forward, whether it's a task, project, or a life decision. Their motto is, "Now that I understand it, I will do it."

S-behaviors care about other people's happiness. They don't like to fail or disappoint people and they don't like to offend people. They want to avoid conflict and confrontation. Sometimes this can make them too agreeable and accommodating and, when communicating, they might have a hard time saying No or confronting people.

A typical S-behavior is: Steady, Supportive, Reliable, Listener, Consistent & Change-Averse.

COMPLIANCE

Lastly, we move on to the C-behavior. The C-behavior is compliant, cautious and conscientious.

Their motto is, "I will do it right no matter how long it takes." The C moves very slowly and cautiously. They are thorough and extremely detail-oriented. They meticulously and logically want to find out the right way to do something first. They want to do things correctly, and they follow a strict adherence to rules, procedures and conventions.

C-behaviors are dispassionate and unemotional in their speech, tonality, gestures, and expressions. They often speak in a monotone, slowly and methodically. They take long pauses in between each of their words and sentences because they like to think before they speak.

A typical C-behavior is: Compliant, Cautious, Thorough, Accurate, Controlling & Risk-Averse.

COMMUNICATING WITH DISC BEHAVIORS

Our DISC behavior highly influences the way that we communicate with other people, whether it's speaking in rapid-fire sentences or in a slow and meticulous monotone. But our behavior also influences the way that we would prefer other people to communicate with us. Some of us prefer to receive long and detailed emails written in full paragraphs, while others prefer to read short bullet-points that get to the bottom line.

Knowing someone's actual behavior type will help you to communicate in a way that's best for that person and provide a superior level of personalized customer-service with your clients. In time, and with some conscientious practice and observation, you will find that you are able to accurately identify and spot a person's behavior within moments of meeting or speaking to them on the phone. You can then adapt and modify your own communication style to suit the needs and preferences of the all-important client.

Often, agents who are serious about utilizing the DISC for business-generation strategies and improved customer-service will note a potential client's behavior type when they meet in person (on the bottom of a Seller Lead Sheet or Buyer Lead Sheet, for example). This is enormously useful for administrative assistants who can take that information and use it to enhance and customize their communication with that client down the line.

Knowing someone's behavior type will help you to communicate in a way that's best for that person and provide a superior level of personalized customer-service with your clients.

The DISC assessment can also be used to improve communication within the office. For those of you who are administrative assistants, knowing your agent's DISC behavior will help you communicate in the best way for them and help you to build an efficient and mutually beneficial working relationship. And solo agents who are eventually in a position to hire administrative support should make sure to utilize the DISC assessment when hiring and training that person.

At ICC, we teach an entire course about the DISC (*BEHAVIOR— Improve Communication & Sales Performance in Real Estate*) that contains a greater level of detail about how to spot behavior and adapt your communication style for each of the different DISC behaviors, especially when dealing with the all-important client.

For now, simply remember that people with different behavior types prefer different forms of communication:

- *Dominance*: prefers concise, direct communication with little to no small talk.

- *Influence*: loves to be social and dislikes impersonal, task-oriented conversation.

- *Steadiness*: likes quiet, personal conversations and dislikes being rushed or pressured into action.

- *Compliance*: dislikes chitchat, prefers to stick to the facts, and also needs time to think before making decisions.

The chart on the following page also has some handy Do's & Don'ts for communicating with each behavior style.

DISC STYLE IDENTIFICATION

D STYLE

- Decisive, tough, impatient
- Strong-willed, competitive
- Demanding, independent
- Direct, does not listen

DO
- Give immediate feedback
- Concentrate on subject
- Maintain result-orientation

DON'T
- Frustrate his/her desire to take action
- Restrict his/her power
- Spend time on non-essentials

I STYLE

- Sociable, talkative, open
- Enthusiastic, energetic
- Persuasive, spontaneous, impulsive
- Emotional, talks more than listens

DO
- Show enthusiasm, smile, chat
- Focus on the positive, make it fun
- Let him/her talk

DON'T
- Put down his/her enthusiasm
- Focus on the details
- React negatively; remain positive

S STYLE

- Calm, steady, laid back
- Caring, patient, amiable
- Listens carefully, sincere
- Modest, indecisive, trustworthy

DO
- Slow down, take your time
- Provide assurance and support
- Give enough time to decide

DON'T
- Be restless, pressure for action
- Make sudden changes
- Fail to deliver on promises

C STYLE

- Precise, exact, analytical
- Logical, systematic
- Quiet, does not express emotions
- Careful, formal, disciplined

DO
- Give detailed information
- Answer questions patiently
- Give time to think and decide

DON'T
- Keep information to yourself
- Pressure for immediate decisions
- Be too chatty

Having said all of this, in real estate we deal with many types of people and situations, from potential clients to third-party vendors and suppliers, and you won't always know the actual DISC behavior of every single person you're communicating with.

While we should always take behavior into account whenever possible, in the next section we will outline some general guidelines for professional office communication as well as tips for communicating with behavior in mind.

COMMUNICATION SKILLS

Good communication skills are vital to the success of every aspect of our lives, from our friendships and familial lives to our business and professional lives. In real estate especially, communication is at the heart of everything we do, from initiating conversations with perfect strangers to maintaining contact with people in our sphere of influence, to scheduling appointments and guiding clients through every step in the transaction.

At every stage, dozens of people are relying on having accurate and timely information that will help them do their various jobs or meet the goals they have set. Effective communication skills make that possible. Ineffective communication results in mistakes, misunderstandings, misinterpretations, and extreme frustration.

While there are some questions and problems that only the agent can answer and solve, clients should primarily be communicating with office administrator(s) when they need help and assistance.

Excellent communication is especially important for those of you in an administrative assistant position, whether you're the sole assistant at your company or whether you're part of a larger administrative support team. If clients are calling the agent to ask basic questions or to clarify the time and date of an appointment, that's a major problem.

While there are some questions and problems that only the agent can answer and solve, clients should primarily be communicating with office administrator(s) when they need help and assistance. It is imperative that administrative assistants take control and ownership of communicating with clients so that the agent is free to spend the majority of their time generating more business.

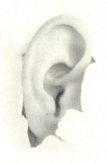 There are many ways to communicate with people. Delivering a message can involve spoken and written language, and it may also include physical gestures. Depending on the exact situation, some communication methods will be more effective or appropriate than others. Perhaps the most essential part of communicating, however, is being a good listener.

Let's take a look at each of these communication skills one by one:

- Speaking
- Writing
- Gesturing
- Listening

SPEAKING

Speaking in person builds rapport, credibility, and helps to develop a more personalized relationship. Your clients are entrusting you with the biggest purchase they will make in their lives, so it's essential to make them feel confident and comfortable while under your care.

When speaking in person, whether face-to-face or over the phone, clients can ask for immediate clarification, and you can provide it. Face-to-face communication improves the likelihood of engagement, which is especially important in real estate sales.

How you speak to people sets the tone for the business. It's important that you are courteous, polite and professional as well as positive and personable without being overly chatty or talking on and on. A smile softens your facial muscles, making your vocal tone sound less stressed and more pleasant. A warm and friendly attitude can brighten the day of a client who's stressed, or help to calm a client who's angry or frustrated.

How you answer the office phone is equally important. People gravitate to happy people. By making your standard greeting upbeat, positive and consistent, you establish yourself and your agent as real estate professionals.

What's more, for administrative assistants, your attitude plays a key role in freeing up the agent's time. If you exude happiness, helpfulness, and positivity, clients will love reaching out to you with their questions and requests. They will know that they can trust you to provide solutions and assistance with a smile.

Of course, everybody has off-days when they're not feeling 100% chipper and upbeat. Standardized greetings are not only professional but they can help you to sound upbeat and optimistic no matter how you're feeling. Always state your name and ask how you can help the person on the phone. For example:

1. "Good morning! This is Sarah. How can I help you?"
2. "Hello, Megan speaking! What can I do for you today?"

It's also important to standardize your out-of-office voicemail greeting. Again, state your name, thank the caller, and tell your callers how quickly they can expect you to return their call. For example:

1. "Hi, you've reached Megan at _____ Real Estate. I'm unable to take your call right now, but if you leave a brief message, I will be back in touch with you as soon as possible."

If you are breaking bad news or trying to secure an agreement, it's essential that you speak to the client in person. Meeting face-to-face is preferable but a phone call is the next best option. We know it's more convenient and efficient for you to email or text, but if you need to have a difficult, urgent, or persuasive conversation, you will be much more successful if you pick up the phone and personally speak with the client or business partner. We'll discuss this in more detail below.

When speaking with people, always remember the following:

In Person

- When greeting people, look them in the eyes and say hello.
- It's usually polite to extend your hand to shake theirs, and if you're sitting behind your desk, it's polite and

professional to get up and come around for the handshake rather than stretching across the desk or reception-area.

- Depending on the protocol in your office, offer your visitors a bottle of water or a cup of tea or coffee.

On the Phone

- Remain professional when speaking, even if the person cannot see you. People can 'hear' what your face is saying. Grimaces show up in your voice and people can tell when you're making faces. Smile.

- There may be times you need to place a caller on hold. Always get their permission first. Doing so shows respect for the client. If the caller cannot be put on hold, such as in an emergency situation, they will tell you, and you can prioritize the calls accordingly.

- If you miss a phone call, be sure to call back quickly, preferably within the same day, but certainly within 24 hours.

WRITING

Communicating ideas in writing can overwhelm some people. They struggle for the right word or phrase to explain what they are trying to say. Sentences don't come easily, and messages are either too brief or overwhelmingly long.

On the other hand, some people prefer putting all of their communications with others in writing. A letter or an email affords them the opportunity to communicate at length on a particular topic. For more introverted, reserved behavior types, it also allows them to avoid meeting with people face-to-face.

However, people that communicate everything in writing may come across as impersonal or passive-aggressive. And another challenge with written communication is that readers misinterpret almost half of what they read. The problem isn't that they can't understand the words. Difficulties arise with syntax, tone, and even word connotation.

Instead of communicating entirely via writing, ask yourself which communications could be told in person or by phone instead. As we've said, while there are advantages to communicating certain things in writing, you should never hide behind an email or a text when delivering a high-priority message or bad news.

For those of you who are assistants, your agent may ask that you refrain from emailing clients and prospective clients, but if you are emailing, try these guidelines when sending written communication to clients and others with whom you work.

EMAIL COMMUNICATION

Administrative assistants should confer with their agent about office guidelines for sending emails and other written forms of communication. The agent may prefer to email clients themselves as it adds a more personal touch. In this case, most of your emails will be intra-office messages between you and the agent, or administrative emails to third-party vendors or office suppliers.

However, for those of you are responsible for emailing clients, the following principles and techniques will help you to modify your written communication style to suit the client's DISC behavior. It will also help you when it comes to communicating and following up with your agent or any other team-members at your particular company.

DISC Behavior & Email

Dominance (D)

With a D-behavior, emails should always be brief and to-the-point. The subject-line should be short and tell them exactly what the issue is and what you need from them. The body of the email can contain a little more detail but, if the overall purpose of your email is that you need the client to sign something or you need more information from them, your subject-line should communicate that.

Don't assume that a D-behavior will read your entire email. Don't ask them a question or request something from them in the last line, as they might not read that far! Any call to action should be upfront.

Always use bullet-points and super short sentences when emailing a D-behavior. Provide a concise, bullet-pointed summary of any attached reports or documents.

Emails from D-behaviors will be blunt and may lack the usual greetings and salutations. Their intention isn't to be unfriendly or rude: they just want to dive in and get directly to the point. When you're emailing a D-behavior, they won't be offended if you skip the formalities either but, at the same time, it's perfectly okay to say a quick Hello if it feels strange to dive right in without at least saying Hi.

Influence (I)

In terms of length, emails from I-behaviors can go either way. I-behaviors are super social and prefer meeting in person and talking on the phone. They can sometimes lack the focus and organizational skills needed to write longer emails. And, when they do write longer emails, they tend to be a little all over the place. Their email won't be as structured as a D-behavior's email. It may be short on punctuation. It may not even be organized into paragraphs and just be a lot of run-on sentences.

When emailing an I-behavior, you can help them to focus by responding to them clearly. While it's generally important to match our client's preferred communication style, you don't necessarily want to match their disorganization or lack of punctuation!

When emailing an I-behavior, emails should have the clarity of D-behavior emails, but they will tend to be a bit longer and much more personable than with the D.

The tone of an I-behavior's email will be very energetic and colorful. They will emphasize their excitement and enthusiasm with a lot of exclamation points or all-caps. They might even highlight sentences or use flamboyant fonts. And, in the same way that we would match their emotion in person or on the phone, we need to mirror and match their emotion in writing too.

If they send you a long email, don't respond back with a single sentence. I-behaviors need recognition and affirmation and you need to be social and engaged with them or you risk breaking rapport. Address all of their points, and match their colorful, energetic style. If they use emojis or happy faces, then you should too.

However, matching your client's behavior and communication style should always be done very subtly. If an I-behavior uses a ton of exclamation points or happy faces, respond to them with just a few exclamation points and one—maybe two— happy faces. If you match them too exactly and include a ton of exclamation points after your sentences, they might think you're making fun of them.

When we're writing emails, we're not consciously thinking about our behavior: an I-profile might not even be aware of how many emojis or happy faces they're using, they're just caught up in the moment. So if you copy them too exactly, they might suddenly realize how emotive they are and become self-conscious, which we definitely do not want.

When matching a client's email style (or any form of communication), our purpose is to validate them. We need to show that person that the way they're communicating is acceptable to us. We never want to match someone in a way that makes him or her feel self-conscious about the way they communicate.

STEADINESS (S)

Like the I-behavior, the S-behavior will have a warm, personable communication-style. However, their emails will be significantly more professional, reserved, and organized. An S-behavior will appreciate a personal greeting and inquiry as to how they are doing. They may ask how you are or they may say something like, "I hope this email finds you well", which is friendly but reserved and professional at the same time. They will end their emails in a similar way, with expressions like "Best Wishes" or "Sincerely", etcetera. When emailing with an S-behavior you should open and close your emails in the same friendly and professional way.

On the one hand, you shouldn't rush headlong into business when emailing an S-behavior, as they do want a more personal relationship with you. However, if you are emailing an S-behavior to communicate bad news or to communicate a change of circumstance, don't wait too long to tell them what you need to tell them. S-behaviors don't like change and your opening remarks should gently prepare them that you're writing because you have some unexpected news. Don't be abrupt. Ease them gradually into the news. Don't wait until the last line to break something to them. This will feel very shocking and misleading to them.

Be supportive and caring but also matter-of-fact and professional when delivering disappointing news. Explain the reasons *why* something is happening and offer them solutions and help. But don't force your opinion on them and don't demand that they make an immediate decision unless

something is truly urgent and time-sensitive. Tell them you're happy to meet with them in person or are available to talk on the phone, but make sure to give them time to digest bad news and come to their own decision.

Having said that, S-behaviors have a tendency to delay making decisions, so consider establishing a gentle deadline if a decision does need to be made sooner rather than later. For example, "I know this is very disappointing and not the outcome we were hoping for, but if you can get back to me by the end of the week that would be really helpful." Give them time and space to respond and always match them in their steadiness.

COMPLIANCE (C)

When a C-behavior emails you, it might look more like a college essay than an email! C-behavior emails will be very carefully composed and structured. Oftentimes it will include bolded headings and will be organized with thesis-style statements ahead of each paragraph. We often see numbered paragraphs with a C-behavior. Sometimes their long, carefully written paragraphs will be followed by bullet-points that reiterate or summarize what they've just said. Their emails will follow a logical, methodical sequence of points. Each paragraph will express a different point or address a different issue and, often, these paragraphs will be interspersed with bullet-pointed questions or requests for more information.

Like the S-behavior, C-behaviors can also take a long time to come to a decision. So email may not be the best communication method if you need a quick answer about something. C-behaviors spend a lot of time gathering all the facts and composing their emails. They will often read their emails over several times before pressing 'Send', or even wait overnight in case new information becomes available. Give them plenty of time to respond to your emails and, if you do need a quicker response, be very specific about what you need and lay out a logical explanation for the urgency. Always approach things logically and factually with a C-behavior. You can include formal greetings but don't use emotional or personal language when you're emailing a C-behavior.

GENERAL EMAIL GUIDELINES

The following guidelines will apply to any email you are sending.

Subject Line

Always include a subject line. The purpose of the subject line is to tell the reader the topic of the email before reading it, so make sure it is specific and accurate.

The subject line can assist people in prioritizing their reading. Carefully crafted subject lines will convey an appropriate level of urgency.

Use concrete and specific nouns in the title line. For example, "Updated Smith Listing on Main St." or "Rescheduling of Friday's Team Meeting".

Timely Response

Reply to every email you receive, even if it's with a two or three-word response that acknowledges receipt or provides the status of a project you're working on.

Carbon Copy (Cc) and Blind Carbon Copy (Bcc)

When appropriate, you will need to Cc or Bcc other people on emails to clients, lenders, escrow/title officers, and other agents and vendors.

For administrative assistants, one of the main purposes of Cc'ing and Bcc'ing is that your agent is never caught off guard with any particular situation. But how do you know when to choose between Cc and Bcc?

Cc stands for carbon copy.

When you Cc someone, they receive a copy of the email you're sending, and their email address appears clearly in the Cc field so everyone can see that that person has been included in the message. Cc is the most common way of sharing the same information between groups of people.

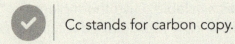 Bcc stands for blind carbon copy or blind courtesy copy.

When you Bcc someone, they also receive a copy of the email you're sending, and *they* will see that they have been Bcc'd rather than Cc'd. However, other recipients will *not* know that a copy has been sent to someone else. Bcc can be used when you want to keep someone in the loop or apprised of a situation but you don't necessarily want to drag that person into the conversation thread.

However, Bcc should be used with caution. If a recipient selects "Reply To All", everyone will be included in the reply—including the previously anonymous Bcc recipient. Depending on the situation, this can cause embarrassment or confusion for readers who were unaware that someone else was looped in on the situation.

 Clients may feel a loss of privacy if they discover that an unexpected person was included in an email exchange, so it's essential that you Bcc with discretion and always ensure that these emails are incredibly polite and professional.

At the same time, Bcc'ing can be used to protect people's privacy. Bcc can be used when you want to keep an email address confidential from other recipients.

Administrative assistants should ask their agent for Cc and Bcc protocols and document these in your Policies & Procedures Manual.

Documents

Documents are also forms of written communication. They can be plats, tax histories, contracts and more.

If you've been asked to forward a document to a client on behalf of an agent, make sure the document page is aligned. Slanted margins and skewed lines represent your office's attention to detail.

Your agent may have a scripted response for each type of email, and the agent should always be Cc'd on the email. If there is no scripted response, create them and have them on file, ready to go.

For example:

"As requested, I have attached copies of the tax history for this property. Please let us know if we can be of further assistance."

Texts

While texting is technically a form of written communication, administrative assistants should avoid texting clients as much as possible. Solo agents can text clients if the client is comfortable with that form of communication, especially when trying to accommodate a client's preferred communication style.

However, texts are far more likely to be misinterpreted than emails and can lead to confusion and misunderstanding.

It's also essential to remember that the real estate industry is bound by many rules and regulations, including strict record-retention laws. Never text anything pertaining to the transaction or that contains a client's sensitive non-public information. Additionally, texting does not provide a reliable historical record of a conversation. Unfortunately, situations do arise where you may need to legally prove that something happened. This is virtually impossible with texting, which is often inadmissible as evidence.

While it is okay to *respond* to a client that initiates a text message, answer politely but briefly and always steer, or transition, the conversation back to email for serious, transaction-based questions and conversations. Simply reply saying, *"Thanks for your message. I'm going to follow up with you by email in just a moment as there is too much information to send in a text."*

Administrative assistants can use texting for communicating important/urgent information to their agent. For example, *"Client will be 15 minutes late"*, *"This property now has two offers"*, or *"Ordering a late lunch; what would you like?"* etc.

GESTURING & FACIAL EXPRESSIONS

Communication isn't always verbal. A highly significant percentage of our communication occurs on a nonverbal and largely unconscious level. Research in Kinesics (the study of the way in which certain body movements and gestures serve as a form of nonverbal communication), estimates that at least 65-70% of the social meaning of a conversation or interaction is achieved not through the words spoken but by facial expressions, gestures, posture and gait, and various arm and body movements.

Behavioral studies show that matching people's gestures, body language, and mannerisms helps to build empathy and trust, and establish rapport. If you know the client's behavior, you can improve your communicate with them by subtly matching their gestures and posture.

Standing over someone who is sitting can come across as domineering or intimidating and create a power differential. Obviously this is the exact opposite of building rapport, so if your client takes a seat then you should sit too. This is especially important when meeting with an S or a C-behavior client who likes to take their time and go over things slowly and thoroughly. Sitting with them creates the sense that you can be trusted to stay with them and give them the attention and level of detail that this type of behavior needs. Conversely, you may find that the more direct and blunt D-behavior client will tend to stand rather than sit down and relax. In this case, you should stand too and create the sense that, like them, you are efficient and aren't going to waste their time with irrelevant chitchat.

As well as posture, we can match other physical movements such as hand gestures. Some people 'talk' with their hands and, generally speaking, if you're interacting with someone who is a hand-talker, it's most likely they are a D or an I-behavior. A D-behavior's hand gestures are often a sign of their impatience, as though they're telling you to get to the point or wrap things up.

Generally you won't need to match these impatient movements as the D will tend to end the conversation quickly and abruptly themselves. (In fact, if you are a D-behavior, you may need to modify this particular hand gesture when talking to clients with slower profiles!)

However, D-behaviors also tend to emphasize their points with strong, swift hand movements and, when talking to a D-behavior, you can match the decisiveness of their hand gestures to demonstrate that, like them, you too are efficient and focused on getting results.

The I-behavior's hand gestures are an extension of their natural optimism. Their hand and arm movements tend to be large and exaggerated—they are a physical reflection of this profile's open, welcoming, and embracing nature. I-behaviors like recognition from people and their peers. Matching their movements and enthusiasm, will make them feel acknowledged and affirmed, which is very important in building rapport with this type of client.

On the other end of the spectrum, S and C-behaviors tend to have very restricted or limited hand movements. S-behaviors are stable and steady and this is reflected in the stillness of their body. They will tend to rest their hands on their lap or away and out of contact. If you are a D or an I-behavior, you will need to modify your hand gestures to match the calmness of the S-client. It's not unheard of for an I-behavior agent to sit on their hands when interacting with an S or a C!

These behaviors take in information very slowly. They are steadier people and do not like distraction or chaos. They really want to focus in on you and, if your hands are moving all over the place, you will struggle to build rapport with them.

Having said that, C-behaviors tend to take control of conversations and will sometimes express their compliant, rule-abiding nature with firm, resolute hand gestures. It is advisable to match these hand gestures very subtly, if at all. If your hand gestures are too strong, they may feel like you are trying to dominate them. However, if you are presenting data and facts to a C-client, you can emphasize the veracity of your information by matching the C-behavior's firm and logical—almost robotic—hand movements.

LISTENING

One of the best ways to communicate is to not say anything at all and simply listen. Listening builds empathy and shows that you value the other person's opinion and perspective.

Good listening involves a variety of skills, some of which we have already discussed.
When listening to another person, gauge their level of eye contact. Does the person look away or look directly at you? What

gestures is he or she using? While listening to them, match their mannerisms and physical gestures to increase the sense that you are in sync with them.

If you are listening to someone on the phone, is the voice confident, upbeat and full of energy or is the person tired? Can you tell if the person is smiling? If the person doing the talking is positive, you'll want to match their energy with the same vibe. But what do you do when the other person is upset?

> *These strategies can help you to listen better.*

1 Summarize

By summarizing what you've heard, you are restating what you have heard. Listen to the speaker's key points then paraphrase them. If you're not sure what the other person is trying to say, ask for clarification. Summarizing helps you determine the main point the other speaker is making. Asking questions makes you seem interested in what's being said.

You can acknowledge what the speaker has said by responding with these sentence starters:

- "I hear you saying . . ."
- "In other words . . ."
- Let me summarize the main points to see if I understand what you're saying . . ."

2 Validate

By validating the feelings of another person, you're not necessarily agreeing with what has been said. You are affirming that this person has the right to feel the way they do. Their emotions are theirs, and they have every right to feel the way they do.

Validating someone shows that you are listening to what's being said. That's important when someone is angry or feels resentment: validating is a way to temper and possibly diffuse a tense situation.

iC

By developing excellent listening skills, you are helping your agent build rapport and relationships with current and prospective clients.

Effective communication creates a stable work environment and helps to build a business. Your job is to help make that happen whenever and however you communicate.

Delivering Bad News

No one likes bad news but, when it occurs, it has to be shared. The worst thing you can do is to ignore bad news in the hopes that it will go away. Bad news usually becomes worse until it is addressed.

The tips below will help you to share bad news, whether it's informing your boss about something that is happening in the office, or breaking bad news to clients.

Typically agents will want to speak with clients personally if there is bad news, such as when a buyer is unable to secure financing. In that case, for administrative assistants, your job is simply to provide the client with immediate access to your boss. But for those of you who are solo agents, the same principles will help you when these difficult conversations arise.

① **Don't Delay**

Give bad news on the same day you learn about it.

Keeping lousy news under wraps allows it to fester and grow. What once may have been a small problem will develop into a monstrosity unless you address it head-on. The sooner you bring bad news into the light, the sooner you can do something about it.

For those of you who are administrative assistants, some agents will set strict timelines for delivering bad news, requesting that nothing negative be shared before a specific time of day. Others may want the news written on a 3 x 3-inch sticky note. Whatever doesn't fit in the space isn't important—they just want the most pertinent information.

If something happens that is super urgent and time-sensitive, always let the agent know as soon as it happens.

② **Use the DISC**

Use what you know about DISC behavior to deliver bad news to clients or your boss.

- **Dominance:** These people work through difficulties quickly. Be courageous, be brief, and get to the point. They may react with anger but don't take it personally.

- **Influence:** Normally optimistic and happy, this person will react very emotionally to bad news and will expect you to provide support. You may be asked to collaborate on a solution, so prepare a few ideas in advance.

- **Steadiness:** People in this category do not like disruption; bad news is disruptive and will be taken pretty poorly. Break the news as gently as possible. Be sensitive to their emotions and apologize if necessary. Validate emotions.

- **Compliance:** Avoid small talk and emotion. Present the information logically and factually. Avoid dictating a single solution. Instead, present some choices for a resolution, as this person will want to take control and make their own decisions.

DISC BEHAVIORAL ASSESSMENT

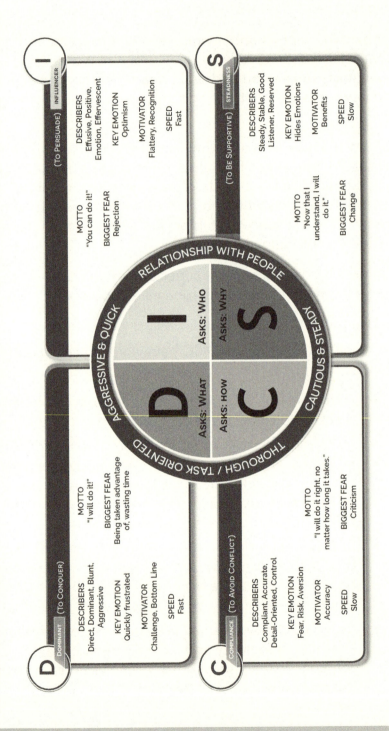

I — INFLUENCER (To Persuade)

DESCRIBERS
Effusive, Positive, Emotion, Effervescent

KEY EMOTION
Optimism

MOTIVATOR
Flattery, Recognition

SPEED
Fast

MOTTO
"You can do it!"

BIGGEST FEAR
Rejection

S — STEADINESS (To Be Supportive)

DESCRIBERS
Steady, Stable, Good Listener, Reserved

KEY EMOTION
Hides Emotions

MOTIVATOR
Benefits

SPEED
Slow

MOTTO
"Now that I understand, I will do it."

BIGGEST FEAR
Change

D — DOMINANT (To Conquer)

DESCRIBERS
Direct, Dominant, Blunt, Aggressive

KEY EMOTION
Quickly frustrated

MOTIVATOR
Challenge, Bottom Line

SPEED
Fast

MOTTO
"I will do it!"

BIGGEST FEAR
Being taken advantage of, wasting time

C — COMPLIANCE (To Avoid Conflict)

DESCRIBERS
Compliant, Accurate, Detail-Oriented, Control

KEY EMOTION
Fear, Risk, Aversion

MOTIVATOR
Accuracy

SPEED
Slow

MOTTO
"I will do it right, no matter how long it takes."

BIGGEST FEAR
Criticism

RELATIONSHIP WITH PEOPLE

AGGRESSIVE & QUICK

CAUTIOUS & STEADY

THOROUGH / TASK ORIENTED

D — ASKS: WHAT
I — ASKS: WHO
S — ASKS: WHY
C — ASKS: HOW

③ Stick to the Facts

Bad news doesn't need a lot of drama. It's already an attention-getter. Avoid embellishing what happened. Instead, provide the facts.

④ Be respectful

When you tell only the facts, you're in a position to show respect for others and preserve everyone's dignity. This means refraining from blaming and name-calling.

⑤ Offer a Solution

Solutions can help to mitigate challenges.

An air conditioning unit that goes out when the outdoor temperatures are reaching three digits is bad news, for sure. If you've already called the warranty company about the situation, say so. If your agent has an appointment and you can stay late to let the service company in, say that too. If overtime could be an issue, offer to flex your schedule.

⑥ Follow Up

Follow up with resolution if it is in your power to do so. If not, follow up with a status update.

If the news affects others, let them know the outcome when the bad news has been taken care of.

For example:

"You may have heard that our air conditioner collapsed yesterday. The service company repaired the equipment and temperatures are cool once again."

A little transparency goes a long way.

Following Up with the Agent

Real Estate Assistants should talk to your agent about how they would like you to follow up on the tasks you've been assigned.

Systems & Timing

You and your agent will need a system for handling the business of the day, from small tasks to more significant activities.

No system works for everyone; keep in mind that different behavior types may need various systems in place. A boss who is a Dominant D-behavior may want quick notes as you complete each task, while an S-behavior boss may prefer a fifteen-minute conversation at the end of each day as a way to summarize what happened.

We recommend that agents meet with their assistants on a daily basis for the first 90 days of hire. It's also important to establish set times to communicate and follow up with each other. Unless it's a true emergency, don't interrupt an agent when they are focusing on lead-generation activities or other tasks that they need to concentrate on.

Creating Your Business Operations Manual

One of your duties as an administrative assistant is to create a Business Operations manual.

This manual communicates the company's policies and step-by-step procedures for performing every aspect of business in the real estate agent's office. If written correctly, it should guide someone who is unfamiliar with your company the day-to-day procedures for operating your business.

Written policies and procedures increase efficiency and organization, and clearly communicate every aspect of the company's ethos and operations. Additionally, a good operations manual saves time during the onboarding process and creates a culture of accountability where employees are largely self-taught, self-managed, and proactive. This is crucial for freeing the agent up to focus on their business-generation activities.

Creating an operations manual may sound daunting for those of you who are brand new to your position, or you solo agents who simply do not have the time to sit down and document every task and process. Don't worry. Like we said in the beginning, we have your backs!

Throughout this book, you will find a wealth of supplemental materials, checklists, forms, and resources to assist you in organizing, categorizing, and assembling your Business Operations manual. Additionally, at the very end of this book, we have also provided you with a robust and comprehensive Real Estate Team Policies & Procedures Handbook. These resources will save you an enormous amount of time and from having to start from scratch.

However, it's important to remember that there is no one-size-fits all operations manual that can be printed out and placed in a binder. The resources and materials we provide you with are a solid starting point, but they should be reviewed and modified to reflect your company's actual policies and procedures. Creating your manual will require some active participation and thoughtfulness on your part.

Format and Layout

A Business Operations manual should be a coherent, organized document that employees can quickly and easily flip through when they need to perform a certain task or to check the company's policy on a particular issue.

Depending on the size and complexity of your company, your operations manual might be a large hundred-page instruction-book, or it could simply be a centralized series of checklists and brief, bullet-pointed "how to" guides.

Your manual can be a physical object like a sturdy 3-ringed binder with tabbed and color-coded index dividers. Or it can be a digital file that everyone has access to on a shared drive. The advantage of a digital file is that it doesn't need to be reprinted every time a procedure changes. However, digital files can quickly become large sprawling documents that are difficult to navigate.

Your Business Operations manual is yet another form of communication, so it's essential that it is written and presented in a way that prevents misunderstanding and misinterpretation.

Divide your manual into clearly defined sections and subsections to facilitate navigation.

For example:

> We suggest that you divide administrative procedures according to the four main components of that role: Administrative Manager, Listing Manager, Transaction Coordinator, and Marketing Director.

Number sections and subsections, and include a table of contents.

Whichever format and layout you choose, it's up to you to ensure that your manual is accurate, up-to-date, easy-to-follow, and user-friendly. Remember that this manual is yet another form of communication, so it's essential that it is written and presented in a way that prevents misunderstanding and misinterpretation.

CONTENT

Operations manuals typically include the following components:

- Important Contact Information
- Emergency Procedures
- Company Organization/Hierarchy and Job Descriptions
- Policies
- Procedures

Think of policies as the rules. These include office hours, dress code, time off, etc.

Procedures describe the process or actual steps your people will need to take in order to follow the rules or policies.

For example:

Company *policy* might state that employees are entitled to X number of days off per year, but a *procedure* would tell them the exact steps they need to take to request that time off in advance.

Likewise, company *policy* might state that employees are expected to communicate professionally and respectfully at all times, but a *procedure* would tell them how to use the particular phone system that the company uses, which email template to use when sending a property plat to a client, or a 'cheat sheet' for how best to communicate with different DISC behaviors.

Generally, policies are static and don't change very often, whereas procedures may need to be updated in line with advances and updates in software, technology, or increased personnel. Not all policies will necessarily connect to a procedure. It's important, however, that your policies and procedures don't contradict each other.

Your Business Operations manual will evolve and develop over time. Don't go overboard creating a phonebook-sized manual for a small company or one-man-show. The purpose of the manual is to help you in your job—creating and maintaining it shouldn't be a full-time job in itself!

For now, your operations manual will be largely comprised of procedures for performing the different components of the administrator role that you encounter through the course of this book. Not only will they be invaluable in doing your job right now, they will also be invaluable for any future-hires that take on aspects of your role as the company expands.

You are not expected to remember everything you need to do your job well. Everything you need for becoming an outstanding administrator will be in the manual, beginning right here with the essential foundations of Communication and the DISC Behavior Profiles.

Now that we have laid those foundations, it is time to delve into the details of your real estate administrative role as well as the role of the agent. See you in the next chapter!

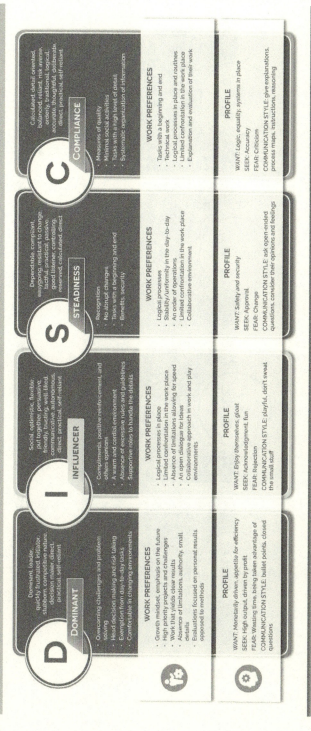

DISC STYLE IDENTIFICATION

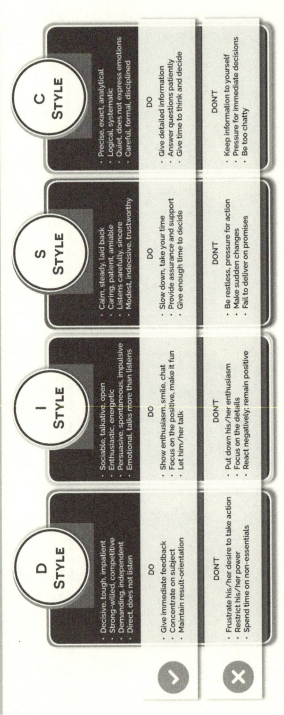

D STYLE

- Decisive, tough, impatient
- Strong-willed, competitive
- Demanding, independent
- Direct, does not listen

DO
- Give immediate feedback
- Concentrate on subject
- Maintain result-orientation

DON'T
- Frustrate his/her desire to take action
- Restrict his/her power
- Spend time on non-essentials

I STYLE

- Sociable, talkative, open
- Enthusiastic, energetic
- Persuasive, spontaneous, impulsive
- Emotional, talks more than listens

DO
- Show enthusiasm, smile, chat
- Focus on the positive, make it fun
- Let him/her talk

DON'T
- Put down his/her enthusiasm
- Focus on the details
- React negatively; remain positive

S STYLE

- Calm, steady, laid back
- Caring, patient, amiable
- Listens carefully, sincere
- Modest, indecisive, trustworthy

DO
- Slow down, take your time
- Provide assurance and support
- Give enough time to decide

DON'T
- Be restless, pressure for action
- Make sudden changes
- Fail to deliver on promises

C STYLE

- Precise, exact, analytical
- Logical, systematic
- Quiet, does not express emotions
- Careful, formal, disciplined

DO
- Give detailed information
- Answer questions patiently
- Give time to think and decide

DON'T
- Keep information to yourself
- Pressure for immediate decisions
- Be too chatty

DISC BEHAVIORAL ASSESSMENT

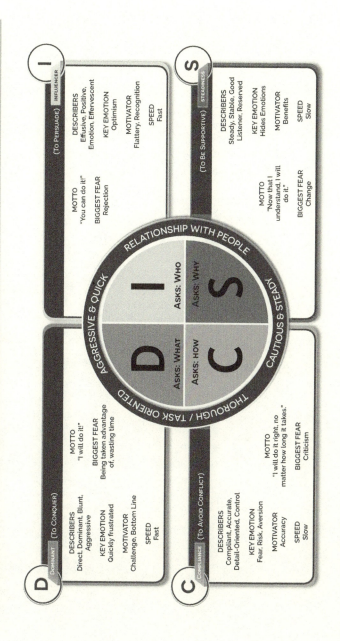

D DOMINANT (TO CONQUER)

DESCRIBERS
Direct, Dominant, Blunt, Aggressive

KEY EMOTION
Quickly frustrated

MOTIVATOR
Challenge, Bottom Line

SPEED
Fast

MOTTO
"I will do it!"

BIGGEST FEAR
Being taken advantage of, wasting time

I INFLUENCER (TO PERSUADE)

DESCRIBERS
Effusive, Positive, Emotion, Effervescent

KEY EMOTION
Optimism

MOTIVATOR
Flattery, Recognition

SPEED
Fast

MOTTO
"You can do it!"

BIGGEST FEAR
Rejection

S STEADINESS (TO BE SUPPORTIVE)

DESCRIBERS
Steady, Stable, Good Listener, Reserved

KEY EMOTION
Hides Emotions

MOTIVATOR
Benefits

SPEED
Slow

MOTTO
"Now that I understand, I will do it."

BIGGEST FEAR
Change

C COMPLIANCE (TO AVOID CONFLICT)

DESCRIBERS
Compliant, Accurate, Detail-Oriented, Control

KEY EMOTION
Fear, Risk Aversion

MOTIVATOR
Accuracy

SPEED
Slow

MOTTO
"I will do it right, no matter how long it takes."

BIGGEST FEAR
Criticism

RELATIONSHIP WITH PEOPLE

AGGRESSIVE & QUICK

CAUTIOUS & STEADY

THOROUGH / TASK ORIENTED

D ASKS: WHAT
I ASKS: WHO
C ASKS: HOW
S ASKS: WHY

iC

LEARNING OBJECTIVES

- Identify key duties in the administrator's job description
- Analyze the job description of the agent
- Develop a master work-schedule
- Formulate strategies to remain on task throughout the day

I.   UNDERSTANDING JOB ROLES

II.   THE ADMINISTRATIVE JOB DESCRIPTION
A.   The Administrator's Four Hats: An Overview
   1.   Listing Manager
   2.   Transaction Coordinator
   3.   Marketing Director
   4.   Administrative Manager
B.   The Administrative Assistant's Job Description
C.   Where to File the Job Descriptions
D.   "And Other Duties as Assigned"

III.   MY JOB, YOUR JOB
A.   The Agent's Job Description
B.   Common Time-Wasters
C.   Rocks, Pebbles, Sand, Water: a Tale of Time-Management

IV.   PERFORMING YOUR ROLE
A.   Task Analysis
   1.   Checklists versus To-Do Lists
B.   Time Blocking
   1.   Big Tasks
   2.   Small Tasks
C.   Using a Timer

V.   HANDLING DISTRACTIONS
A.   Email
B.   Social media
C.   Solo Agents

VI.   THE SOLUTION TRIANGLE
A.   Asking For Help
B.   Always Find a Who!
C.   Who Are Your Who's?
   1.   DISC and the Solution Triangle

VII.   NEXT STEPS

VIII.   APPENDIX

UNDERSTANDING JOB ROLES

As you saw in the first chapter, excellent communication is the foundation of any real estate business. Good communication helps to prevent confusion and misunderstanding, and within your real estate company, it's essential that there is no confusion or misunderstanding about your role and your responsibilities.

This is especially important when solo agents hire their first administrative assistant. For so long, the agent has been in adrenaline-mode, doing everything themselves. In that time, they have developed deeply engrained habits and workflows (however inefficient and chaotic), and it can be difficult for them to delegate and let go of certain tasks. Written job-descriptions help everyone to understand the scope and details of their position and perform their role at the highest level.

In this chapter, we will further examine the real estate administrative role as well as the role of the agent. The agent/assistant relationship is a symbiotic relationship. It's impossible for either party to perform their role unless they are intimately familiar with the unique tasks, duties, and responsibilities of the other person. In order to be of benefit to each other, you must understand each other.

Again, we would like to emphasize that the administrative role at your company may be structured in slightly different ways. At larger real estate companies, the administrative role might be heavily subdivided, and several individuals might perform specific portions of this overall role. In smaller operations, it's more common to see a single assistant who manages every administrative duty and responsibility. And solo agents, of course, must perform the tasks and duties of both the administrative role and the agent role.

Understanding the duties and responsibilities of each job role helps you to systematize those roles and increase efficiency and productivity. One of the primary tasks of a real estate administrator is to create systems when they do not already exist, and to streamline and improve chaotic systems and inefficient  processes that simply do not work. In this chapter, we provide you with techniques and strategies for managing your time and dealing with the innumerable distractions that come your way each and every day.

In short, this chapter has been designed to help you:

- Identify key duties in the administrator/administrative assistant job description

- Analyze the job description of the agent

- Develop a master work schedule

- Formulate strategies to remain on task throughout the day

THE ADMINISTRATIVE JOB DESCRIPTION

For those of you have been hired as administrative assistants, you probably read your job description when you applied for the position and understood immediately that an administrator's role is actually made up of several roles. Those of you who are solo agents know this all too well.

Real estate administrators wear many different hats. This well-known expression dates back to a time when people in official positions would literally wear the appropriate hat for their position when appearing at an event or acting in an official capacity. Often, civil servants or employees in the military had more than one official role or position and, so, the image emerged of the same person wearing different hats when acting in different roles or capacities.

As the administrator of a real estate office, you will be acting in several capacities on a daily, weekly, and monthly basis. Many of your duties fall under the broad tasks of coordinating, managing, and supervising, but there are four critical roles that an administrator assumes in any real estate office. They are: the *Listing Manager*, the *Transaction Coordinator*, the *Marketing Director*, and the *Administrative Manager*.

The Administrator's Four Hats: An Overview

As you can see from the image below, each general area of responsibility is one of four distinct quadrants. However, these quadrants do not exist in isolation. They overlap, and you will find yourself moving fluidly between each quadrant in the course of performing your different duties each day and week.

Paying close attention to your four responsibilities keeps the office running smoothly while your agent generates business.

The real estate business that comes in will drive your daily and weekly duties. Some days, the company will have a lot of new listings so, naturally, you will spend more time wearing your *Listing Manager* and *Transaction Coordinator* hats that week. However, in real estate we are always looking forward and preparing for the future, so you should not let too much time pass before allocating some time for your *Marketing Director* role, as this will help bring in more leads and listings down the line.

Of course, for solo agents who are primarily responsible for generating business, it can be tricky to dedicate time to each of these administrative quadrants. We completely understand how overwhelming and distracting this can be and, later in the chapter, we will share our strategies for managing and coping with that.

For now, let's keep things simple and take a closer look at the four hats a real estate administrator wears each and every day. For those who are brand-new to the business, don't worry if you don't understand certain words or terminology; they will all become clear in later chapters that examine each role in more detail and, of course, they will become even clearer once you are actually performing the role.

LISTING MANAGER

As the Listing Manager, you oversee every aspect of the real estate transaction, from pre-listing to listing, and from listing all the way to contract.

When you first learn of a listing appointment, your pre-listing tasks and duties revolve around preparing the agent for that appointment. A successful listing appointment results in a signed listing-agreement and, from here, you will be responsible for following through with each detail that leads to the executed contract or purchase agreement.

 You will not be dealing with too many other people at this stage. Your work here is very task-oriented and includes a great deal of marketing activities, as well as consulting and coordinating home-cleanings, inspections, repairs, and staging. You'll also be responsible for coordinating showings and open houses as well as inputting and updating listings. For each home listed, you will compile a comparative market analysis and conduct a variety of research such as property tax information, comparables, and old Multiple Listing Service (MLS) listings.

TRANSACTION COORDINATOR

As Transaction Coordinator, you will take the listing from contract to closing. When a buyer's offer to purchase a property has been accepted by the seller, you are under contract. At that point there will be many contingencies that need to be performed and addressed by both parties before the sale closes and the buyers can take possession of the home and move in.

 Again, your responsibilities include coordination, but this time you'll be working with the title/escrow process and the mortgage loan and appraisal processes. You will also help facilitate buyer inspections and repair negotiations. Once that's done, you'll

handle moving schedules for when the buyer takes possession of the house. You will also take care of sale follow-ups. We will explore these individual tasks and duties in greater detail later in Chapter 5.

As *Transaction Coordinator,* the client you're representing could be the buyer or the seller. Either way, the process will be fairly similar as you work through the contingencies in order to achieve the successful sale of the property.

MARKETING DIRECTOR

Of all the hats you'll wear in your administrative role, Marketing Director is the most fun. In smaller companies where a single person performs the entire administrator role, most of an assistant's time will be spent working in the capacity of Listing Manager and Transaction Coordinator where you're help is most needed. As the company expands, a great deal more of your time will be spent on marketing and handling public relations for the business.

Typical duties include managing the company's client database or Customer Relationship Management (CRM) system, updating social media and web pages, creating print and digital sales materials, gathering testimonials, obtaining favorable online reviews, and planning appreciation events.

However, those things are only the tip of the iceberg, so you can see how it can get very busy and complicated when you are also acting as the company's Listing Manager and Transaction Coordinator.

The most important hat you will wear, therefore, is in your capacity as the Administrative Manager that oversees and commands the entire operation.

ADMINISTRATIVE MANAGER

The Administrative Manager is the office taskmaster who makes sure everything gets done, and we mean everything!

Duties in this quadrant include maintaining the company's financial systems, preparing profit and loss statements, overseeing the budget, paying bills, reviewing bank accounts, and coordinating all purchases.

As Administrative Manager, you will also take on the job of hiring all future administrative assistants should the need arise. In essence, you are launching, managing, maintaining, and expanding business operations from the ground up. Your role focuses on the day-to-day operations of the business, which you will help your agent build when an existing system is not already in place.

Most importantly, you'll create and maintain seamless systems that keep the business running while the agent focuses exclusively on sales.

As the Administrative Manager, you must ensure that all agent activities are limited to listing property, showing property, negotiating contracts and lead-generation. You are also responsible for holding the agent(s) accountable. We'll discuss this in more detail in just a moment.

The Administrative Assistant's Job Description

Now that you understand the four main areas of responsibility, Icenhower Coaching & Consulting has developed a thorough and detailed Administrative Assistant Job Description that outlines each category's duties.

1. Listing Manager (Listing to Contract)

- Oversee all aspects of sellers transactions from initial contact to executed purchase agreement.
- Prepare all listing materials: pre-listing presentation, Listing Agreement, sellers' disclosures, comparative market analysis, pull online property profile, research old multiple listing service (MLS) listings and etc.
- Consult & coordinate with sellers all property photos, staging, repairs, cleaning, signage, lockbox, access requirements & marketing activities.
- Obtain all necessary signatures on listing agreement, disclosures and other necessary documentation.
- Coordinate showings & obtain feedback.
- Provide proactive weekly feedback to sellers regarding all showings and marketing activities.
- Coordinate all public open houses and broker open houses.
- Input all listing information into MLS and marketing websites and update as needed.
- Submit all necessary documentation to office broker for file compliance.
- Input all necessary information into client database and transaction management systems.

2. Transaction Coordinator (Contract to Closing)

- Oversee all aspects of buyer & seller transactions from executed purchase agreement to closing.
- Coordinate title/escrow, mortgage loan and appraisal processes.
- Coordinate inspections, assist in negotiations regarding repairs, and coordinate completion of repairs.
- Regularly update & maintain communication with clients, agents, title officer, lender etc.
- Submit all necessary documentation to office broker for file compliance.
- Coordinate moving/possession schedules.
- Schedule, coordinate & attend closing process.
- Input all client information into client database system.
- Schedule 30 Day, 90 Day & 120 Day client customer service follow up calls to assist with any home improvement provider recommendations and to ask for referrals.

3. Marketing Director

- Manage client database management program & system.
- Create & regularly prepare all buyer & seller consultation packages.
- Coordinate the preparation of all listing & open house flyers, graphics, signage and all other marketing materials.
- Manage & update agent website(s), blog(s) and online listings.
- Regularly assist agent to manage & enhance agent's social media presence.
- Track & coordinate all inbound leads from websites, social media & other online sources.
- Coordinate all client & vendor appreciation events.
- Regularly obtain client testimonials for websites, social media & other marketing materials.
- Coordinate & implement agent marketing videos & property videos on website(s), blog(s), social media and client database email campaigns.

4. Administrative Manager

- Oversee all aspects of the administration of the agent's business.
- Create & manage all systems for sellers, buyers, client database management, lead generation tracking, lead follow-up & all office administration.
- Maintain all agent financial systems, profit & loss statement, bill payment, budget(s), bank accounts, and business credit card(s).
- Coordinate the purchasing of any office equipment, marketing materials and any other business related supplies and materials.
- Create & update a business operations manual and all job descriptions/employment contracts for any future hires.
- Manage the recruiting, hiring, training and ongoing leadership of all future administrative hires.
- Hold agent(s) accountable for conducting all agreed upon lead generation activities.
- Ensure that all agent activities are limited to listing property, showing property, negotiating contracts & lead generation.

You may notice that your duties, for the most part, must occur in the office. Every listed duty begins with a powerful action word, and all of these tasks support one of the four responsibilities in the agent's job description. We will look at each area in-depth in the next four chapters of the book.

Your ability to tend to the tasks and responsibilities of *your* job helps the agent to do *their* job. That means you must complete everything on this list.

WHERE TO FILE THE JOB DESCRIPTIONS

File a copy of your job description and your agent's job description in your Business Operations Manual.

"AND OTHER DUTIES AS ASSIGNED"

Although it's not mentioned in the administrative assistant job description, "Other Duties As Assigned" is a standard part of most people's job. Essentially, this is a catchall phrase that means you must also attend to other duties that come up even though they were not explicitly addressed in your job description.

In a nutshell: if you see something that needs to be done—do it. Don't wait to be asked, and don't expect someone else to do it just because it's not mentioned in your job description. While written job descriptions help everyone stay within the parameters of their position, some people can be slaves to their job description and become disgruntled when asked to do something that isn't specifically stated, word for word, in their job description.

For real estate administrator's, keeping the business running means keeping your agent's focus on business-generation, which means you must handle *anything* that might take their time and attention away from that. The goal is to make sure that your agent takes on NO other duties or tasks.

Real estate agents have four responsibilities: listing property, showing property, negotiating contracts, and generating leads.

The agent is the rainmaker. Everything else is your responsibility. Always remember that your relationship is mutually beneficial and symbiotic: the more business that your agent can generate, the more income everyone earns.

MY JOB, YOUR JOB

Administrative assistants are hired to be the backbone of the real estate office. You provide the fundamental structural support and balance that keeps everything upright. You enable flexible motion and help to coordinate everything.

Never forget that this is your job.

Agents, on the other hand, are the muscle—the engine that propels the business forward and keeps it moving in a different way. Muscles turn fuel into motion and agents turn leads into clients and income. It's impossible for us to do anything without our muscles and, likewise, your real estate company will collapse financially if the agent is inactive and stops moving.

Never forget that this is their job.

THE AGENT'S JOB DESCRIPTION

As we've stated several times, the agent has four primary responsibilities:

1. Business-Generation: Prospecting for New Leads

2. Lead Follow-Up: Nurture and Convert Leads

3. Conduct Listing Appointments and Buyer Consultation Appointments

4. Write Offers and Negotiate Contracts

We say this not to be repetitive but to drive home the fact. There is a big difference between knowing what your job description is on paper and actually sticking to those things once you walk into the office. Agents and their assistants will need to remind themselves often that, "This is *my* job, and this is *your* job".

As we mentioned before, it can be difficult for agents to delegate and let go of certain duties and tasks. Agents tend to find it especially challenging to focus on business-generation and lead follow-up. These activities require an enormous amount of energy and a thick skin. There can be quite a lot of rejection involved, and real estate assistants often discover that agents find ways to procrastinate and avoid these activities—despite being very good at them.

Oftentimes, though they know they hired an assistant for a very good reason, agents resume their old habits and wind up getting lost in administrative and customer-service tasks that they should be delegating.

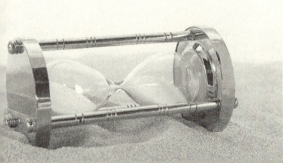

"I had fifteen minutes, so I thought I'd help," they'll say; or they'll use excuses like, "There's not enough time left before lunch/the next appointment/ this week, so I'll just do this instead."

For those of you who have been hired as an assistant, your agent may want to 'help' you do your job, but you cannot allow that to happen. You must take care of everything else related to the business. Every minute the agent spends outside his or her job description is time not spent on generating business.

Don't permit them to perform your duties, no matter how much they try to, whether they want to update a spreadsheet or just water the plants. It might not come naturally for some of you (especially those of you with more reserved behavior-profiles), but you will have to become insistent and unswerving about your job duties. You will need to be possessive and protect your position from being usurped!

Of course, for those of you who are solo agents, you're in the trickier position of being the business's muscle as well as its backbone. When juggling administrative duties along with your primary responsibilities, you will especially have to watch out for common time-wasters that can sneak into the day.

Common Time-Wasters

Time-wasters tend to fall into these broad categories:

- *Wasting time on unqualified buyers*

  Real estate agents know they should spend time with people. Sometimes, however, agents choose to spend time with unqualified buyers because they think spending time with anyone is better than spending time with no one.

  An agent's time is better spent prospecting or nurturing serious buyers.

- *Poorly scheduled appointments*

  Agents should never schedule appointments during time they have blocked for lead-generation activities. This is the most important time to protect.

  Agents who spend half the day driving between appointments or hanging around lengthy meetings after they are finished waste too much precious time.

  Maximize time by scheduling appointments in close geographical proximity to each other.

- *Anything to do with Operations*

  If your agent wants to organize files, coordinate an open house, or even update social media, she or he is doing *your* job. The agent must work on generating sales.

  Operations keep the business running, but sales supports operations.

- *Writing (and checking off) elaborate to-do lists*

  Lists have a mesmerizing attraction. Checking off tasks can be satisfying. It's a way to measure successes. Each check gives the owner a sense of accomplishment, as well as a shot of dopamine—the brain-induced chemical that reinforces doing pleasurable acts.

Check off another item on the to-do list and receive more dopamine. Before long, compulsive list-makers break their duties into smaller and smaller tasks, creating more boxes to tick off and more opportunities to generate dopamine.

Unfortunately, simply listing tasks does not equal productivity. In fact, it often results in accomplishing less.

- *Nesting*

  Often, agents want to spend a considerable amount of time in the office. If he or she is working on leads or negotiating contracts, that's fine. A pleasant desk and comfortable chair, however, can lure an agent into lingering in the office much longer than they should.

  Administrative Assistants should use their communication skills to ask their agent what can be taken off their plate to get them back on track with prospecting, nurturing and converting, conducting appointments, and writing/negotiating offers.

 Administrative Assistants may notice that their agent has control or trust issues that make them hesitant about delegating anything at all, or they possibly have a fear of being successful. Their real estate coach will help them work through this.

In the meantime, remain diligent about your duties, demonstrating that you are competent in their execution. Most importantly, stand your ground and maintain control of your duties.

If the agent isn't generating income, you can't be paid, and the company won't exist. It's in both of your best interests to ensure that the agent focuses only on prospecting, nurturing and converting, conducting appointments, and writing/negotiating offers.

To do this, a real estate administrator must become a master planner and an expert in time-management.

Rocks, Pebbles, Sand, Water: a Tale of Time-Management

There's a well-known story about a wise professor who wanted to teach his class about the importance of priorities and time-management.

On the table in front of him, he placed a huge, clear container. The professor asked the students if it was empty, and they said that it was. Next, he carefully placed large rocks inside the jar. When the rocks were nearly at the top, the professor asked his students if the jar was full. They said it was.

The professor picked up another container. This one was full of small pebbles, and he poured these into the larger container among the big rocks. Again he asked his students, "Is the container full?" Again, they said, "Yes, it is full."

Next, the professor picked up a sack of sand. He poured the grains of sand among the rocks and the pebbles. When the sand had reached the top of the container, the professor asked again, "is the container full now?" The students were certain that it was.

The professor picked up a pitcher of water and poured the liquid over the rocks, pebbles, and sand.

"Each time I filled this jar, you thought it was full," he said. "Yet each time I was able to add more to the container."

This jar is a metaphor for how we prioritize and organize our time.

If the professor had poured the sand in first, and then the pebbles, there would have been no room for the big rocks. The big rocks are the large tasks in your day—the things that absolutely have to get done. The pebbles are smaller chores, though still important, that can be done quickly throughout the day. The sand represents the day-to-day interruptions, like a ringing phone and incoming emails.

You must take care of and attend to everything. Similar to putting these items in a jar, you'll need to plan your schedule in a way that allows you to take care of big tasks, small chores, and day-to-day interruptions.

Returning to the story, the professor asked the students one more time, "Is the container full *now*?" Confident in their answer, the students said that the jar was indeed full.

The professor smiled and reached for one last thing. He held up a bag of water containing a beautifully colored fish, and poured it into the container of water, sand, pebbles, and rocks.

The students gasped in delight.

"You must always make room in your schedule for that which is beautiful and provides joy. Then I say, your container is full," said the professor.

You have been tasked to coordinate your day as well as that of your agent. You have to fit everything in. By scheduling your essential tasks (the rocks) first, you can fit the daily chores (the pebbles) around them. Smaller things like emails and other communications are more fluid, like the sand and water surrounding the pebbles and rocks.

And, as the professor said, you'll also want to allow some room for joy.

PERFORMING YOUR ROLE

How, exactly, do you go about fitting everything in? When you have a to-do list as long as your arm, what techniques and strategies can you use to perform your role in the best way possible?

For starters, you should tear up that long and haphazard to-do list and, instead, adopt a two-pronged approach of Task Analysis and Time Blocking.

To some extent, this is somewhat a 'chicken and egg' process— it's difficult to say which comes first. In order to perform a task analysis, you will need to block off time in your schedule to do so; but in order to block off time in your schedule, you will need to estimate how long it will take you to perform the task analysis!

Since we must start somewhere, however, let's first take a look at task analysis.

TASK ANALYSIS

Task analysis is, unsurprisingly, the analysis of how a task is completed and accomplished. Essentially, it is nothing more than breaking tasks into smaller, more manageable steps.

Depending on the complexity of the task, performing a task analysis could involve: a detailed description of both the physical and mental activities required to complete the task; documenting the frequency of the task, or the estimated time it will take to complete the task; documenting any equipment or materials needed to complete the task; noting any other unique factors involved; noting any other people or parties involved in completing the task.

A well-executed task analysis should result in an orderly, hierarchical representation of steps and actions needed to perform the task.

As you saw a moment ago, the Administrative Assistant Job Description includes large tasks such as "overseeing all aspects." The best way to approach each task is to determine how it can be broken into more manageable chunks or actions.

> "Overseeing all aspects of seller's transactions from initial contract to executed purchase agreement" includes:
>
> - Obtaining a blank copy of the contract
> - Preparing a client folder with appropriate checklists
> - Organizing documentation
> - Identifying due dates
> - Scheduling inspections
> - Keeping a record of all communications with attorneys, lenders, and clients
> - Getting necessary signatures

In turn, each of these tasks can be further analyzed and broken down into steps.

Real estate administrators should perform a task analysis for any task or activity you perform on a regular, repeated basis. Breaking tasks into their component parts can help you identify inefficiencies and create procedures for performing tasks in the most logical order and way.

When performing a task analysis, however, be careful that you don't give in to a mindless to-do list mentality. Each of your tasks is a goal to be fully completed rather than rushed through haphazardly and merely checked off a list.

CHECKLISTS VERSUS TO-DO LISTS

As we just mentioned, a well-executed task analysis should result in an orderly, hierarchical representation of steps and actions needed to perform a task. In other words, when you perform a task analysis, you are essentially creating a checklist.

Understand that a checklist is not a to-do list.

With a to-do list, you write down all of your tasks and—in theory—work your way through them one by one. As you cross things off, you add new to-dos to the list. The problem is that to-do lists can become an ad-hoc jumble of unrelated activities with varying levels of importance. Often we skip over tasks, promising ourselves we'll come back to them, but each day brings new tasks, our to-do list grows and grows, and we forget to revisit what we've missed.

With a checklist, you write down all of the steps and actions needed to complete a certain task or process. The list of tasks never changes. You use the same checklist every time you perform that particular task.

Throughout this book ICC provides you with many checklists to assist you in each of your various roles, from 'Pre-Listing' checklists to 'Listing to Contract' checklists, 'Buyer' and 'Seller' checklists, 'Inspection' checklists, and more.

Each of our checklists is formatted in a logical, hierarchical fashion that often includes an inbuilt timeline for additional structure and efficiency. Each of our checklists also contains a status column so that you have a clear visual of what has been requested or completed and what remains to be done.

To-do lists can be useful in certain circumstances, but checklists are far better for busy administrators whose role largely consists of recurring activities, repeated from property to property and from client to client.

Checklists create accountability and discipline. Checklists create an organized timeline. Checklists ensure that everything gets done. Checklists prevent mistakes.

TIME BLOCKING

Another purpose of a task analysis is to determine how much time it takes to complete something. Everyone has the same amount of time each day, but the reason some people get more done is because they are much better at using their time for maximum benefit to themselves and to others.

Time blocking is a type of scheduling that can help you to manage your time better and get more done. Whether you're an assistant or a solo agent, a good real estate administrator is a master planner who can strategize what must get done and coordinate schedules seamlessly.

To time block effectively, you will need to identify your rocks and pebbles and further sort these on a daily, weekly, monthly, and even yearly basis.

BIG TASKS

Often this means scheduling big events and meetings first—and well ahead of time. Any meeting or appointment that involves multiple people should be scheduled well in advance as you will need to factor in response times from several parties as well as coordinating any rescheduling in the event that someone cannot make the appointment.

Solo agents must manage their own scheduling and time blocking, of course. For those of you who are administrative assistants, scheduling meetings and appointments is your responsibility and a key component in freeing up your agent's time and keeping them on track each day and week.

Once your tasks have been categorized, set aside the most significant portions of the day for tasks requiring more of your undivided time. You will find that first thing in the mornings is when you will typically have the most uninterrupted time to focus on more difficult or lengthy tasks.

Most of the real estate world doesn't get busy until 10:00 am, so take advantage of the mornings to knock out tasks that require more concentration. Additionally, the morning is typically when the agent is (or should be) focusing on their lead-generation activities. If you align your time blocks to that of your agent's, this will ensure that neither of you are interrupting the other during that time.

SMALL TASKS

Next you'll want to schedule smaller tasks—the little pebbles that will fit in and around the bigger tasks. If you've chosen to segment your time, you might be able to get through two or three medium-sized tasks in a 25-minute period.

Next, fill in your time with the sand and water—the smaller items you can take care of quickly and without interruption to the rest of the schedule.

Interestingly, as you develop systems and become more efficient, you will find that your big tasks wind up becoming your smaller tasks.

The first few client folders you prepare will be tedious work, for example, but once you've established your systems, the assembly of each folder will be quicker. You'll have more time for other duties as you find ways to support your agent's focus on prospecting, nurturing and converting, conducting appointments, and writing/negotiating offers (or, in the case of solo agents, you'll have more time to get back out there and do what you do best).

What once was a longer 20-minute task will soon become the sand and water that you can quickly fit in around your major time blocks. When you have a few extra minutes during the day, you can prep a few folders to have ready and waiting for those days when you are busier than usual.

Using a Timer

Some people swear by using a timer to stay focused and finish on time.

Popular methods include working on a big project for 25 or 45 minutes. When the timer goes off, take a quick break or work on a smaller task. By alternating between large and small tasks on a regular schedule, you are helping your brain stay focused and sharp throughout the day.

Again, this emphasizes the importance of knocking out your most important and difficult tasks first thing every morning. Avoid the natural temptation of responding to less-important emails, texts, voice messages, etc. when you first arrive at the office. Instead, utilize this uninterrupted time to accomplish your 'big rocks' that need attention.

Handling Distractions

Distractions are part of any job, and this is true in a real estate office. Two of the biggest offenders are email and social media.

Email

Email is a double-edged sword. Electronic communication is critical for the operation of the business, but it can also prevent you from doing anything else.

Administrative Assistants will be responsible for both their own email and those of their agent.

Remember that next to texting, emails are one of the worst ways to communicate with clients. The content can easily be misunderstood, so it's best to use email only for delivering electronic documentation unless the client has asked for something else.

Responding to every individual email as it comes in is not the best use of an agent's time. It is highly recommended that agents set a schedule for responding to emails. Many managers and executives only look at email two or three times a day, but assistants will need to review all Inboxes at least every hour.

Be aware of how much time you spend reading emails that are not business related. Either send the emails to the junk or trash folder and delete them at the end of the day, or flag them for later reading.

Social media

Like email, social media enables task avoidance.

Part of your job will be to update the company website, post in a variety of social media platforms, and coordinate inbound leads from the agent's online presence.

Don't allow yourself to become distracted when performing online tasks and activities. This is work—not an opportunity to get caught up in cute pictures of puppies or laughing at the latest memes.

The standard rule for engaging in social media at work is to get in and get out quickly.

Solo Agents

Speaking of getting in and getting out quickly, we have a few words for you solo agents who wear multiple hats and must divide your time among so many different tasks and activities. As always, these tips and techniques can be adapted for every team-member, so please read on no matter your role!

Unfortunately, there is no magical one-size-fits-all schedule for solo agents who are also juggling administrative tasks and customer-service. We cannot tell you exactly how to structure your day on a minute-by-minute basis.

However, at ICC, we encourage you to highly prioritize income-producing activities over business-servicing activities. When you are wearing your administrator hat, you need to perform those tasks as efficiently and systematically as possible, so that you can wear your agent hat for as long and as often as possible.

When we say that you are your own personal assistant, we don't mean that you should spend hours and hours each day in that persona. You must prioritize business-generation over business servicing. Specifically, you can prioritize it in these three ways:

① Follow the 80/20 Rule

Spend 80% of your time on tasks and activities that generate income, and spend 20% of your time (or less!) servicing the business the 80% efforts created. Spend four times more time creating new business than servicing existing business.

An alternative approach would be to spend more time on income-producing activities that will account for 90% of your goals and hire an assistant to perform the 10% that is rote, administrative, and non-income-producing.

Understand, however, that work expands to fill the time available for its completion. Unless you follow strict scheduling, a single task can wind up taking an entire day to complete. Whether you follow an 80/20 rule, a 90/10 rule, or a 70/30 rule, you must prioritize specific times to perform specific activities. For this reason, I'm afraid you're no longer free in the mornings.

② You're No Longer Free in the Mornings

Prioritize and perform your lead-generating calls and activities first thing each morning. For starters you'll be fresh and have more energy, but there are also generally fewer distractions in the morning. Buyers typically don't want to see properties first thing in the morning and sellers usually want to conduct listing appointments in the afternoon or early evening.

 So start adopting a new mindset that you are no longer available in the mornings. Block out that time on your calendar or it will get gobbled up by less important obligations.

Then, when inspectors want to schedule their inspections, when an appraiser wants to be let into a home, or even when buyers want to view a property, simply respond with:

"I have an appointment at that time, but how about 3pm that afternoon?"

Believe us, nothing is ever that urgent that it cannot wait a few hours. Don't feel that you are not being truthful when you tell people you have an appointment. You do—you have an appointment with yourself and your future success. As long as you hold yourself accountable to actually performing income-generating activities during that time, there is absolutely nothing wrong with prioritizing and protecting this time of day.

③ Erase and Replace

Of course, situations do sometimes arise that are genuinely urgent and more important than lead-generation. Sometimes, you will truly have to do something else during the time you had blocked off for income-producing activities.

However, don't develop a mindset that you had to something else *instead*. Rather, you have to do something else *as well*. You still need to hold yourself accountable for those two hours of activity. When something comes up, you erase your time block for that day, but you extend your time blocks an hour each on the next two days. Never erase your tasks without replacing them somewhere else in your schedule.

THE SOLUTION TRIANGLE

Even if you had all the time in the world to get your job done, you might still fall behind, especially if you're not quite sure *how* to do a task—or if you're asking yourself *why* the task even needs doing at all.

How do you get the right help?

In our many years of coaching, ICC has used the Solution Triangle tool when working with administrative assistants and managers.

If you're new on the job, and particularly if you're new to the real estate industry in general, you're going to use and rely on this tool a lot.

ASKING FOR HELP

Ideally, all assistants—even new and inexperienced assistants—should be largely self-managed and self-sufficient. Of course, you should go to your agent when you need help, but understand that each time you seek the assistance of the agent is time taken away from their business-generation priorities. It's important, then, to have alternative sources of help and assistance.

 Often, however, not only are assistants new and inexperienced, but they are typically an SC behavior-type that dislikes asking for help.

At ICC, we highly recommend that a Real Estate Assistant be an SC behavior. If you're an administrative assistant reading this, it's highly likely that you some sort of SC behavior blend.

S-profiles are professional, thorough and reliable. They're reserved and quiet but are pleasant and personable to communicate with. On the administrative side of the business, S-behaviors are able to put their head down and work steadily at tasks that might bore or frustrate a D or an I-behavior. This is the reason that we also like to see a fairly prominent C-profile for this role. As an agent, you need to trust that your assistant is not going to make sloppy mistakes or drop the ball throughout the entire transaction process. C-behaviors are extremely detail-oriented, accurate and compliant.

However, as we mentioned in the previous chapter, S-behaviors don't like to bother people or be perceived as incompetent or a pest. They like to gather lots of information before proceeding with something or making a decision. They spend a long time in preparation mode before moving forward. Likewise, C-behaviors meticulously and logically want to find out the right way to do things and can become paralyzed gathering facts and data without taking concrete action.

These people often spend too much time asking *What, How,* and *Why,* when they should be asking *Who?*

No matter your behavior profile, it's important that you modify your natural traits and tendencies and learn to seek out help.

Always Find a Who!

As you can see in the image below, the Solution Triangle is divided into four levels with *Why* at the base followed by *How* and *What* then, finally, *Who* at the very top. The sooner we move up the triangle, from *Why* all the way to *Who*, the sooner we move into taking concrete action and finding a solution.

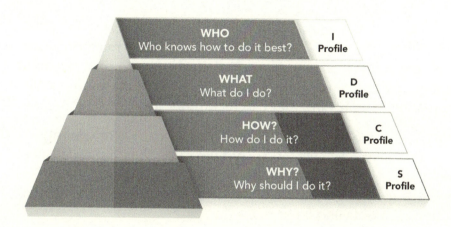

Now, don't get us wrong. Of course we should ask ourselves a range of questions when problem-solving and approach difficult situations with a variety of strategies. Like we said, assistants should be largely self-managed and self-sufficient. However, on the administrative side of real estate, you're not generally dealing with large, philosophical or conceptual problems. The problems you will encounter will be more concrete, tangible, and matter-of-fact. Oftentimes, either you will know what to do, and how to do it, or you won't!

Spending too much time researching an answer delays completing the job. Over-thinking your next steps can have you caught up in analysis paralysis. When we remain in the *What* and *How* levels, and ponder a problem for too long, we c risk falling down the triangle into *Why*, which can sometimes lead us to asking ourselves why we should even be doing something at all! We risk procrastinating, delaying action, and finding reasons why we should give up.

The sooner we move up the triangle, from *Why* all the way to *Who*, the sooner we move into taking concrete action and finding a solution.

WHO ARE YOUR WHO'S?

Finding a *Who* is always your best solution, but who are your *Who's* that you can turn to?

If you work at a large real estate company, the office broker or one of the office managers can probably tell you which person in the office is the best person to help you. Sometimes we don't automatically go to the right *Who*. Instead we find a *Who* that can recommend another *Who*.

We call this the Who-Tree and, yes, we realize we're starting to sound a little like Dr. Seuss, but we often find that assistants are extremely reluctant to approach people, and we cannot emphasize enough that, in real estate, other people are always your best assets and allies.

The people who have come before you have already been through trial-and-error experiences, and will have identified methods and strategies that do and do not work. Other people will speed you towards a solution—you need to use this spreadsheet, or you should use this title company rather than that title company.

Solutions will come a lot quicker if someone shows us a system or model that's already been proven successful and emulate, rather than reinvent, it.

Seek out and marshal a group of *Who's* around you, so that you're not always going to the agent. Quite frankly, the agent often isn't the best person to ask anyway. They hired you for a reason! Agents may know a little more than you, but they're not so great on the administrative side of things and are not your best resource.

Build relationships and develop rapport with office brokers, administrative managers, and other people in leadership positions. Social media platforms like Facebook often have Administrative Manager Groups that can offer technical support and strategic advice. If you have access to your agent's coach, you can also ask them for guidance. Build a network of subject-matter experts who can help you. You have our permission to seek the empowerment you need by going immediately to your *Who*.

What's more, understanding DISC behavior will help you to find a *Who* that can also tell you *How*, *Why*, and *What*.

DISC AND THE SOLUTION TRIANGLE

Normally, when discussing the DISC, we tend to present each behavior in the order it appears in the acronym: D.I.S.C.

When discussing the Solution Triangle, however, we begin our discussion with *Why* at the base and quickly work our way towards the *Who* at the top.

As you will see, each level of the Solution Triangle corresponds to one of the four DISC behaviors.

WHY: THE S-BEHAVIOR

Why should I do it?

Why forms the base of the Solution Triangle. A steady, supportive S-behavior will help you understand the rationale behind a particular function. Knowing why something has to be done—an Open

House, for example—can help you stay the course in getting your job done.

It also provides a focus so that you can align all your activities to meeting the goal. In the case of an Open House, the goal—or the why—is to generate more leads.

An S-behavior will spend a lot of time with you to help and support you. Everyone loves an S-behavior, and this is why! They are service-oriented people by nature, so consider yourself fortunate if an *S* happens to be your *Who*.

HOW: THE C-BEHAVIOR

How do I do it?

The next level in the Solution Triangle is *How?* To get the specifics on how to prepare a contract or conduct that Open House, ask a rule and data-oriented compliant behavior. C-behaviors will be sure every box is ticked off, and they've likely developed checklists for their checklists!

C-behaviors know every intricacy in getting a task done right the first time, and they'll take the time to show you how it's done because they will want to make sure it gets completed correctly, and that you follow their system exactly. In fact, they have likely already prepared detailed workflows, spreadsheets or checklists that you can use to really speed things up.

WHAT: THE D-BEHAVIOR

What do I do?

As we move up the Solution Triangle, we ask ourselves *What?* When we don't know what to do, or a daunting task presents itself, the person to reach out to is the blunt, no-nonsense D-behavior.

Dominant personalities love to give directions. They know a lot because they've done a lot, and they're more than happy to advise you.

D-behaviors are leaders who confidently point the team in the right direction. This will be the person who says, "We need to hold an Open House." They clearly see what must happen next.

Just don't ask them for the specifics. They're too busy to sit down and walk you through the Open House checklist, and the tediousness of it would drive them crazy anyway.

When asking for their help, be respectful of their time by sending them a text or an email. If you must speak to them, first ask them when a good time would be to do so. Always give D-behaviors the choice of how they spend their time.

WHO: THE I-BEHAVIOR

Who knows how to do it best?

Finally, at the very top of the Solution Triangle is *Who?* You're not alone when you work as an administrative assistant. You can, and you should, tap into the resources around you. You'll get the most cooperation in providing assistance on how to do something from a social, influential I-behavior.

I-behaviors are very good at moving directly to *Who*. I-behaviors are extremely social, they know a lot of people, and their natural instinct is to ask someone that they know and trust.

I-behaviors have the inside scoop on the talents of everyone in the office, and this person knows who is best at particular parts of the job, whether it's building a presentation packet or posting in social media.

Need help with coordinating that Open House? If an I-behavior doesn't know what or why or how to do it, an I-behavior will know *who can.*

Next Steps

Taking the reins as the administrator for a busy real estate agent can be exceptionally rewarding. As you learn how to perform each of the duties in your job description, you'll find yourself developing new skills that allow you and your agent to handle more business, while solo agents will develop the skills they need to handle that business along with everything else they need to do.

Applying your knowledge of DISC behaviors will assist you in getting your job done, especially if you're not afraid to reach out and ask other people for help. By optimizing your time and coordinating all aspects of the business, you'll become an invaluable cornerstone of a growing company.

In the next four chapters, we'll take an in-depth look at each of the hats you'll be wearing in your administrative capacity, beginning with the fundamentally important *Administrative Manager* role.

1. Listing Manager (Listing to Contract)

- Oversee all aspects of sellers transactions from initial contact to executed purchase agreement.
- Prepare all listing materials: pre-listing presentation, Listing Agreement, sellers' disclosures, comparative market analysis, pull online property profile, research old multiple listing service (MLS) listings and etc.
- Consult & coordinate with sellers all property photos, staging, repairs, cleaning, signage, lockbox, access requirements & marketing activities.
- Obtain all necessary signatures on listing agreement, disclosures and other necessary documentation.
- Coordinate showings & obtain feedback.
- Provide proactive weekly feedback to sellers regarding all showings and marketing activities.
- Coordinate all public open houses and broker open houses.
- Input all listing information into MLS and marketing websites and update as needed.
- Submit all necessary documentation to office broker for file compliance.
- Input all necessary information into client database and transaction management systems.

2. Transaction Coordinator (Contract to Closing)

- Oversee all aspects of buyer & seller transactions from executed purchase agreement to closing.
- Coordinate title/escrow, mortgage loan and appraisal processes.
- Coordinate inspections, assist in negotiations regarding repairs, and coordinate completion of repairs.
- Regularly update & maintain communication with clients, agents, title officer, lender etc.
- Submit all necessary documentation to office broker for file compliance.
- Coordinate moving/possession schedules.
- Schedule, coordinate & attend closing process.
- Input all client information into client database system.
- Schedule 30 Day, 90 Day & 120 Day client customer service follow up calls to assist with any home improvement provider recommendations and to ask for referrals.

3. Marketing Director

- Manage client database management program & system.
- Create & regularly prepare all buyer & seller consultation packages.
- Coordinate the preparation of all listing & open house flyers, graphics, signage and all other marketing materials.
- Manage & update agent website(s), blog(s) and online listings.
- Regularly assist agent to manage & enhance agent's social media presence.
- Track & coordinate all inbound leads from websites, social media & other online sources.
- Coordinate all client & vendor appreciation events.
- Regularly obtain client testimonials for websites, social media & other marketing materials.
- Coordinate & implement agent marketing videos & property videos on website(s), blog(s), social media and client database email campaigns.

4. Administrative Manager

- Oversee all aspects of the administration of the agent's business.
- Create & manage all systems for sellers, buyers, client database management, lead generation tracking, lead follow-up & all office administration.
- Maintain all agent financial systems, profit & loss statement, bill payment, budget(s), bank accounts, and business credit card(s).
- Coordinate the purchasing of any office equipment, marketing materials and any other business related supplies and materials.
- Create & update a business operations manual and all job descriptions/employment contracts for any future hires.
- Manage the recruiting, hiring, training and ongoing leadership of all future administrative hires.
- Hold agent(s) accountable for conducting all agreed upon lead generation activities.
- Ensure that all agent activities are limited to listing property, showing property, negotiating contracts & lead generation.

SOLUTION TRIANGLE

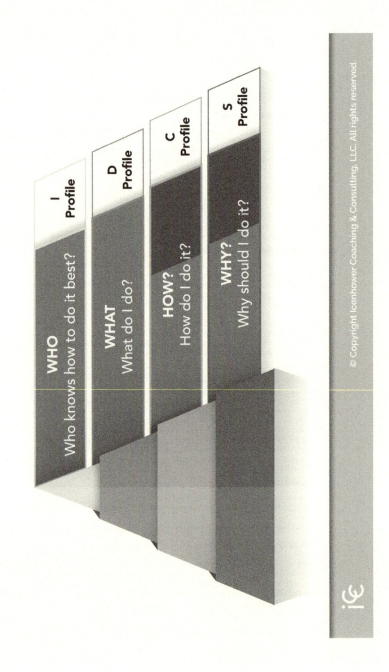

I
Profile

WHO
Who knows how to do it best?

D
Profile

WHAT
What do I do?

C
Profile

HOW?
How do I do it?

S
Profile

WHY?
Why should I do it?

CHAPTER 3:

THE ADMINISTRATIVE MANAGER: CREATING STRUCTURE

ICENHOWER
COACHING & CONSULTING

LEARNING OBJECTIVES

- Demonstrate understanding for the need to communicate
- Propose daily, weekly, and monthly meeting schedules
- Design report templates
- Develop ways to evaluate personal and team effectiveness

I. **THE ADMINISTRATIVE MANAGER: CREATING STRUCTURE**

II. **CREATING SYSTEMS AND MANAGING THEM**

III. **YOU ARE WHAT YOU DO**
   A. Organizing for the Day Ahead
   B. Developing a Routine

IV. **ESTABLISHING WORKFLOW**
   A. Daily
   B. Weekly

V. **COMMUNICATION AGENDAS**
   A. Daily Meeting Agendas
   B. Weekly Meeting Agendas
   C. Quarterly & Annual Meeting Agendas

VI. **CONDUCTING WEEKLY TEAM MEETINGS**
   A. Real Estate Team Meeting Agenda Items

VII. **MAINTAINING AGENT FINANCIAL SYSTEMS**
   A. Receivables and Payables
   B. Banking

VIII. **COORDINATING OFFICE PURCHASES**
   A. Making Purchases
   B. Keeping Track of Receipts

IX. **HIRING ADDITIONAL ADMINISTRATIVE ASSISTANTS**

X. **KEEPING AGENTS FOCUSED**
   A. Time Block Agent Lead-Generation
   B. Use Contact Forms
   C. Agent Scoreboard
   D. Listing and Pending Inventory Pipeline
   E. Lead Sourcing and Showing Results

XI. **NEXT STEPS**

XII. **APPENDIX**

THE ADMINISTRATIVE MANAGER: CREATING STRUCTURE

N ow that you have a broad idea of what to expect in your overall administrator role, the next four chapters will examine each of the four hats individually.

As you have seen, there are an enormous amount of tasks and responsibilities to take care of, and the most important hat you will wear is in your capacity as the company's Administrative Manager that oversees and organizes the entire operation. It makes sense, therefore, to start with this fundamental and indispensable role.

i€

As the administrative manager, you will be responsible for the following tasks and duties:

- Oversee all aspects of the administration of the business.

- Create & manage all systems for sellers, buyers, client database management, lead-generation tracking, lead follow-up, and all office administration.

- Maintain all financial systems, profit and loss statements, bill payment, budget(s), bank accounts, and business credit-card(s).

- Coordinate the purchasing of any office equipment, marketing materials and any other business-related supplies and materials.

- Create and update a Business Operations manual, including all job descriptions and employment contracts for any future-hires.

- Manage the recruiting, hiring, training and ongoing leadership of all future administrative hires.

- Manage agent accountability for conducting all agreed-upon lead-generation activities.

- Ensure that all agent(s) activities are limited to listing property, showing property, negotiating contracts & lead-generation.

Each of these duties is a part of the systems and procedures that create an office structure. In essence, you will be creating the ways that your office conducts business. Every procedure you put in place must support the agent in generating sales and closing contracts. Remember to document the procedures you create in your Business Operations manual.

In this chapter, you will:

- Learn how to create systems and establish workflows including, daily, weekly, and monthly meeting schedules.
- Learn the importance of Communication Agendas and the need to communicate regularly.
- Design report-templates.
- Develop ways to evaluate personal and team effectiveness.

CREATING SYSTEMS AND MANAGING THEM

As you establish office procedures, keep in mind that a large part of your job will include documenting communications, transactions and finances. You will routinely handle a variety of inquiries, and will need to put your master scheduling skills to work.

Organization and structure will make all of these tasks easier, and you will be creating every system from 'formulated' to 'filed away'.

ICC has provided you with many of our forms for your regular agendas and reports, but there may be some additional forms that you will want to make for yourself. If it enhances or streamlines business procedures, do it. Keep in mind, however, that creating forms for the sake of having them is 'busy work' that may prevent you from doing your actual job.

Creating forms for the sake of having them is 'busy work' that may prevent you from doing your actual job.

You Are What You Do

Organizing for the Day Ahead

 When you plan your day, begin with the biggest tasks first. These were the large rocks we talked about in the last chapter. By setting aside ample time to take care of the most important activities, you can be sure that they'll get done.

If you can, schedule these activities at the time of day when you can do your best thinking, without interruptions, typically first thing in the mornings. Arrange smaller tasks around them until you fill up 80% of your available time.

Leave the remaining 20% open for routine tasks like answering the phone and responding to emails.

Developing a Routine

As you build your office systems and procedures, you'll find yourself creating routines that make the most sense.

For example:

> If fewer clients want to see houses on Mondays, that might become the day for agents to intensively focus on generating leads. Administrative assistants will need to support the agent in protecting that time. Solo agents will need to protect that time themselves and minimize the amount of time they spend on non-generation activities.

Administrative assistants should take advantage of days when agents are away from the office at scheduled meetings and appointments. If agents tend to show houses on Wednesdays, that might be the best day for focusing on paperwork or reconciling bank statements.

As natural work patterns emerge, administrative assistants should adapt their schedule to fit the needs of the agent.

Likewise, you solo agents must remember to think of yourself as being your own personal assistant and, like any assistant, establish systems and routines that make your life easier. As natural work patterns emerge, solo agents should adapt their administrative alter ego's schedule to fit the needs and priorities of their sales agent self!

Establishing Workflow

Soon you will discover that your duties will begin to fall into a fairly regular schedule. Although there will be occasional emergencies that require your immediate attention, most days in the office will be somewhat routine, and you can organize your schedule accordingly.

Depending on the size of your company and the scope of your operation, some of the following items may or may not currently apply to you. As your business continues to grow and you reach a point of expansion, a typical daily and weekly workflow will look very much like this:

Daily

- ✓ Scan emails for urgent and emergency items
- ✓ Work on important or longer term projects
- ✓ Check emails: respond, file, delete or forward
- ✓ Answer the phones
- ✓ Prepare client folders
- ✓ Maintain accurate listing information
- ✓ Update social media with posts on Facebook, Instagram, etc.
- ✓ Hold the daily agent/administrative assistant meeting
- ✓ Hold the daily meeting and file the agenda afterward

WEEKLY

- ✓ Plan the week's schedule
- ✓ Schedule agent appointments, including showings, closing, etc.
- ✓ Replenish supplies and materials if necessary
- ✓ File away receipts
- ✓ Prepare listing reports
- ✓ Prepare client folders
- ✓ Complete listing forms and checklists
- ✓ Research comparables, tax histories, etc.
- ✓ Update company webpage with blog, events, etc.
- ✓ Coordinate schedules
- ✓ Gather testimonials
- ✓ Write the agenda for the weekly meeting
- ✓ Hold the weekly meeting and file the agenda afterward
- ✓ Maintain the client database
- ✓ Prepare weekly team-meeting agenda
- ✓ Update team scoreboards for lead-generation activities

Remember that many of these tasks and activities can be broken down into smaller, more manageable steps. When appropriate, document these steps in your Business Operations manual.

COMMUNICATION AGENDAS

In every real estate office, employees have an enormous amount of work and responsibilities on their plates.

When every day is so busy, and when some of them are downright insane, it's easy to say, "Oh we can take care of that tomorrow," or the next day, or next week. In reality, though, next week can easily become the week after that, and before you realize it, the month has gone by and you have missed important checkpoints.

What gets monitored gets done, and you have a lot to get done every day. One of the best ways to ensure that business is taken care of is by maintaining regular communication about it—and then documenting that it happened.

One of the first things you'll need to do is create an Agenda Binder with a few tabbed sections:

- Daily Agendas
- Weekly Agendas
- Annual Agendas, or Business Plan

ICC has templates you can use for these agendas, or you may create your own.

The Agenda Binder serves to document your meetings and helps to keep the business focused on real estate. Every agenda should be about the supports in place to assist the agent in generating leads, attending to appointments, and closing sales.

From the daily meeting to the annual meeting, the purpose of all team communication and interaction is to evaluate everyone's performance, both on the sales side and on the administrative and operations side.

Agendas provide the team with a way to hold each other accountable and make changes that will better serve clients and generate sales. The ongoing process of communicating is an evaluation of how well your systems work.

Be sure to file the agendas in their respective sections of a binder so that you can maintain documentation of what was discussed at the meetings. At the end of each year, remove the agendas and store them in a large folder or filing box for five years.

DAILY MEETING AGENDAS

For companies that have administrative support staff, the agent and the assistant must meet daily to review their plan.

Often easier said than done, those of you who are assistants will need to get your agent's attention every day for no more than 10 minutes to check schedules and appointments, inform them of anything new that has come up, and make sure that the agent's schedule consists of selling and closing.

Decide together on the best time of day for this. Some agents may prefer to meet first thing in the morning with a cup of coffee in hand, or they might want to close the day with the meeting. There may be times that you'll have to conduct the meeting over the phone. If so, the assistant should initiate the call and take notes during the meeting.

Whatever the two of you decide, it will be up to you to make the meeting happen.

WEEKLY MEETING AGENDAS

There are few things more important than the productivity and success of your weekly team meetings.

A weekly meeting moves beyond the day-to-day routine and looks at the bigger picture for the week. Some people prefer to have them on Friday so they can prepare for the following week ahead, while others prefer first thing on Monday mornings. However, most prefer to hold them on Tuesday, Wednesday, or Thursday to avoid the constant rescheduling associated with vacations and holidays around long weekends.

Schedule the meeting for when the agent is least likely to have showings, appointments, or other commitments. For many agents and administrative assistants, that's sometime before noon.

These meetings should provide accountability for the agent to complete his or her regular lead-generation activities.

Did he or she meet their weekly goal for telephone contacts to their Sphere of Influence (SOI)? How many listing appointments did they conduct?

If goals were not met, formulate a strategy to bring them to completion that week. You'll need to monitor these during the week so they are completed before the next weekly meeting. Verify at the next meeting that the goals have now been met.

QUARTERLY & ANNUAL MEETINGS AGENDAS

Some real estate offices hold quarterly meetings in addition to the weekly meetings. These meetings are especially appropriate if the agent plans to pay taxes on a quarterly basis.

The annual meeting focuses on:

- ✓ Profit & Loss Statement
- ✓ Financial Review
    - ✓ Gross Earnings
    - ✓ Net profits
    - ✓ Taxes
- ✓ Annual Business Plan

We will cover the annual team-meeting agenda items in much greater detail in Chapter 9.

CONDUCTING WEEKLY TEAM MEETINGS

The following team meeting agenda ideas can be used to create a positive culture of growth and skill development within the members of a real estate team.

Teams that want to increase production understand the importance of carving out time for income-producing activities. Similarly, they realize that tracking these activities is crucial for accountability, motivation and development.

Teams that experience difficulty with growth often focus solely on business-servicing activities, leaving no time or focus for business-generation efforts. These are busy teams, not productive ones.

In turn, this puts a lid on their growth, which causes significant problems with team morale. Growing organizations are healthy organizations, and successful teams understand that focusing on growth must start with their weekly team meeting agenda.

> Teams that experience difficulty with growth often focus solely on business-servicing activities, leaving no time or focus for business-generation efforts. These are busy teams, not productive ones.

REAL ESTATE TEAM MEETING AGENDA ITEMS

Use the 5 team-meeting agenda items below to ensure that your real estate team maintains a growth-oriented focus in alignment with hitting its annual goals.

① Emotional Capital Introduction

Team members are more productive when they get to know each other on a personal level. This icebreaker engages everyone on the team as each member checks in with the group by briefly telling everyone else what has been going on in their lives over the past week and how they are doing.

Whether it is a personal or business update that is shared, this emotional capital item provides a forum for everyone to speak and be heard. Some teams share their 'Ups and Downs.' Others state something that they are grateful for, etc.

Beginning each meeting with a personal introduction brings team members closer together over time. However, the business agenda should not be derailed with chitchat and small talk, so it's essential to limit each person's speaking time, especially on larger teams. We suggest 20-30 seconds per person.

② Business Activity Log

A quick run through of all existing business might include the following: (1) Active Listings; (2) Pending Contracts; (3) Buyers w/ Signed Exclusive Agency Agreements; (4) Upcoming Listings; and (5) Upcoming Closings.

All of this information should be displayed on a spreadsheet or team activity-log for everyone to review, update and ensure its accuracy.

③ Sales Agent Updates

Each member of the team should be listed as a separate item on the real estate team meeting agenda in order to review their lead-generation activities in front of the group.

For example, buyer's agents might report their number of: (1) Prospecting Contacts; (2) Buyer Consultation Appointments; (3) Buyer Agency Agreements Signed; (4) Pending Contracts; and (5) Closings.

They also should compare these numbers to their weekly, monthly and year-to-date goals as they report.

Listing Specialists, Showing Assistants and Inside Sales Agents (ISAs) also report their income-producing activities in a similar fashion. To further enhance accountability, all of these numbers should also be inputted by each of the agents a day or two prior to the meeting so that they can be displayed to everyone at the meeting on the team scoreboard.

SAMPLE SALES AGENT UPDATE OF LEAD GENERATION ACTIVITIES

WEEKLY LEAD GEN	LEADS & ATTEMPTS	CONTACTS	APTS	CONTRACTS	CONTACT GOAL	OPEN HOUSES	# ADDED TO DATABASE
Agent #1	156	86	2	2	80	0	5
Agent #2	123	65	1	0	50	2	10
Agent #3	188	95	3	2	100	1	12

YTD LEAD GEN	LEADS	CONTACTS	APTS	CONTACTS	YTD OPEN HOUSES	TOTAL IN DATABASE	DATABASE GOAL
Agent #1	1,560	516	22	21	3	950	1,100
Agent #2	738	390	13	6	9	124	250
Agent #3	1,128	570	35	19	6	275	450

Notes:

_____
_____
_____
_____
_____
_____
_____
_____
_____
_____
_____

④ Administrative Staff Updates

Position by position, each administrative staff member reports their progress on developing systems, marketing activities, and other annual business plan items that the team wants to accomplish over the course of the year.

At larger companies with multiple administrative staff, the Administrative Manager, Transaction Coordinator, Marketing Director and Listing Manager should all participate and report separately on their activities and progress.

Please note that these updates should not include any information pertaining to active listings or transactions. This meeting represents the one hour per week that the team focuses on growth and generating new business together. The rest of the week is available for handling issues with pending transactions and etc., so it is crucial to protect this time.

⑤ Growth & Development

A real estate team that is truly growth-oriented makes time to focus on learning-based activities. Here, the team plans and discusses any upcoming training classes, conferences or team-building events they might attend. Senior members of the team might schedule one-on-one coaching appointments or role-play sessions with other team members to help speed up learning curves.

Again, simply including Growth & Development on the team-meeting agenda focuses everyone on their own growth. It sets the tone that the team does not just provide leads and income to its members. It demonstrates an expectation that they will continuously improve themselves as well.

MAINTAINING AGENT FINANCIAL SYSTEMS

In every real estate operation, a good administrator will maintain accurate and highly organized financial systems. At larger companies with additional administrative support, it is feasible that the administrative manager could handle every aspect of the company's financial systems. Often, administrative assistants will be tasked with this responsibility and, obviously, solo agents must manage this system by themselves.

Depending on your level of comfort and expertise, it may be more cost and time effective in the long run to utilize an experienced accountant for at least some portions of the company's finances, particularly when it comes to tax time. The money coming in and going out of your business creates your company's financial footprint, and it is essential to maintain detailed and precise systems and records.

Receivables and Payables

Accounts Payable (AP) is the amount of money a company owes because it purchased goods or services from a creditor, supplier, or vendor. Amounts payable are liabilities, because you still need to pay it.

Accounts Receivable (AR) is the amount of money owed to your business. Accounts receivable are assets, because it is money you will receive.

Simply put, this is the money coming in and going out of your business. The nature of the transaction (AP or AR) will dictate how it is recorded in your company's financial books/ledger or software system.

As the Administrative Manager, creating regular and accurate accounts receivable and accounts payable entries will keep track of incoming and outgoing income and help to balance the books. You will need to record precise details of each transaction, making note of who it is from or for, what date it occurred on, and in what dollar amount.

You can choose to attend to transactions on a daily or weekly basis, or even as they come in. How often you enter these transactions may depend on the amount of business the company generates.

Your ledger may be an electronic app, a digital spreadsheet, or even an old-fashioned sheet of paper. Regardless of which version you choose, be sure to keep a printed copy of the file. This will become part of your documentation system.

By establishing a system that is not only quick but also easy to maintain, you'll find that completing profit and loss statements and preparing for filing taxes will be a snap.

Many agents track income received and expenses paid in a software program like Quickbooks or Quicken. If so, a profit and loss statement can easily be generated on a monthly basis or as needed.

If taxes are paid quarterly, and your agent's tax preparer or accountant is provided with bank statements and ledgers on a regular basis, this finance-professional can easily generate a profit and loss statement quickly and inexpensively.

BANKING

Most banks automatically provide you with electronic access to your bank account. If you also receive a paper version, save it and compare it with the electronic version. A good rule of thumb is to look at your bank account at least weekly. This allows you to check for irregularities, identify transactions that might not have been recorded, and note any service-fees for the month.

Document procedures for maintaining financial systems in the Administrative Manager section of your Business Operations manual.

COORDINATING OFFICE PURCHASES

Whether you're an assistant or a solo agent, as the company's administrator, it's your job to stock the office with the necessary supplies for conducting business.

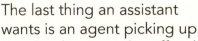
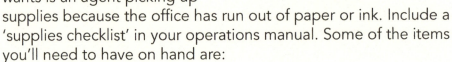

The last thing an assistant wants is an agent picking up supplies because the office has run out of paper or ink. Include a 'supplies checklist' in your operations manual. Some of the items you'll need to have on hand are:

- Three-ring binders
- Tabbed inserts
- Markers
- Pens
- Pencils
- Highlighters
- File folders
- Filing cabinets
- Paper clips
- Sticky notes
- White paper for printing
- Ink for the printer(s)

You may wish to also consider the following seasonal items:

- Holiday cards
- Note cards (blank, thank-you, and congratulations)
- Calendars
- Printed Listing and Buyer Consultation Packets

And, of course, you'll need postage. You can make regular trips to the post office, but you can also take care of your postage needs through usps.com, stamps.com and other online services.

Making Purchases

As well as file folders, pens and paper, the office will also need furniture, computers, and a printer/copier/scanner. Where you purchase these items can be as significant as the items themselves.

Many office supply stores offer discounts for purchases, and some will deliver your order if it is over a certain amount, which saves you the time in having to go pick it up. Wholesale membership clubs may also offer attractive savings.

Keeping Track of Receipts

Those little scraps of paper are easy to lose, but keeping receipts can keep you out of hot water.

Always get a receipt.

The reason for this is to keep track of all purchases and show a record of them. This is important for itemizing business expenses, and a numbering system helps to keep everything in order for the year. If your real estate business is ever selected for an audit, you will be eternally grateful that you took the time to create and maintain this system.

Assistants should make sure that your agent always has a receipt for anything they may have purchased. If the receipt was forgotten, call the company. Restaurants, gas stations and office supply stores can print an electronic copy of the receipt and email it to you if you know the day on which the transaction took place.

One of the easiest ways to keep track of receipts is to tape it to a blank piece of 8-1/2 x 11" paper. Number the receipt, note what the purchase was for (for example, "client lunch"), and make a photocopy of the page (thermal receipts fade over time). There are also a number of mobile apps and software programs that allow you to scan and sort receipts for future use as well.

Place the receipt in a binder or a folder, and number the transaction in the company checkbook or on the credit card statement when it comes in.

HIRING ADDITIONAL ADMINISTRATIVE ASSISTANTS

Congratulations!

If it's time to hire another administrative assistant, it means that you and your agent have created a synergy between the two of you and the business is going from strength to strength. Clients recognize professionalism, and their testimonials—along with your business practices—increases your ability to reach more clients and make more sales. Of course, you'll need another pair (or more) of hands helping out in the office.

When it's time to hire another real estate administrative assistant, pull out the copy of the job description you filed in the Business Operations manual. You'll need the description of duties for the ad you post in your local newspaper or in an online job forum.

Remember to post a mention of the job in Facebook as well; your network of friends and clients may know someone who would fit in well with everyone in your real estate office.

Be sure to refer to ICC's training course, *HIRE – The Complete Hiring Process for Real Estate Agents,* which includes a complete how-to for hiring administrative staff members. This course will provide you with a detailed and thorough system for identifying, interviewing, and hiring talented candidates for this role, including all of the necessary forms, documentation, and tools to follow this step-by-step process.

KEEPING AGENTS FOCUSED

As we have repeatedly stated, it is your job to completely own the administrative side of your agent's business. This can be easier said than done. Despite the fact that you were hired to service existing clients so that agents can focus more time and energy being the rainmakers that generate more business, it doesn't necessarily mean that they will naturally let you.

Agents tend to unconsciously gravitate back to client servicing activities even though they know they need to let go of them. It is part of your job to keep them out of your kitchen and not allow them to use customer-service as an excuse to avoid their own lead-generation activities.

Sometimes it's hard to tell the boss what to do, but this what you were hired for. Therefore it is essential that you hold agents accountable to the rainmaking tasks they've committed to perform.

In the same way many of us know that we need to exercise or eat healthily, but can't manage to do it consistently, agents know that they need to lead-generate for business, but they aren't always willing to do it. When it comes to accountability, every agent needs it. There isn't a more crucial duty on your job description.

iℰ

TIME BLOCK AGENT LEAD-GENERATION

There are a number of ways to hold your agents accountable.

For example, suppose they commit to contacting all of their past clients to check in on how their homes are coming along, offer preferred vendors to help with needed repairs and improvements, and ask for referral business. An administrative manager might get the agent to time block 2 hours each morning to make past client phone calls for a month. Imagine the referral business they could generate with this type of focus!

Notice how "Marketing/Business Generation" time is blocked from 9:00am-11:00am each weekday on the sample weekly calendar shown below. Also notice that "Lead Conversation and Follow Up" is blocked from 1:00pm-2:00pm as well. Once it's calendared, the two of you have a commitment; now it's your job to hold them accountable for doing it.

	Mon 3/13	Tues 3/14	Wed 3/15	Thu 3/16	Fri 3/17
6a					
7a					
8a					
	8:30 - Prepare for Business	8:30 - Prepare for Business	8:30 - Prepare for Business	8:30 - Prepare for Business	8:30 - Prepare for Business
9a / 10a	9 — 11 Marketing/Business Generation	9 — 11 Marketing/Business Generation	9 — 11 Marketing/Business Generation	9 — 11 Marketing/Business Generation	9 — 11 Marketing/Business Generation
11a	11 — 12p Business Servicing	11 — 12p Business Servicing	11 — 12p Business Servicing	11 — 12p Business Servicing	11 — 12p Business Servicing
12p	12p-1p Lunch	12p-1p Lunch	12p-1p Lunch	12p-1p Lunch w/ Wife	12p-1p Lunch
1p	1p — 2p Lead Conversion & Follow-Up	1p — 2p Lead Conversion & Follow-Up	1p — 2p Lead Conversion & Follow-Up		1p — 2p Lead Conversion & Follow-Up
2p	2p — 3p Business Servicing	2p — 3p Business Servicing	2p — 3p Business Servicing	2p — 3p Lead Conversion & Follow-Up	2p — 3p Business Servicing
3p			3:30p — 6p Watch David's T-Ball Game	3p — 4p Business Servicing	
4p / 5p	4p — 5:30p Listings Presentation - 123 Cottonwood Ct	4p — 6p Show Homes to Johnsons		4:30p — 5:30p Buyer Consultation w/ Taylors	4p — 6p Listings Presentation - 456 Spring Creek Way
6p					
7p		6:30p — 8p Family Dinner			6:30p — 8:30p Family Birthday Party
8p					
9p					

Use Contact Forms

Many top administration managers have their agents submit weekly contact forms to document how many contacts an agent makes each day, week, or month. Accordingly, in the appendix to this chapter, we have included a couple different versions of these contact forms for your use in holding agents accountable to their lead-generation activities.

Agent Scoreboard

Showing agent scoreboards at weekly team meetings is a great way to promote peer accountability among multiple agents. Everyone feels the responsibility of their own part in ensuring that the team hits its goals. Nothing creates a higher level of accountability than making weekly lead-generation activity results public in front of all of the team's members on a regular basis.

We have included two examples of real estate team scoreboards for your review. Of course, everyone on the team will need to buy in, and commit to, these activities, along with agreed-upon deadlines for reporting these numbers weekly to administrative staff.

Listing and Pending Inventory Pipeline

You should also cover your Listing Inventory, Buyer Inventory, and Pending Inventory List during your weekly and team meetings. Examples of these three lists are included for your review, and we will cover them in further detail in later chapters.

LISTING INVENTORY

Active Listings

#	Client	Buyer too?	Address	City, Zip	Agent	Source	List Price	List Date	DOM	LA Expires	Today
1	Mark Fisher	Yes	1701 S. Crumal St.	Visalia 93292	Robyn	Robyn SOI	$159,900.00	11/14/17	235	11/14/18	7/7/2018
2	Steve Ensslin	Yes	143 Carmelita St.	Pville 93257	Kari	Kari SOI	$329,000.00	11/17/17	232	6/4/18	7/7/2018
3	Dan & Karen Holloway	Maybe	2067 Linda Vista Ave.	Pville 93257	Kari	Open House	$495,000.00	2/26/18	131	6/26/18	7/7/2018
4	Maria Focha	No	1104 S Whitney	Visalia 93277	Robyn	Agent Referral	$225,000.00	3/13/2018	116	6/8/18	7/7/2018
5	Matt Kelly	Yes	763 Park Place Ct	Exeter 93221	Robyn	Robyn SOI	$514,900.00	3/16/2018	113	5/9/18	7/7/2018
6	Ricardo Mora & Sylvia Lopez	No	996 E San Joaquin	Tulare 93274	Kari	Website	$210,000.00	3/22/18	107	9/18/18	7/7/2018
7	Brian and Kara Martinez	Yes	1955 W Wall Ave	Pville 93257	Kari	Kari SOI	$208,000.00	3/28/2018	101	9/21/2018	7/7/2018

Listing Agreement Signed & Waiting to Go Active

#	Client	Buyer too?	Address	City, Zip	Agent	Source	LA Signed	LA Expires	Notes
1	Hayley Tashjian	Yes	216 N. Orange Ave.	Exeter 93221	Robyn	Melissa SOI	3/25/18	3/24/19	Active on 4/15
2	April Black	No	2720 W. Caldwell Ave.	Visalia 93277	Kari	Kari SOI	1/31/18	12/31/18	Active on 4/26
3	Barbara (Heather Saddler)	Yes	3529 W. Howard	Visalia 93277	Robyn	Robyn SOI	3/5/2018	9/4/18	Waiting for yard renovation
4	Miguel Sanchez	Yes	39 Brook Street	Visalia 93291	Robyn	Rob PC Ref	3/15/2018	12/31/18	Active on 5/1

Listing Leads - No Listing Agreement Signed Yet

#	Client	Buyer too?	Address	City, Zip	Agent	Source	Status
1	Andrew Serna	Yes	794 Sheffield Ave.	Exeter 93221	Robyn	Rob SOI Ref	Still can not make contact to reschedule
2	Thomas and Sherry Ferreira	Yes	1704 Cotton Ct.	Visalia 93291	Robyn	Website Lead	Still deciding between us and Uncle who is an agent
3	David & Lindsay Johnson	Yes	2822 W. Border Links	Ivanhoe 93292	Kari	Open House	Still remodeling bathroom. Ready to list when done
4	Susan and Terry Malhman	Yes	15016 Avenue 312	Visalia 93291	Robyn	Robyn SOI	Waiting for summer school break.
5	Bill and Marina Meek	No	5837 W. Stewart Ave.	Visalia 93291	Robyn	Farm	May/June
6	Terra Walker	Maybe	1802 Marroneto Circle	Tulare 93274	Robyn	Zillow Lead	Canceled/Reschedule
7	Jerry Davis	No	24006 Road 224	Lindsay 93247	Kari	Open House	Waiting on tenants to vacate
8	Jerry Davis	No	1825 E Fir St	Lindsay 93247	Kari	Open House	Waiting on tenants to vacate
9	Miguel and Crystal Sanchez	Maybe	2823 W Brooke Ave	Visalia 93291	Robyn	Robyn SOI	Sellers unsure if moving forward at this point
10	Rafael and Sylvia Arzate	Yes	3613 E. Harvard Ct.	Visalia 93292	Robyn	Robyn SOI	early to mid May
11	Albert Limon	Yes	1032 E. Academy Ave.	Tulare 93274	Robyn	Website Lead	Dead for now. Waiting till next year or so
12	Brad Vickers	No	4106 S. Bridge St.	Visalia 93277	Robyn	Robyn SOI	Canceled & rescheduled for 4/15
13	Daniel Snead	No	3145 W. Ashland Ave.	Visalia 93277	Kari	Kari SOI	May 3rd appointment

BUYER INVENTORY

Buyer Agency Agreements (BAA) Signed

	Client	Agent	Pre-Qualified/Lender	City/Area	Source	Price Target	BAA Signed	BAA Expires	Status
1	Mark Fisher	Melissa	Yes- HomePlus Mortgage	NW/SW Visalia	Robyn SOI	$400,000	11/14/17	11/14/18	Actively looking
2	Steve Ensslin	Melissa	No- HomePlus trying to contact	Visalia	Melissa SOI	$550,000	11/17/17	6/4/18	Shown 15 homes. Actively looking
3	Dan & Karen Holloway	Kari	Yes- CC Mortgage	Springville	Open House	$495,000	2/26/18	6/26/18	Actively looking
4	Maria Focha	Melissa	Yes- CC Mortgage	NE Tulare	Agent Referral	$225,000	3/13/2018	6/8/18	Looking for 2 acre lot
5	Matt Kelly	Jessica	Yes- HomePlus Mortgage	Exeter	Robyn SOI	$514,900	3/16/2018	5/9/18	Still can not make contact to reschedule
6	Ricardo Mora & Sylvia Lopez	Kari	No- Trying to connect w/ CC Mortgage	NW Visalia	Website	$210,000	3/22/18	9/18/18	Still deciding between us & agent Uncle
7	Brian and Kara Martinez	Melissa	Cash	Visalia	Melissa SOI	$208,000	3/28/2018	9/21/18	Still remodeling bathroom. List when done
8	Ron & Linda Watts	Kari	Yes- CC Mortgage	Tulare	Website	$350,000	2/26/18	2/25/19	Waiting for summer school break.
9	Don Evans	Kari	Yes- CC Mortgage	W Visalia	Kari SOI	$425,000	3/13/2018	3/12/19	May/June
10	James & Maggie Wilson	Melissa	Yes- CC Mortgage	Visalia	Website	$310,000	3/16/2018	3/15/19	Canceled/Reschedule
11	Debra Mattoon	Melissa	Yes- CC Mortgage	Tulare	Robyn SOI	$475,000	3/22/18	10/21/18	Waiting on tenants to vacate
12	Dan & Abbie Johnson	Kari	Cash	Visalia	Robyn SOI	$850,000	3/28/2018	3/27/19	Waiting on tenants to vacate
13	Jerry Washington	Melissa	Yes- Valley Credit Union	Visalia	Website	$500,000	2/26/18	2/25/19	Sellers unsure if moving forward at this point
14	Jim & Cindy Stephens	Jessica	Yes- HomePlus Mortgage	Porterville	Open House	$285,000	3/13/2018	3/12/19	early to mid May
15	Sarah Watson	Logan	No - Trying to connect w/ HomesPlus	Visalia	Website	$350,000	11/14/17	11/13/19	Dead for now. Wating till next year or so
16	Maggie Henderson	Tasha	Yes- HomePlus Mortgage	SW Visalia	Website	$500,000	11/17/17	11/16/18	Canceled & rescheduled for 4/15
17	Jessica Tulane	Melissa	Yes- HomePlus Mortgage	W Visalia	Open House	$285,000	2/26/18	2/25/19	May 3rd appointment
18	Mike & Angela Fountain	Melissa	Yes- CC Mortgage	Three Rivers	Melissa SOI	$350,000	3/13/2018	3/12/19	Actively looking
19	Terry Wilkenson	Jessica	No - appointment w/ CC mortgage set	Visalia	Website	$425,000	3/16/2018	3/15/19	Meeting Lender this week
20	Brandon Ames	Kari	Yes- CC Mortgage	NW Visalia	Robyn SOI	$400,000	3/22/18	3/21/19	Actively looking

Totals - BAA Signed & Active	
Melissa	10
Kari	5
Jessica	3
Logan	1
Tasha	1
TOTAL	20

Active Buyer Leads - No BAA Signed, But Actively Looking

	Client	Agent	Pre-Qualified/Lender	City/Area	Source	Price Target	Status
1	Andrew Sema	Melissa	No	Exeter	Rob SOI Ref	$375,000	Still can not make contact to reschedule
2	Thomas and Sherry Ferreira	Kari	No	Porterville	Website Lead	$425,000	Still deciding between us and Uncle who is an agent
3	David & Lindsay Johnson	Melissa	Yes- HomePlus Mortgage	NW/SW Visalia	Open House	$400,000	Still remodeling bathroom. Ready to list when done
4	Susan and Terry Malhman	Melissa	No- HomePlus trying to contact	Visalia	Robyn SOI	$550,000	Waiting for summer school break.
5	Bill and Marina Meek	Kari	Yes- CC Mortgage	Springville	Farm	$495,000	May/June
6	Terra Walker	Melissa	Yes- CC Mortgage	NE Tulare	Zillow Lead	$225,000	Canceled/Reschedule
7	Jerry Davis	Jessica	No	Exeter	Open House	$514,900	Waiting on tenants to vacate
8	Jerry Davis	Kari	Yes- Cousin is a lender	NW Visalia	Open House	$210,000	Waiting on tenants to vacate
9	Miguel and Crystal Sanchez	Melissa	No	Visalia	Robyn SOI	$208,000	Sellers unsure if moving forward at this point
10	Rafael and Sylvia Arzate	Jessica	Yes- CC Mortgage	Visalia	Robyn SOI	$425,000	early to mid May
11	Albert Limon	Tasha	No	Tulare	Website Lead	$310,000	Dead for now. Wating till next year or so
12	Brad Vickers	Logan	Yes- HomePlus Mortgage	Visalia	Robyn SOI	$475,000	Canceled & rescheduled for 4/15
13	Daniel Snead	Melissa	No	Visalia	Kari SOI	$850,000	May 3rd appointment
14	Christine Akers	Kari	Cash	Porterville	Website	$500,000	Sellers unsure if moving forward at this point
15	Neil & Paula Brockmeier	Jessica	No	Visalia	Website	$285,000	early to mid May
16	Jake & Winsome Ullman	Logan	No	SW Visalia	Website	$360,000	Dead for now. Wating till next year or so
17	Dan & Debie Cote	Jessica	Yes- CC Mortgage	W Visalia	Website	$425,000	Canceled & rescheduled for 4/15
18	Julian Werts	Kari	Yes- CC Mortgage	Three Rivers	Kari SOI	$400,000	May 3rd appointment
19	Tom & Christy Blue	Melissa	No	Exeter	Open House	$650,000	Actively looking
20	Ryan Atkinson	Jessica	Cash	Visalia	Jessica SOI	$550,000	Meeting Lender this week

PENDING INVENTORY PIPELINE

	Client	B or S	Address	City, Zip	Agent	Source	Price	Open	Close Date	Total GCI	Notes
1	William and Erica Pine	Buyer	1600 Palm Dr.	Exeter 93221	Melissa	Melissa SOI	$500,000	12/21/18	4/19/18	$13,500	
2	Luis Guerrero	Buyer	2148 W. Union Ave.	Porterville 93257	Melissa	Website	$255,000	1/9/18	4/11/18	$5,558	
3	Chris and Crystal Smith	Buyer	14663 Avenue 344	Visalia 93292	Melissa	Robyn SOI	$685,000	2/12/18	4/12/18	$12,813	
4	Carly Heinzen-Woods	Seller	813 W. Reese Ct.	Visalia 93277	Robyn	Robyn PC	$224,900	2/15/18	4/13/18	$6,900	Ray Jones (Uncle) 949-555-1243
5	Jennifer De Mascio	Buyer	813 W. Reese Ct.	Visalia 93277	Melissa	Robyn PC	$350,000	2/15/18	4/13/18	$6,900	
6	Henry Hash	Seller	644 W. Loyola Ave.	Visalia 93277	Kari/Robyn	Kari Expired	$249,700	2/22/18	3/23/18	$6,250	
7	Henrique Guerreiro	Seller	1000 Belmont	Porterville 93257	Robyn	Robyn SOI	$205,000	2/23/18	4/9/18	$6,150	
8	Jessica De Mascio	Seller	1025 Princeton Ave.	Visalia 93277	Robyn	Robyn SOI	$219,900	3/1/18	4/13/18	$6,810	
9	Gary Garret	Seller	1331 Laura Ct	Visalia 93292	Kari	Kari FARM	$389,000	3/15/18	5/21/18	$6,900	Also buying
10	Gary Garret	Buyer	381 S Beverly	Porterville 93257	Kari	Kari FARM	$310,000	3/21/18	5/1/18	$5,125	Also listing/selling
11	Florence Ann Webster	Seller	2400 W Midvalley	Visalia 93277	Kari	Kari PC	$885,500	9/21/18	12/31/19	$14,000	
12	Daniel Snead	Seller	3145 W Ashland	Visalia 93277	Kari	Open House	$249,000	9/22/18	12/31/19	$7,100	
13	Donnie Brandon	Seller	401 N. Powell	Visalia 93291	Robyn	Robyn SOI	$814,900	3/13/18	12/31/19	$16,200	
14	Scott and Kirsten Hyder	Buyer	131 W Putnam	Porterville 93257	Kari	Kari PC	$750,000	3/27/18	5/21/18	$18,400	
15	Samuel Velasquez	Buyer	893 San Ramon	Visalia 93292	Melissa	Website	$350,000	3/28/18	4/26/18	$8,900	Melissa's cousin
16	David & Mel Johnson	Seller	2822 Border Links	Visalia 93291	Robyn	Robyn SOI	$750,000	2/25/18	4/16/18	$14,750	
17	Kimmy Berkley	Seller	236 Feemster Ct	Visalia 93277	Robyn	Open House	$550,000	2/29/18	4/13/18	$9,550	
18	John & Dani Kale	Buyer	145 Beverly Glen	Visalia 93277	Kari	Website	$350,000	3/1/18	4/1/18	$7,525	
19	Mark & Donna Griffel	Seller	856 N. Fairway	Visalia 93291	Robyn	Robyn SOI	$655,500	3/5/18	4/25/18	$11,500	
20	Omar & Katie Vaz	Seller	435 Keogh Dr.	Visalia 93291	Robyn	Website	$450,000	2/15/18	4/6/18	$7,000	
21	Katherine Florentine	Buyer	231 Park Place	Porterville 93257	Kari	Kari SOI	$350,000	3/13/18	5/12/18	$6,250	
22	Larry Burke	Buyer	259 Hyde Way	Tulare 93234	Melissa	Melissa SOI	$250,000	3/18/18	5/2/18	$6,800	Tenant's occupying property
23	Larry Burke	Buyer	1342 Ames Ct.	Exeter 93221	Melissa	Melissa SOI	$259,000	3/26/18	5/14/18	$7,450	

LEAD SOURCING AND SHOWING RESULTS

For motivational purposes, it is equally important to show how the results of our lead-generation activities are coming along throughout the year. Agents are inspired to see things like how many homes they have sold, what their year-to-date sales volume numbers are, and how many contracts they have currently pending under contract. Contact forms and scoreboards track the activities, but it's also important to *show* the results so they know and remember that the activities are worth the discipline and effort.

It's also important to know what's working. Lead Sourcing is the practice of tracking where each transaction comes from. Did it come from an open house, sphere of influence, or maybe a website lead, for example?

We have included two different versions of our year-to-date check-up forms as examples you can use to identify source leads and show year-to-date results.

NEXT STEPS

As important as it is to keep the real agent's focus on selling and closing real estate transactions, it is equally important that your focus be on your duties in running the real estate office.

As you establish the routines and procedures that create a seamless and efficient business environment, keep in mind these tips:

- All procedures must support and/or enhance the business.
- Systems for the sake of having systems wastes time.
- Prior planning and attention to detail in the beginning saves delays later.
- Organization matters.

And remember, as much as the agent may want to help you with these administrative duties, you must take them over so he or she can focus on their own job duties.

Your regular communication with the agent and delivery of all reports will assure him or her that you're on top of your job. You are handling the day-to-day operations of the business.

As the Administrative Manager, you have all the necessary systems and procedures under control. That means you can concentrate on the next two important tasks, your duties as the Listing Manager and Transaction Coordinator.

We will look at these roles in chapters 4 and 5.

SAMPLE SCOREBOARD

TEAM SCOREBOARD	1/8 - 1/12	1/15 - 1/19	1/22 - 1/26	1/29 - 2/4	Weekly Goal	Monthly Actual	Monthly Goal	Yearly Goal
CONTACTS								
Robyn	15	38	23	15	25	91	100	1200
Melissa	20	36	26	12	25	94	100	1200
Kari	26	22	8	3	25	59	100	1200
Logan	4	6	5	3	5	18	20	240
SOI GROWTH								
Robyn	3	3	2	1	3	9	13	150
Melissa	4	7	7	4	3	22	13	150
Kari	6	1	2	2	2	11	9	100
Logan	2	3	1	2	1	8	4	48
Jessica	4	4	6	6	5	20	20	240
Adrianna	2	2	2	2	5	8	20	240
LISTING APPOINTMENTS SET								
Robyn	3	3	4	5	2	15	6	70
Kari	1	1	3	3	2	8	4	43
LISTING APPOINTMENTS HAD								
Robyn	3	3	2	4	2	12	6	70
Kari	0	1	1	3	1	5	4	43
LISTINGS SIGNED								
Robyn	2	3	2	0	2	7	6	63
Kari	0	1	0	1	1	2	4	38
BUYER APPOINTMENTS SET								
Robyn	2	2	6	2	1	12	4	46
Kari	1	3	2	1	2	7	7	75
Logan	4	2	3	2	1	11	4	48
BUYER APPOINTMENTS HAD								
Kari	2	1	2	2	1	7	3	34
Melissa	1	4	2	2	1	9	6	67
Logan	2	2	0	1	1	5	4	48
BUYER AGENCY AGREEMENTS SIGNED								
Melissa	0	4	3	2	1	8	5	50
Kari	1	1	2	2	1	6	3	25
Logan	2	2	0	1	1	5	3	30
CONTRACTS WRITTEN								
Kari	1	2	6	1	1	10	3	28
Melissa	1	3	3	0	1	8	5	56
ONLINE LEAD CONTACTS								
Logan	162	171	147	140	200	620	800	9600
Jessica	60	90	110	160	150	420	600	5400
RECRUITING APPOINTMENTS								
Robyn	3	1	3	0	1	7	4	50

SAMPLE SCOREBOARD

John Smith Real Estate Team DATE: March 15

TEAM DASHBOARD	MONTH	MONTHLY GOAL	YTD	ANNUAL GOAL	YTD LISTINGS CLOSED	YTD BUYERS CLOSED
Closed Units	8	11	20	130	11	9
Closed Volume	$4,506,876	$8,000	$10,850,455	$401 Million	$6,324,112	$4,526,343
Pending Units	6					
Pending Volume	$3,110,500					
Active Listing	12	9	< March			
Upcoming Listings	5					

WEEKLY LEAD GEN	LEADS & ATTEMPTS	CONTACTS	APTS	CONTRACTS	CONTACT GOAL	OPEN HOUSES	# ADDED TO DATABASE
Agent #1	156	86	2	2	80	0	5
Agent #2	123	65	1	0	50	2	10
Agent #3	188	95	3	2	100	1	12

YTD LEAD GEN	LEADS	CONTACTS	APTS	CONTACTS	YTD OPEN HOUSES	TOTAL IN DATABASE	DATABASE GOAL
Agent #1	1,560	516	22	21	3	950	1,100
Agent #2	738	390	13	6	9	124	250
Agent #3	1,128	570	35	19	6	275	450

AGENT LEAD MEASURES

AGENT PRODUCTION	ANNUAL UNITS GOAL	YTD CLOSED UNITS	BUYERS AGENCY PENDING	UNDER CONTRACT PENDING	# OF TEAM GENERATED CONTRACTS	# OF AGENT GENERATED CONTRACTS	YTD CLOSED GCI
Agent #1	55	12	0	2	2	12	$172,956
Agent #2	35	2	8	1	8	3	$11,240
Agent #3	40	6	12	3	11	10	$72,550

AGENT LAG MEASURES

LEAD SOURCING YTD	COI	FSBO	EXPIRED	JUST LISTED & SOLD	FARMING	OPEN HOUSES	VENDOR REFERRALS
Closed Units	12	3	0	0	2	2	1
Closed Volume	$7,910,430	$980,000	0	0	$835,200	$774,825	$350,000
Listings	6	3	0	0	1	0	1
Buyers	6	0	0	0	1	2	0

ACTIVE LISTINGS	JAN	FEB	MARCH	APRIL	MAY	JUNE
NEEDED EACH	8	15	20	20	25	25
MONTH TO REACH	JULY	AUG	SEPT	OCT	NOV	DEC
ANNUAL GOAL	30	25	20	15	15	15

CLOSED UNITS	JAN	FEB	MARCH	APRIL	MAY	JUNE
NEEDED EACH	5	7	9	11	14	19
MONTH TO REACH	JULY	AUG	SEPT	OCT	NOV	DEC
ANNUAL GOAL	18	15	12	8	7	5

One Day – 20 Contacts

Name: _____

Date: _____

	Type*	Name	Ask for Appt?	Appt?	Ask for Referral	Referral?	Follow Up/Notes
1.			☐ Y / ☐ N	☐	☐ Y / ☐ N	☐	
2.			☐ Y / ☐ N	☐	☐ Y / ☐ N	☐	
3.			☐ Y / ☐ N	☐	☐ Y / ☐ N	☐	
4.			☐ Y / ☐ N	☐	☐ Y / ☐ N	☐	
5.			☐ Y / ☐ N	☐	☐ Y / ☐ N	☐	
6.			☐ Y / ☐ N	☐	☐ Y / ☐ N	☐	
7.			☐ Y / ☐ N	☐	☐ Y / ☐ N	☐	
8.			☐ Y / ☐ N	☐	☐ Y / ☐ N	☐	
9.			☐ Y / ☐ N	☐	☐ Y / ☐ N	☐	
10.			☐ Y / ☐ N	☐	☐ Y / ☐ N	☐	
11.			☐ Y / ☐ N	☐	☐ Y / ☐ N	☐	
12.			☐ Y / ☐ N	☐	☐ Y / ☐ N	☐	
13.			☐ Y / ☐ N	☐	☐ Y / ☐ N	☐	
14.			☐ Y / ☐ N	☐	☐ Y / ☐ N	☐	
15.			☐ Y / ☐ N	☐	☐ Y / ☐ N	☐	
16.			☐ Y / ☐ N	☐	☐ Y / ☐ N	☐	
17.			☐ Y / ☐ N	☐	☐ Y / ☐ N	☐	
18.			☐ Y / ☐ N	☐	☐ Y / ☐ N	☐	
19.			☐ Y / ☐ N	☐	☐ Y / ☐ N	☐	
20.			☐ Y / ☐ N	☐	☐ Y / ☐ N	☐	

TOTALS: _____

*Type:
SOI, FSBO, Expired/Cancelled, Circle Prospecting, etc.

Total Contacts Made: _____

Total Appointments Made: _____

ICENHOWER COACHING & CONSULTING

Lead Tracking

Name: ______________________ Date: ______________

Type*	Name	Phone Number	Email	Address	Price Point	Bed/ Bath	Subdivision	Notes

Calls Made: FSBO: ________ EXPIRED: ________ CANCELLED: ________ CIRCLE: ________ SPHERE: ________

Contact Made: FSBO: ________ EXPIRED: ________ CANCELLED: ________ CIRCLE: ________ SPHERE: ________

Total Contacts Made: ________ **Total Appointments Made:** ________

ICENHOWER
COACHING & CONSULTING

ICC Year-to-Date
Check-Up Form

Client Name: Insert Client Name here

YEAR TO DATE NUMBERS	
Closed Units	42
Closed Volume	$10,072,334
Closed GCI	$312,536
Pending GCI	$63,820
Pending Volume	$2,099,000
Active Listings	5

BUYER / SELLER RATIO	
Percent of Buyers	40
Percent of Sellers	60

CLOSED LEAD SOURCES	
Sphere of Influence (SOI)	24
Expired Listings	7
Agent Referrals	3
Online	7
Open House/Sign/ Office	1

CLOSED LEAD SOURCES

- Spehere of Influence (SOI)
- Expired Listings
- Agent Referrals
- Online
- Ophen House/Sign/ Office

iC

ICC Year-to-Date
Check-Up Form

Client Name: Insert Client Name here

YEAR-TO-DATE NUMBERS		
Closed Units		42
Closed Volume		$10,072,334
Closed GCI		$312,536
Pending GCI		$63,820
Pending Volume		$2,099,000
Active Listings		5

BUYER / SELLER RATIO	
Percent of Buyers	40%
Percent of Sellers	60%

CLOSED LEAD SOURCES	
Sphere of Influence (SOI)	24
Expired Listings	7
Agent Referrals	3
Online	7
Open House/Sign/ Office	1

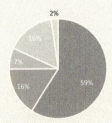

CLOSED LEAD SOURCES

- Spehere of Influence (SOI)
- Expired Listings
- Agent Referrals
- Online
- Ophen House/Sign/ Office

CHAPTER 4:

THE LISTING MANAGER: FROM LISTING TO CONTRACT

LEARNING OBJECTIVES

- Prepare your agent for listing consultations
- Create and customize a Pre-Listing Checklist
- Create and customize a Listing Checklist
- Put listings up for sale
- Manage and maintain active listings
- Assemble files and maintain them
- Organize research and documents
- Integrate communication loops in daily business
- Create a plan of action

I. LISTING FORMS AND CHECKLISTS: FILE PREPARATION AND MAINTENANCE

A. Your Property-File Folder
B. The Pre-Listing Checklist
C. The Listing Checklist
D. Essential Listing Forms and Tasks
1. Prequalification & Preapproval
2. Seller Lead Sheets
3. Pre-Listing Presentation
4. Listing Agreement
5. Seller's Disclosures
6. Comparative Market Analysis (CMA)
7. Seller Net Sheet
8. Property Profile
9. Older MLS Listings

II. CONTINUAL COMMUNICATION LOOPS

III. BE PREPARED AND ORGANIZED

IV. SAY THIS, NOT THAT

V. APPENDIX

LISTING FORMS & CHECKLISTS:
FILE PREPARATION AND MAINTENANCE

With the systems and procedures you have put in place as the Administrative Manager, you're now ready to get down to the business of real estate. You duties here will fall into two broad categories: Transaction Coordinator and Listing Manager, which is the focus of this chapter.

As the Listing Manager for your real estate office, you will support the agent in getting a property listed and taking it to the contract stage. Within this role, you will be responsible for the following tasks and activities:

- Overseeing all aspects of sellers' transactions from initial contact to executed purchase agreement.

- Preparing all listing materials: pre-listing presentation, listing agreement, sellers' disclosures, comparative market analysis, online property profiles, research old multiple listing service (MLS) listings, etc.

- Consulting & coordinating with sellers on property photos, staging, repairs, cleaning, signage, lockbox and access requirements, as well as marketing activities.

- Obtaining all necessary signatures on listing agreement, disclosures and other necessary documentation.

- Coordinating showings and obtaining feedback.

- Providing proactive weekly feedback to sellers regarding all showings and marketing activities.

- Coordinating all public open houses and broker open houses.

- Inputting all listing information into the MLS and marketing websites, and updating as needed.

- Submitting all necessary documentation to office broker for file compliance.

- Inputting all necessary information into client database and transaction management systems.

 As you read through the list, you likely noticed that many of these tasks are anticipatory in nature. You will assist in preparing everything necessary to list the sale and promote it. You'll also maintain performance documentation.

These duties help the real estate agent focus on what matters most: showing and selling houses. By having the files and pertinent documents ready to go, you will free your agent up to focus exclusively on securing the listing. For those of you who are solo agents, it is essential that you employ all of the task-analysis and time-blocking strategies we discussed in Chapter 2.

Chapter 4 shows you what you need to do to initiate the listing process. In this chapter, you will learn how to:

- Prepare your agent for listing consultations.
- Create and customize a Pre-Listing Checklist.
- Create and customize a Listing Checklist.
- Put listings up for sale.
- Manage and maintain active listings.
- Assemble files and maintain them.
- Organize research and various documents.
- Integrate communication loops in daily business.
- Create a plan of action.

YOUR PROPERTY-FILE FOLDER

Typically, all property-file documentation and information will be stored in an online shared-drive or similar software program that is also accessible to your agent(s).

Each folder will be labeled by property address. Each folder will also contain three checklists: the *Pre-Listing Checklist*, the *Listing Checklist*, and the *Closing Checklist*.

These three checklists will essentially serve as both to-do lists and a table of contents for the file documents that will eventually be placed in the folder.

The use of a shared (or "cloud") drive enables all members of the team to access a property folder's contents when needed.

THE PRE-LISTING CHECKLIST

The first of our checklists is the Pre-Listing Checklist.

This will be the first item that is placed in your property-file folder—typically when the agent sets a listing consultation to be conducted with the sellers of a home at some point in the near future.

The moment the agent sets the appointment to meet the sellers, all of the items contained on the Pre-Listing Checklist will need to be completed in order to (a) prepare the agent for the listing consultation and (b) to help ensure that the agent ultimately secures the listing by getting the listing agreement signed.

An example of a Pre-Listing Checklist is shown below. Remember to include this checklist in the Listing Manager section of your Business Operations manual.

After the listing agreement is signed by the sellers, you will then

Property Address: _____

Days Prior to Listing Appt	Date Completed	Description	Requested	Complete
3		Create new listing file with all forms & templates		
3		Schedule listing appointment in agent's calendar		
3		Locate & save old MLS listings for subject property		
2		Obtain property profile, assessments & taxes		
2		Call title & request legal description & deed		
2		Obtain parcel map & survey info		
2		Print agent's pre-listing presentation materials for consultation		
2		Prepare seller net sheet(s)		
2		Prepare CMA for agent's review		
2		Prepare map & directions to property		
2		Fill out & print seller's disclosures for listing consultation		
1		Prepare listing packet		
1		Fill out MLS input sheet w/ missing info still needed		
1		Input client into CRM database		
1		Pre-listing packet hand delivered to client		
1		Prelisting packet & video emailed to client		
0		If listing is NOT signed, schedule a follow-up call for agent		
0		If listing IS signed, start "Listing to Contract Checklist"		

move to the Listing Checklist and start taking the steps required to put the property up for sale and manage the active listing going forward.

THE LISTING CHECKLIST

As soon as the listing agreement has been signed by the seller(s), it is time to switch to the Listing Checklist. The first half of the checklist contains tasks needed to get a property ready to go up for sale, and the second half focuses on duties to market and manage the active listing.

Every home your agent lists will have a list of marketing activities, and you can stay on top of these with a checklist similar to the one ICC provides. This checklist also contains all of the previously mentioned items and documentation to ensure that each of them has been completed and are contained in the property-file folder.

Most homes will need similar marketing activities: photos, a property description, an MLS listing, social media updates, and more. Some of the houses may be presented in the form of an open house. In this case, you will need to schedule the open house with the sellers, prepare flyers and make sure that outside signs are ready, etc.

Property photo-shoots will also need to be scheduled. The seller may need to remove clutter and personal items, paint or clean the home, make repairs, address curb appeal issues, and more.

'For Sale' signs will need to be placed in the yard. Information about the home will need to be inputted into the MLS database and possibly in other online websites and locations.

Administrative assistants will be an important part of the process because you will coordinate and schedule the preparations as well as the marketing activities. It will also be your responsibility to continuously communicate with the sellers about buyer feedback, marketing activities, and MLS status changes of other homes that are listed and sold in the neighborhood.

An example of our very thorough Listing Checklist is shown below. For your convenience, there is also a copy of this checklist in the Appendix of this chapter. Before you include this checklist in the Listing Manager section of your Business Operations manual, you may wish to confer with your agent and modify this checklist if necessary. Remember that your operations manual should reflect your company's actual practices and procedures.

After all offers and/or counter-offers for the purchase of the property are accepted, we then move to the Closing Checklist which will be covered in detail in the next chapter.

Property Address: _____

Days After Listing Agmt	Date Completed	Description	Requested	Complete
0		Admin intro call to sellers - immediately after listing signed		
0		Receive signed listing agreement		
0		Did Agent ask for referrals at listing appointment?		
1		Schedule Open House(s) with Sellers/Agent		
1		Create property file and/or upload all pre-listing documents		
1		Obtain all signed & completed sellers disclosures		
1		Obtain showing instructions from agent/sellers		
1		Obtain seller mortgage statement or loan info		
1		Put seller on MLS listing auto-alert email drip for home(s) to buy		
1		Put seller on MLS listing auto-alert drip- MLS status changes in neighborhood		
1		Get seller pre-qualified for loan to purchase next home		
1		Order preliminary title report, HOA Documents & CCRs		
1		Call stager to schedule staging consultation		
1		Call photographer to schedule photo shoot		
1		Order & schedule yard sign		
1		Add sellers to admin weekly update call list		
1		Add sellers to agent's weekly update call list		
1		Enter listing into MLS as incomplete for agent to proof		
1		Assign lock box to MLS listing		
1		Add client to CRM database		
1		Add new listing to Team Scoreboard		
1		Turn listing contract/disclosures in to brokerage compliance		
2		Get MLS listing edits/approval from Agent		
2		Upload MLS Client Detail Report to property file		
2		Email MLS Client Detail Report to all team members		
2		Add/Enhance Listing on all other websites		
2		Add listing to broker tour/caravan		
2		Calendar Listing Expiration Date		
2		Prepare property flyer template (& Open House flyer)		
2		Create "Just Listed" Facebook & social media posts		
2		Obtain Neighbo...		
2		Get 2 sets of ke...		
2		"Just Listed" ma...		
2		"Open House" r...		
2		First Open Hous...		
2		Add clients as f...		
2		Order Seller Co...		
3		Claim listing on...		
4		Sign up at prop...		
4		Lockbox on at p...		
4		Flyers delivered...		

5		**LISTING GOES ACTIVE on MLS**		
5		Send Thank You/Gift Card to Person who Referred Listing		
5		Start agent prospecting calls around new listing		
5		"Just Listed" email to neighborhood & SOI		
5		"Just Listed" posted on Facebook & social media		
7		Email Activity Report to sellers		
7		Weekly Activity Report Call to sellers		
7		Agent ask for referrals on weekly call?		
8		Order "Open House" Mailers/Flyers for neighborhood		
8		"Open House" email to neighborhood & SOI		
8		"Open House" posted on Facebook & social media		
14		Email Activity Report to sellers		
14		Weekly Activity Report Call to sellers		
15		Schedule 2nd Open House?		
21		Email Activity Report to sellers		
21		Weekly Activity Report Call to sellers		
28		Email Activity Report to sellers		
28		Weekly Activity Report Call to sellers		
35		Email Activity Report to sellers		
35		Call to sellers for PRICE REDUCTION APPOINTMENT?		
42		Email Activity Report to sellers		
42		Weekly Activity Report Call to sellers		
49		Email Activity Report to sellers		
49		Weekly Activity Report Call to sellers		
56		Email Activity Report to sellers		
56		Weekly Activity Report Call to sellers		
63		Email Activity Report to sellers		
63		Weekly Activity Report Call to sellers		
70		Email Activity Report to sellers		
70		Call sellers for RE-LISTING APPOINTMENT? Price Reduction?		
		Once Offer(s) Received		
71		Prepare summary(s) of key offer terms to present to sellers		
71		Prepare net sheet(s) for offer(s) to present to sellers		
72		Draft response(s) to offers for sellers to sign- acceptance/counter offer		
72		Send counter offer (or acceptance) to buyer's agent		
		Once Offer Accepted - Start Seller Closing Checklist		

Essential Listing Forms and Tasks

The following are descriptions of some of the more important documents and tasks in both the Pre-Listing and Listing checklists.

Prequalification & Preapproval

Prequalification and preapproval are the first serious steps in the mortgage loan process. Buyers with a prequalification or preapproval letter tend to be more prepared and determined than buyers who are "just looking", and less likely, therefore, to waste the agent's time or, indeed, their own.

Sometimes, mortgage lenders use the terms 'prequalification' and 'preapproval' interchangeably but, generally speaking, prequalification differs from preapproval in the following way.

A prequalification is an *estimate* of how much a buyer *might* be eligible to borrow from a given lender. Generally, the buyer's financial information is self-reported and has not been verified by a mortgage underwriter, so a prequalification is very much an approximation.

A preapproval letter is, generally, a firmer commitment to lend a specific loan amount based on an in depth review and verification of the buyer's financial information  by a mortgage underwriter. A preapproval letter generally states that as long as nothing changes financially for the borrower/buyer, and as long as the property appraisal is successful, the lender will guarantee an interest rate and loan amount.

A preapproval letter gives potential buyers a distinct advantage in a competitive marketplace. A prequalification letter is the minimum document that any serious buyer should obtain as soon as possible.

Keep a copy of the prequalification or preapproval letter in the client folder.

Seller Lead Sheet

This is a form that your agent will fill out based upon questions and answers received from the prospective client, usually over the phone, prior to the in-person listing consultation appointment at the home.

This sheet provides important information about the seller's motivation, as well as property details, contact information and other details that can be useful throughout the transaction process, including the client's presumed DISC behavior.

An example Seller Lead Sheet is provided in the Appendix to this chapter.

Pre-Listing Presentation

A Pre-Listing Presentation answers some of the most commonly asked questions from sellers, including:

- How do I know you'll fairly assess the sales value of my home?
- What kind of photos will you provide?
- Can you help me sell my home quickly?
- What marketing strategies do you use?
- What experience do you have?
- Do you have any recommendations?

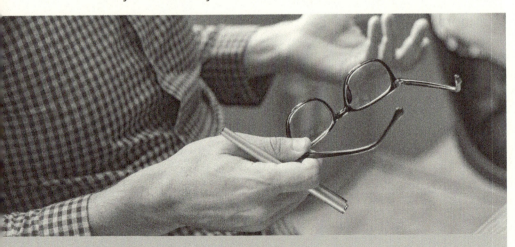

Having a Pre-Listing Presentation in place saves the agent's time when it comes to discussing a potential listing. Most of the basic questions have been answered in the presentation, and agents can focus on one thing: the price at which the house should be listed. This document is not only a time-saver; it's also a reassurance for potential clients.

Pre-Listing Presentations can also be given to potential clients who drop by the office. Or it can be delivered to potential home-sellers a day or two prior to the actual Listing Consultation appointment, either electronically in PDF format or by hand/mail to the home.

Savvy agents will have already created a Pre-Listing Presentation with answers to the questions that most sellers have. If a Pre-Listing Presentation is not already in place, make sure that this document is produced as soon as possible.

ICC will provide you with a sample Pre-Listing Presentation packet and help you to create one in Chapter 6 of this course. If your company has administrative support, this task can easily be delegated to the administrative assistant.

Administrative assistants should also ensure that Pre-Listing Presentations are printed in advance of the agent's meeting with their clients.

LISTING AGREEMENT

Real estate agents cannot represent an interested seller unless there is a Listing Agreement in place. The Listing Agreement is sometimes referred to as a contract. In essence, it is a legally binding document that authorizes the agent to list a property for sale and get paid a commission for doing so.

The multi-page document allows an agent to act on the seller's behalf in selling the property. Because it is a legal document, everything written in it must be accurate and true. In general, the Listing Agreement includes the listing price of the property, the duration of the agreement (i.e. the date upon which the contract expires), and any fees that the agent will charge.

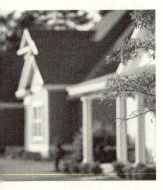

The suggested listing price is determined by researching neighborhood 'comps' or 'comparables'—recently-sold homes that are similar in size, condition, and location to the client's property—and completing a Comparative Market Analysis (CMA). Needless to say, solo agents must conduct this research themselves, but this task should absolutely be the responsibility of any administrative assistant.

The agreement will need signatures from the sellers and the agent, and it will have to be dated. The Listing Agreement goes in the seller's property-file folder.

SELLER'S DISCLOSURES

The Seller's Disclosure is a statement about the known condition of the sale property. Although it is considered anecdotal in nature, it is required for the sale of real estate in the United States.

The Seller's Disclosure identifies, or discloses, any potential problems with the home that the seller *knows about*, such as a broken air conditioner, seasonal flooding, a cracked foundation, or a history of termite eradication. The Seller's Disclosure does not replace an actual home inspection or property survey, and it will not validate warranties on equipment.

While many mortgage lenders do not require a home-inspection (as opposed to an appraisal which is a requirement), they can be required in certain geographic locations. Either way, most buyers choose to conduct one for their own protection, as the sellers might be unaware of problems in their home. Home inspections occur within a set period of time after the buyer's offer to purchase is accepted by the seller.

The Seller's Disclosure document goes in the seller's property-file folder.

COMPARATIVE MARKET ANALYSIS (CMA)

When a seller is ready to put their home up for sale, they want the most money they can get for their property, and rightly so. However, sellers are not always realistic about the true value of their home; they tend to overestimate what their home is actually worth, and determining a property's sale price can be an emotionally charged experience.

Conducting a Comparative Market Analysis (CMA) is an objective way to determine the value of a home.

The Comparative Market Analysis will include the prices of nearby homes (active listings), the prices of any neighboring homes that are under contract (pending listings), the purchase price of any properties that have been sold in the last 180 days, and any homes removed from the market.

The idea is to compare homes that are similar to each other. Look for homes that were built in the same year, that have similar square footage, and are in the same condition, etc.

Once you have compiled neighborhood 'comparables', your agent will be able to determine the fair market value of the property and suggest a listing price to the homeowner.

SELLER NET SHEET

The Seller Net Sheet is an itemized breakdown of all anticipated costs associated with selling the property, with an estimated amount of proceeds that the seller will receive from the sale quoted at the bottom. Note that this is only an estimate, as sales prices and other terms frequently change during contract negotiations later on.

However, a Seller Net Sheet helps to prevent big surprises and seller frustrations later on. Many agents prepare these with their own software programs, or have title and escrow companies provide them.

PROPERTY PROFILE

A Property Profile is another facet of the property listed for sale. Think of it as a financial check up.

County Appraisal Districts (CAD) offer a wealth of property information, including the history of the home from the time it was built to the present, including liens, judgments and taxes owed. You'll also find the legal description for the property, and it should match the property being sold.

Potential buyers realize that the purchase price of a home is just the beginning of their property expenses. The Property Profile may also include expenses for the operation of the property. This will include estimated insurance costs and projected utility expenses. A home with an elevator or a pool will include annual costs for maintenance that give the potential buyer an idea of what to expect financially.

Another important aspect of the Property Profile is determining who owns the property, because only the legal owner can sign sale documents.

Place the Property Profile in the seller's property-file folder.

Older MLS Listings

A quick online search can reveal if the property has any older MLS (Multiple Listing Service) listings if the property was previously listed for sale. These listings provide agents with valuable insights about property details and history prior to conducting the in-person listing consultation. Therefore, it is a useful practice to save copies of old MLS listing e-reports in the property-file folder for later use.

Continual Communication Loops

With this much going on, you can see the importance of communication and everything we taught you in the opening chapter. For those of you have been hired as administrative assistants, you and your agent need to stay in regular communication with each other.

However, creating a continual communication loop goes beyond the two of you. Once a seller agrees to list their property, they also become part of the communication loop, as do potential buyers, agents and other vendors.

With every showing of a home, you have an opportunity to gather feedback that can help sell a home. Do prospects complain about the smell of pets? If so, the carpets may need cleaning. Do they dislike the yellow walls in the kitchen? Paint can be a quick but dramatic fix. Is the lawn unkempt? Hire a gardening service.

One of the best places to gather feedback is during an open house. You'll have plenty of visitors willing to offer insights that you can act on for a quicker sale. You can also report the number of online views the property has received on the numerous websites where the property is advertised for sale on the Internet.

We recommend that administrative assistants proactively call the sellers of active listings once a week, on the same day and at the same time, to provide feedback from these marketing activities.

BE PREPARED AND ORGANIZED

Imagine a siren going off at a fire station when a house fire is reported. That's what it can feel like when an agent sets up a listing consultation appointment. Listing appointments are often scheduled unexpectedly, with only a few days to prepare in advance, so it's best to have your fire engine gassed up and your equipment ready to go.

In other words, now that you know what you need for listing a property, there is no reason why you can't be as prepared as possible beforehand. Preparation and organization is especially important for you solo agents who don't have the advantage of an administrative assistant.

Make sure you have several copies of your Pre-Listing Presentation packets printed in advance, along with copies of blank Listing Agreements for sellers to sign on the spot.

You should also have copies of the Seller Lead Sheet printed and ready to use at all times. This way, agents can call potential clients in advance of the listing appointment and quickly run through all the necessary, routine questions concerning the property and the seller's needs and motivations. A copy of our Seller Lead Sheet can be found at the end of this chapter for your review and use.

Create a property-file folder the minute you learn of the listing consultation appointment date and time. This way you can upload your Pre-Listing Checklist into the folder and start completing pre-listing tasks while uploading all pre-listing documents in the folder going forward.

Creating a file folder is only the beginning. You'll also need a calendar to coordinate all of the activity surrounding the listing, from getting the property ready to be shown to putting it under contract.

Whether you use a traditional calendar or a shared digital calendar, you need a system for identifying marketing activities. This will help you make sure you don't have overlapping activities. For those of you who are administrative assistants, we strongly recommend a digital calendar that is shared with your agent(s).

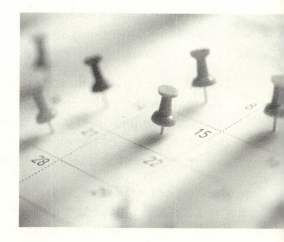

SAY THIS, NOT THAT

Prospective clients, sellers and buyers will have plenty of questions while you are working with them. It's only natural for a seller to question comparables or agonize over expenses in readying a house for the market. You'll even find that sellers will call you to vent about having to take the dogs to the park again while the house is being shown.

Naturally, you lucky solo agents will have to field every situation and scenario by yourself. Typically, however, an administrative assistant who is always in the office is the obvious and easiest person to answer client questions and take their calls.

As an Administrative Assistant, if you can answer questions like, "What time is the Open House?" you should certainly do so. Or if they want something straightforward such as a Presentation Profile, you can send it on the agent's behalf.

For questions that only your agent can answer, write down the information the caller is requesting, as well as their name and contact information. If your agent will be back in the office, place the note on top of the client folder so the agent has all of the information on hand when returning the call.

If the agent won't be back in the office, text a picture of the message, and leave the message on your desk until you can confirm that it has been addressed. Once the matter has been taken care of, document the call in your log and file the written documentation in the client folder.

There will be times you're tempted to say things you know you shouldn't. Instead of promising what you can't deliver, be honest about what you can and cannot do. Avoid sarcastic humor: not everyone gets it, and clients and potential customers may be offended, especially when you are still getting to know each other during the listing process.

Below are some examples of the best way to communicate with clients.

Say This	Not That
We'll do everything we can to remove the smell of smoke.	Yes, I guarantee we can make the smell go away.
I'll pass along the offer to the agent.	That's a crazy offer!
I'll have the documents ready for your signatures.	We'll sign the documents for you.
Getting an inspection may allay any fears about the home's quality.	You'll never have problems with this house.
We can take your request into consideration. I'll be sure the agent is aware of your request.	We can't do that.
Oh, the house at X location?	Oh, that house? The money pit?

You get the idea. Be honest and professional. Place yourself in the client's shoes and be the real estate company that you would want guiding you through one of the most expensive commitments of your life.

As you see clients go through the next part of the sales process, from contract to closing, you'll be glad that you were a vital part of an exciting process.

PRE-LISTING CHECKLIST

Property Address: _____

Days Prior to Listing Appt	Date Completed	Description	Requested	Complete
3		Create new listing file with all forms & templates		
3		Schedule listing appointment in agent's calendar		
3		Locate & save old MLS listings for subject property		
2		Obtain property profile, assessments & taxes		
2		Call title & request legal description & deed		
2		Obtain parcel map & survey info		
2		Print agent's pre-listing presentation materials for consultation		
2		Prepare seller net sheet(s)		
2		Prepare CMA for agent's review		
2		Prepare map & directions to property		
2		Fill out & print seller's disclosures for listing consultation		
1		Prepare listing packet		
1		Fill out MLS input sheet w/ missing info still needed		
1		Input client into CRM database		
1		Pre-listing packet hand delivered to client		
1		Prelisting packet & video emailed to client		
0		If listing is NOT signed, schedule a follow-up call for agent		
0		If listing IS signed, start "Listing to Contract Checklist"		

LISTING TO CONTRACT CHECKLIST

Property Address: _____

Days After Listing Agmt	Date Completed	Description	Requested	Complete
0		Admin intro call to sellers - immediately after listing signed		
0		Receive signed listing agreement		
0		Did Agent ask for referrals at listing appointment?		
1		Schedule Open House(s) with Sellers/Agent		
1		Create property file and/or upload all pre-listing documents		
1		Obtain all signed & completed sellers disclosures		
1		Obtain showing instructions from agent/sellers		
1		Obtain seller mortgage statement or loan info		
1		Put seller on MLS listing auto-alert email drip for home(s) to buy		
1		Put seller on MLS listing auto-alert drip- MLS status changes in neighborhood		
1		Get seller pre-qualified for loan to purchase next home		
1		Order preliminary title report, HOA Documents & CCRs		
1		Call stager to schedule staging consultation		
1		Call photographer to schedule photo shoot		
1		Order & schedule yard sign		
1		Add sellers to admin weekly update call list		
1		Add sellers to agent's weekly update call list		
1		Enter listing into MLS as incomplete for agent to proof		
1		Assign lock box to MLS listing		
1		Add client to CRM database		
1		Add new listing to Team Scoreboard		
1		Turn listing contract/disclosures in to brokerage compliance		
2		Get MLS listing edits/approval from Agent		
2		Upload MLS Client Detail Report to property file		
2		Email MLS Client Detail Report to all team members		
2		Add/Enhance Listing on all other websites		
2		Add listing to broker tour/caravan		
2		Calendar Listing Expiration Date		
2		Prepare property flyer template (& Open House flyer)		
2		Create "Just Listed" Facebook & social media posts		
2		Obtain Neighborhood Contact Information		
2		Get 2 sets of keys made - for lockbox & office		
2		"Just Listed" mailers/flyers created & ordered		
2		"Open House" mailers/flyers created		
2		First Open House day/time scheduled with sellers/agents?		
2		Add clients as friends on Facebook/Social Media		
2		Order Seller Coverage Warranty		
3		Claim listing on Zillow/Trulia & set up reporting		
4		Sign up at property		
4		Lockbox on at property		
4		Flyers delivered to property		

5		LISTING GOES ACTIVE on MLS		
5		Send Thank You/Gift Card to Person who Referred Listing		
5		Start agent prospecting calls around new listing		
5		"Just Listed" email to neighborhood & SOI		
5		"Just Listed" posted on Facebook & social media		
7		Email Activity Report to sellers		
7		Weekly Activity Report Call to sellers		
7		Agent ask for referrals on weekly call?		
8		Order "Open House" Mailers/Flyers for neighborhood		
8		"Open House" email to neighborhood & SOI		
8		"Open House" posted on Facebook & social media		
14		Email Activity Report to sellers		
14		Weekly Activity Report Call to sellers		
15		Schedule 2nd Open House?		
21		Email Activity Report to sellers		
21		Weekly Activity Report Call to sellers		
28		Email Activity Report to sellers		
28		Weekly Activity Report Call to sellers		
35		Email Activity Report to sellers		
35		Call to sellers for PRICE REDUCTION APPOINTMENT?		
42		Email Activity Report to sellers		
42		Weekly Activity Report Call to sellers		
49		Email Activity Report to sellers		
49		Weekly Activity Report Call to sellers		
56		Email Activity Report to sellers		
56		Weekly Activity Report Call to sellers		
63		Email Activity Report to sellers		
63		Weekly Activity Report Call to sellers		
70		Email Activity Report to sellers		
70		Call sellers for RE-LISTING APPOINTMENT? Price Reduction?		
		Once Offer(s) Received		
71		Prepare summary(s) of key offer terms to present to sellers		
71		Prepare net sheet(s) for offer(s) to present to sellers		
72		Draft response(s) to offers for sellers to sign- acceptance/counter offer		
72		Send counter offer (or acceptance) to buyer's agent		
		Once Offer Accepted - Start Seller Closing Checklist		

Seller Questionnaire & Lead Form

Date: _____

Name: _____ Spouse Name: _____

Property Address: _____ City: _____ State: _____ Zip: _____

Phone #s – Mobile: _____ Spouse Mobile: _____ Home: _____ Work: _____

Email: _____ Spouse Email: _____

Family / Children (include ages): _____

1. Have you spoken with any other agents? ☐ Yes ☐ No
2. Have you considered selling the home yourself? ☐ Yes ☐ No
3. Why do you want to move? _____
4. Do you know where you want to move to? _____
5. What date do you want to be moved by? _____
6. Are there any negatives to not moving by then? (suggest lifestyle sacrifices, job, costs, schools, family, etc.) _____

7. Tell me all the negatives of not moving at all? (same suggestions above) _____

8. Tell me all the benefits of buying a new home: (dig deep & find out WHY?) _____

9. On a scale of 1 to 10, how would you rank your motivation to move? With 10 being highly motivated: _____
10. When did you buy your home? _____ What price did you pay? _____
11. Do you know how much you still owe on it? _____
12. Have you made any major improvements to the home since? ☐ Yes ☐ No _____

13. Do you happen to have an idea as to what you think it's worth, or should sell for? _____
14. Do you have a price you won't sell your home below? _____
15. Tell me about the positive & negative features of your home: _____

16. How many BR: ____ Baths: _____ SqFt: _____ Stories: _____ Other: _____
17. How did you hear about me/us? _____
18. Are you interviewing any other agents? ☐ Yes ☐ No Who? _____ When? _____
19. "Thank you! The next step is for me to take a quick look at your home and I can answer any other questions you may have. Then you can decide what we do next. How does that sound?" (pause)
    "Great! Does 4:30 tomorrow or 5:00 Wednesday work for you?"

Appointment Date/Time: _____

DISC Behavioral Profile: _____ Why? _____

LEARNING OBJECTIVES

- Arrange and oversee purchase transactions
- Develop strategies that increase communication
- Organize deadline schedules
- Assemble follow up materials and documents

I. THE TRANSACTION COORDINATOR: FROM CONTRACT TO CLOSING

II. SELLER AND BUYER CLOSING CHECKLIST

A. Where to Store Closing Checklists
B. When to Complete Closing Checklists: Contingency Dates and Deadlines

III. KEY CONTRACT-TO-CLOSE TERMS AND TASKS

A. The Purchase Agreement
B. Title/Escrow
C. Mortgage Loan and Appraisal Processes
D. Inspections
E. Repair Negotiations
F. The Buyer Lead Sheet

IV. THE IMPORTANCE OF COMMUNICATION

A. Communicating With Your Agent
    1. Active and Pending Inventory Lists
    2. Shared Drives & CRM Systems
B. Communicating With the Buyer/Seller

V. KEEPING UP WITH CRITICAL DEADLINES

VI. CLOSING WITH CONFIDENCE

A. Scheduling Closing
B. Coordinating Moving Schedules
C. File Maintenance
D. 30-Day/90-Day Follow-Ups and Anniversary Date

VII. APPENDIX

The Transaction Coordinator: from Contract to Closing

As soon as a buyer makes an offer on a property and the home is under contract the real work begins.

The property that has just gone "under contract" (also known as "sale pending" or simply "pending") isn't quite sold yet. For the home to close, the seller and the buyer must meet every contingency required in the contract (also known as the "purchase agreement"). Your clients will need your help with removing these contract contingencies to close the transaction.

Depending on the housing market and the desirability and condition of the home, the listing may have been on the market for a few days or several weeks. Either way, the closing process will be the same. Once the purchase price and other major terms have been agreed upon and are outlined in writing, you'll be using your organizational skills to coordinate everything from inspections to the closing meeting.

Savvy administrators maintain communication with all stakeholders and keep everyone informed and up-to-date on any and all changes that occur throughout the process.

And, once the transaction is closed and the new owners have taken possession of the home, there will be plenty of follow-up work to do.

Whether you are an assistant or a solo agent, real estate administrators perform the following routine duties to take the transaction from contract to closing:

- Oversee all aspects of buyer & seller transactions from executed purchase agreement to closing.

- Coordinate title/escrow, mortgage loan, and appraisal processes.

- Coordinate inspections, assist in negotiations regarding repairs, and coordinate completion of repairs.

- Regularly update & maintain communication with clients, agents, title officer, lender, etc.

- Submit all necessary documentation to office broker for file compliance.

- Coordinate moving/possession schedules.

- Schedule, coordinate & attend closing process.

- Input all client information into client database system.

- Schedule 30 Day, 90 Day & 120 Day customer-service follow-up calls to assist with any home-improvement provider recommendations and to ask for testimonials/ referrals.

Your performance as the Transaction Coordinator can help the process go smoothly for everyone, and ICC has the checklists and tools you need to stay organized and on top of it all. By taking over the coordination duties, you are freeing your agent up to generate more sales.

Chapter 5 will help you understand each step of the closing process, and you'll also learn strategies to sharpen your organizational and communication skills. In this chapter, you will learn how to:

- Arrange and oversee purchase transactions.
- Develop strategies that increase communication.
- Organize deadline schedules.
- Assemble follow-up materials and documents.
- Create and customize seller and buyer closing checklists.

SELLER AND BUYER CLOSING CHECKLISTS

The first step in successfully closing a home sale involves knowing what actions, approvals, inspections, and reports must be completed. The second step is in knowing when they must take place. Finally, you must follow up and verify that they have happened, so you will need to organize and maintain all documentation of the transaction and any follow-ups.

To help manage all of the steps and actions that you are responsible for completing, you will need to implement various Closing Checklists for each property transaction you oversee.

When your client is the party that listed their property for sale, you will use a Seller Closing Checklist. When your client is the party purchasing a property, you will use a Buyer Closing Checklist.

You might even use both checklists at once if you reside in a state or province that permits dual agency and you represent both the buyer and the seller in the same transaction. It is important to have and use two different checklists for sellers and buyers since there are different tasks and responsibilities required depending on which side of the transaction you're on.

WHERE TO STORE CLOSING CHECKLISTS

Much like your Pre-Listing and Listing Checklists, your Closing Checklists should be digital so that it can be placed in your property file folder upon initiation of the transaction. From there your checklist can be used like a table of contents for you to regularly update while overseeing the process. When the property-file  folder is kept on an online shared, or "cloud" drive, all other agents and members of your team can be permitted access to the file and checklist to stay up-to-date on the progress of the transaction.

WHEN TO COMPLETE CLOSING CHECKLISTS: CONTINGENCY DATES AND DEADLINES

Your Closing Checklists should be implemented immediately upon an offer or counter-offer being accepted by one of the parties. Upon acceptance, we now have a legally binding contract for the purchase and sale of the property. Ownership of the property will formally transfer from the seller to the buyer at closing, after all of the contingencies of the sale are satisfied by each of the parties to the transaction.

Many of these contingencies must simply be completed by the closing date. For example, the buyer must provide monetary 'funds to close' before the closing date, whether via a loan or cash. A seller must typically transfer 'clear title' without any liens or encumbrances against the property (i.e. unpaid taxes or loans) prior to the close date mandated in the purchase agreement.

However, many contingencies must be removed at specified times prior to the closing date. Typically, these include seller-disclosures, inspection(s), appraisal, and loan contingencies. As Transaction Coordinator, it is crucial that you note all contingency expiration and removal dates on your calendar.

All Closing Checklists should clearly highlight key contingency deadline dates, along with all of the necessary property inspections required by the contract and/or buyer to close the sale. For this reason, the first step you must take is to *thoroughly examine the purchase agreement* to extract all contingency deadlines and note them on the Closing Checklist.

Examples of both our Seller Closing Checklist and our Buyer Closing Checklist are shown below. We have also attached large versions of these checklists at the end of this chapter for your future use in creating your own versions.

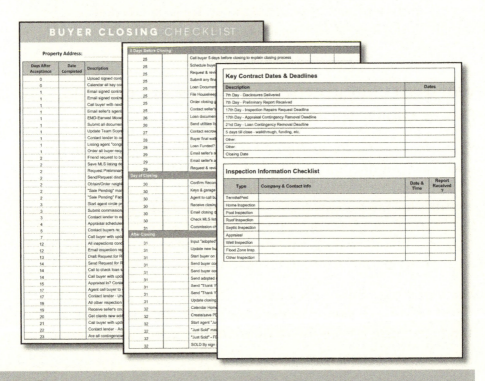

As you review each checklist, you will see that they are organized somewhat chronologically and hierarchically. When the contract is initially accepted, there are dozens of tasks to complete in the following days and weeks. Five days before closing, you will complete all of the tasks and activities in that section of the checklist as you prepare for the all-important day of closing.

However, you will also see that your duties do not end at that point. Each checklist contains a list of important 'after closing' follow-up tasks that you will need to complete.

The Key Contract Dates & Deadlines and Inspection Information Checklists are shown at the bottom of each checklist.

Please also note that Contract-To-Close processes and dates vary dramatically in different geographic locations. Some areas use escrow companies, title companies or attorneys to administer and close transactions. Different locations also require different inspections and report: some call for earthquake disclosures, others require radon testing, while others customarily perform roof inspections, etc. Consequently, administrative assistants should make sure to work with your agent to edit and customize these checklists before using them as your templates moving forward.

KEY CONTRACT-TO-CLOSE TERMS AND TASKS

The following are some of the more important items, terms, and tasks involved in the contract to closing process.

THE PURCHASE AGREEMENT

Arguably the most critical document in the purchase transaction, the executed Purchase Agreement initiates the purchase of the property. This contract stipulates that the seller has agreed to transfer the property and any rights to it for a specified price, and the buyer has agreed to pay that price. However, price is not the only negotiable term in a purchase agreement. The parties might also negotiate the amount of the buyer's initial deposit, how closing costs are paid, the closing date, and any number of other deal points.

Once both parties have signed the document, it is a legal and binding agreement.

Depending on the contract your agent uses, there will likely be multiple pages requiring the initials of each party, their signatures and the date of the sale. When you receive the contract, you'll need to go through each page, verifying that it is complete and that everything has been attended to.

A completed contract will include these considerations:

- **Legal Property Description:** The property must be clearly and legally identified on the contract.

- **Names:** The agreement will contain the full legal names of the buyers and sellers; make sure they are spelled correctly.

- **Purchase Price & Payment Method:** The purchase price is written on the contract, and so are other specific terms to which the seller and buyer have agreed. The terms may include everything from who may be paying points and other closing costs or whether the swing-set and refrigerator convey with the house. Additionally, the buyer will put up an initial earnest money deposit to show commitment; earnest money is 'held' by an attorney or an escrow officer, not the real estate agent.

- **Inspection, Survey, Warranty:** An inspection will tell a prospective homebuyer if repairs need to be made, and which party makes those repairs may become part of the negotiation process in the purchase of the home. As previously stated, a buyer may wish to conduct any number or types of inspections on the property. The survey confirms property lines and alerts the buyer to possible infringements. In addition, there may be a warranty plan purchased for appliances, air conditioning, and other potentially expensive systems. Usually the buyer pays for these services.

- **Contingency Deadlines:** All deadline dates for loan, appraisal, inspections, disclosures etc. must be noted on the closing checklist, and calendared.

- **Closing Date & Possession:** The contract will indicate the final date of sale and when the property officially belongs to the new owners (typically right after the closing meeting), at which point they can take possession of the house. Sometimes, however, if both parties are in agreement, the date of possession occurs after the closing date, and the seller pays rent to the new owner for a specified period of time.

If any of these items are wanting from the contract, confer with your agent about securing them.

Clients may ask you if it's a good idea to have their attorney read over the contract. Purchasing a home is a binding and significant expense. It's always a good idea to allow clients the opportunity to have an attorney look over the terms of a contract, and the buyer and the seller are usually allowed a predetermined amount of time for the review.

TITLE/ESCROW

The title of a property will not be conveyed to the buyer until all contractual obligations are met. Even when the buyer places earnest money in escrow, the sale is not final. There is usually a period during which the buyer can cancel the contract if the inspection points to repairs that neither party is willing to correct.

A property is 'in escrow' when a third-party such as the title company, lender or attorney holds the earnest money from the buyer. The escrow serves as a deposit, and it is held by a neutral party.

As the transaction coordinator, your responsibilities include making sure that the earnest money gets deposited and accounted for by that third-party person. Although you may sometimes have to take the deposit to the company for depositing and obtain a receipt for your client, it is always advisable to encourage your clients to deliver funds to the neutral closing company themselves. This avoids triggering real estate licensing authority trust-fund handling regulations.

MORTGAGE LOAN AND APPRAISAL PROCESSES

Although some buyers may pay cash for a property, the vast majority of buyers will need to obtain a mortgage loan from a lender to pay the agreed-upon purchase price in the contract. Most lenders require that an appraisal of the property be completed to ensure that there is enough equity in the home to serve as security, or collateral, for the loan amount being borrowed.

Although cash-buyers aren't required to conduct or pay for an appraisal, some still elect to do so anyway, just to ensure they aren't overpaying for the property.

If the appraisal report reveals that the appraised value of the home is far below the agreed-upon purchase price, the lender will likely lend only the amount for which the property appraised. The buyer will have to renegotiate the contract or pay a more substantial deposit in cash to purchase the home.

As the transaction coordinator, you will be coordinating the appraisals and making sure that everyone gets the copies they need.

INSPECTIONS

Some states require home inspections before a real estate sale can be completed. It is always a good idea to advise buyers to obtain a general home inspection, and any other inspections that are customary in your local area.

You can rely on your real estate contacts to select a home inspector; you'll likely know several inspectors and have their contact information on file because of your agent's networking.

You will help to coordinate the home inspection. This inspection must be done by a licensed inspector who will provide the buyer with a detailed report of findings in the home.

REPAIR NEGOTIATIONS

The information gathered from property inspection reports may affect the purchase price and subsequent negotiations. For example, if the roof needs repair, the seller may be willing to make the necessary repairs or reduce the purchase price so the buyer can make the repair. If the foundation is cracked, the buyer may decide to walk away from the sale. If the decision to cancel the sale occurs within a specific amount of time, the earnest money may be returned to the buyer.

It's critical that you help clients stay on top of deadlines, or they may lose a significant amount of money. Good calendaring and communication is key.

THE BUYER LEAD SHEET

If your agent represented the buyer in the purchase of the property, your agent should have used a Buyer Lead Sheet to ask a variety of important questions regarding their best contact information, motivation, and needs in a home. Although this sheet is typically used prior to even looking for a home to buy, it contains important information about your client that will help you coordinate the transaction on their behalf. Therefore, it should be uploaded to the property-file folder for future use. We have also provided our copy of a Buyer Lead Sheet for your agents use at the end of this chapter.

THE IMPORTANCE OF COMMUNICATION

Every chapter has stressed the importance of communication, but nowhere is it more important than taking a transaction from contract to closing.

The seller who is hoping the contract will close is, naturally, very anxious. So too is the buyer, who likely is preparing to commit a significant portion of money to the home. Even your agent will be a little anxious about the sale. Everyone wants the sale to go through, but they are also aware that it might not.

It's easy to fret over what's happening—or not happening—during the process, but you can help to alleviate everyone's concerns by staying in touch with them and remembering the importance of communication.

COMMUNICATING WITH YOUR AGENT

You and your agent will develop a communication system for sending updates regarding a property that is under contract, but these properties should also be discussed in your daily and weekly communication meetings.

For example, you'll need to tell the agent when the home inspection will take place or what the closing date is. The agent will also want to know about any hiccups along the way. Informing the agent of possible challenges that may prevent the sale from going through will give him or her the time necessary to intervene. For example, explaining that a termite infestation does not necessarily mean the home is unsalvageable can save the sale.

Of course, the real estate agent might not be in the office often enough for you to provide regular updates about clients and prospects. Some agents prefer reviewing updates at the end of the day or early the next morning before you get to the office.

You can also communicate with your agent through the use of Inventory Lists, Shared Drives, and your Customer Relationship Management (CRM) system.

ACTIVE AND PENDING INVENTORY LISTS

At any given time, you will have multiple properties in various stages of the overall transaction. Inventory Lists help you to keep track of, and communicate, the details and listing-status of each property and/or client.

Inventory Lists are also important communication tools that help you to identify leads that your agent needs to nurture and follow up with.

As you can see, a *Listing Inventory* includes client information and property details in the following categories:

- Active Listings
- Listing Agreement Signed & Waiting to Go Active
- Listing Leads—No Listing Agreement Signed Yet

LISTING INVENTORY

Active Listings

	Client	Buyer too?	Address	City, Zip	Agent	Source	List Price	List Date	DOM	LA Expires	Today
1	Mark Fisher	Yes	1701 S. Crumall St.	Visalia 93292	Robyn	Robyn SOI	$159,900.00	11/14/17	235	11/14/18	7/7/2018
2	Steve Enstein	Yes	143 Carmelita St.	Pville 93257	Kari	Kari SOI	$329,000.00	11/17/17	232	6/4/18	7/7/2018
3	Dan & Karen Halloway	Maybe	2067 Linda Vista Ave.	Pville 93257	Kari	Open House	$495,000.00	2/26/18	131	6/26/18	7/7/2018
4	Marla Focha	No	1104 S Whitney	Visalia 93277	Robyn	Agent Referral	$225,000.00	3/13/2018	116	6/6/18	7/7/2018
5	Matt Kelly	Yes	763 Park Place Ct	Exeter 93221	Robyn	Robyn SOI	$514,900.00	3/16/2018	113	5/9/18	7/7/2018
6	Ricardo Mora & Sylvia Lopez	No	896 E San Joaquin	Tulare 93274	Kari	Website	$210,000.00	3/22/18	107	9/18/18	7/7/2018
7	Brian and Kara Martinez	Yes	1955 W Walt Ave	Pville 93257	Kari	Kari SOI	$208,900.00	3/28/2018	101	9/21/2018	7/7/2018

Listing Agreement Signed & Waiting to Go Active

	Client	Buyer too?	Address	City, Zip	Agent	Source	LA Signed	LA Expires	Notes
1	Hayley Tashjian	Yes	216 N. Orange Ave.	Exeter 93221	Robyn	Melissa SOI	3/25/18	3/24/15	Active on 4/15
2	April Black	No	2726 W. Caldwell Ave.	Visalia 93277	Kari	Kari SOI	1/31/18	12/31/18	Active on 4/26
3	Barbara (Heather Saddler)	Yes	3529 W. Howard	Visalia 93277	Robyn	Robyn SOI	3/5/2018	9/4/18	Waiting for yard rennovation
4	Miguel Sanchez	Yes	39 Brook Street	Visalia 93291	Robyn	Rob PC Ref	3/15/2018	12/31/18	Active on 5/1

Listing Leads - No Listing Agreement Signed Yet

	Client	Buyer too?	Address	City, Zip	Agent	Source	Status
1	Andrew Serna	Yes	704 Sheffield Ave.	Exeter 93221	Robyn	Rob SOI Ref	Still can not make contact to reschedule
2	Thomas and Sherry Ferreira	Yes	1704 Cotton Ct.	Visalia 93291	Robyn	Website Lead	Still deciding between us and Uncle who is an agent
3	David & Lindsay Johnson	Yes	2822 W. Border Links	Ivanhoe 93292	Kari	Open House	Still remodeling bathroom. Ready to list when done
4	Susan and Terry Matheman	Yes	15016 Avenue 312	Visalia 93291	Robyn	Robyn SOI	Waiting for summer school break.
5	Bill and Marina Meek	No	5837 W. Stewart Ave.	Visalia 93291	Robyn	Farm	May/June
6	Terra Walker	Maybe	1802 Mammoth Circle	Tulare 93274	Robyn	Zillow Lead	Canceled/Reschedule
7	Jerry Davis	No	24006 Road 224	Lindsay 93247	Kari	Open House	Waiting on tenants to vacate
8	Jerry Davis	No	1825 E Fir St	Lindsay 93247	Kari	Open House	Waiting on tenants to vacate
9	Miguel and Crystal Sanchez	Maybe	2823 W Brooke Ave	Visalia 93291	Robyn	Robyn SOI	Sellers unsure if moving forward at this point
10	Rafael and Sylvia Arzate	Yes	3613 E. Harvard Ct.	Visalia 93292	Robyn	Robyn SOI	early to mid May
11	Albert Limon	Yes	1032 E. Academy Ave.	Tulare 93274	Robyn	Website Lead	Dead for now. Waiting till next year or so
12	Brad Vickers	No	4106 S. Bridge St.	Visalia 93277	Robyn	Robyn SOI	Canceled & rescheduled for 4/15
13	Daniel Snead	No	3145 W. Ashland Ave.	Visalia 93277	Kari	Kari SOI	May 3rd appointment

The *Buyer Inventory* is divided into two sections:

- Buyers that have signed exclusive Buyer Agency Agreements (BAA) with your agent(s)
- Active Buyer Leads that have not signed a BAA but are actively looking for a property

As you can see, *Buyer Inventory* lists also include an at-a-glance 'status' column. This clearly communicates which clients are actively looking at properties, which clients have cancelled appointments and need to be rescheduled, and other pertinent information for both you and the agent.

BUYER INVENTORY

Buyer Agency Agreements (BAA) Signed

	Client	Agent	Pre-Qualified/Lender	City/Area	Source	Price Target	BAA Signed	BAA Expires	Status
1	Mark Fisher	Melissa	Yes- HomePlus Mortgage	NW/SW Visalia	Robyn SOI	$400,000	11/14/17	11/14/18	Actively looking
2	Steve Ensslin	Melissa	No- HomePlus trying to contact	Visalia	Melissa SOI	$550,000	11/17/17	6/4/18	Shown 15 homes. Actively looking
3	Dan & Karen Holloway	Kari	Yes- CC Mortgage	Springville	Open House	$495,000	2/26/18	6/26/18	Actively looking
4	Maria Focha	Melissa	Yes- CC Mortgage	NE Tulare	Agent Referral	$225,000	3/13/2018	6/8/18	Looking for 2 acre lot
5	Matt Kelly	Jessica	Yes- HomePlus Mortgage	Exeter	Robyn SOI	$514,900	3/16/2018	5/9/18	Still can not make contact to reschedule
6	Ricardo Mora & Sylvia Lopez	Kari	No- Trying to connect w/ CC Mortgage	NW Visalia	Website	$210,000	3/22/18	9/18/18	Still deciding between us & agent Uncle
7	Brian and Kara Martinez	Melissa	Cash	Visalia	Malissa SOI	$208,000	3/28/2018	9/21/18	Still remodeling bathroom. List when done
8	Ron & Linda Watts	Melissa	Yes- CC Mortgage	Tulare	Website	$350,000	2/26/18	2/25/19	Waiting for summer school break.
9	Don Evans	Kari	Yes- CC Mortgage	W Visalia	Kari SOI	$425,000	3/13/2018	3/12/19	May/June
10	James & Maggie Wilson	Melissa	Yes- CC Mortgage	Visalia	Website	$310,000	3/16/2018	3/15/19	Canceled/Reschedule
11	Debra Mattoon	Melissa	Yes- CC Mortgage	Tulare	Robyn SOI	$475,000	3/22/18	10/21/18	Waiting on tenants to vacate
12	Dan & Abbie Johnson	Kari	Cash	Visalia	Robyn SOI	$850,000	3/28/2018	3/27/19	Waiting on tenants to vacate
13	Jerry Washington	Melissa	Yes- Valley Credit Union	Visalia	Website	$500,000	2/26/18	2/25/19	Sellers unsure if moving forward at this point
14	Jim & Cindy Stephens	Jessica	Yes- HomePlus Mortgage	Porterville	Open House	$285,000	3/13/2018	3/12/19	early to mid May
15	Sarah Watson	Logan	No - Trying to connect w/ HomesPlus	Visalia	Website	$350,000	11/14/17	11/13/19	Dead for now. Wating till next year or so
16	Maggie Henderson	Tasha	Yes- HomePlus Mortgage	SW Visalia	Website	$500,000	11/17/17	11/16/18	Canceled & rescheduled for 4/15
17	Jessica Tulane	Melissa	Yes- HomePlus Mortgage	W Visalia	Open House	$285,000	2/26/18	2/25/19	May 3rd appointment
18	Mike & Angela Fountain	Melissa	Yes- CC Mortgage	Three Rivers	Melissa SOI	$350,000	3/13/2018	3/12/19	Actively looking
19	Terry Wilkenson	Jessica	No - appointment w/ CC mortgage set	Visalia	Website	$425,000	3/16/2018	3/15/19	Meeting Lender this week
20	Brandon Ames	Kari	Yes- CC Mortgage	NW Visalia	Robyn SOI	$400,000	3/22/18	3/21/19	Actively looking

Totals - BAA Signed & Active	
Melissa	10
Kari	5
Jessica	3
Logan	1
Tasha	1
TOTAL	20

Active Buyer Leads - No BAA Signed, But Actively Looking

	Client	Agent	Pre-Qualified/Lender	City/Area	Source	Price Target	Status
1	Andrew Serna	Melissa	No	Exeter	Rob SOI Ref	$375,000	Still can not make contact to reschedule
2	Thomas and Sherry Ferreira	Kari	No	Porterville	Website Lead	$425,000	Still deciding between us and Uncle who is an agent
3	David & Lindsay Johnson	Melissa	Yes- HomePlus Mortgage	NW/SW Visalia	Open House	$400,000	Still remodeling bathroom. Ready to list when done
4	Susan and Terry Maltman	Melissa	No- HomePlus trying to contact	Visalia	Robyn SOI	$550,000	Waiting for summer school break.
5	Bill and Marina Meek	Kari	Yes- CC Mortgage	Springville	Fam	$495,000	May/June
6	Terra Walker	Melissa	Yes- CC Mortgage	NE Tulare	Zillow Lead	$225,000	Canceled/Reschedule
7	Jerry Davis	Jessica	No	Exeter	Open House	$514,900	Waiting on tenants to vacate
8	Jerry Davis	Kari	Yes- Cousin is a lender	NW Visalia	Open House	$210,000	Waiting on tenants to vacate
9	Miguel and Crystal Sanchez	Melissa	No	Visalia	Robyn SOI	$208,000	Sellers unsure if moving forward at this point
10	Rafael and Sylvia Arzate	Jessica	Yes- CC Mortgage	Visalia	Robyn SOI	$425,000	early to mid May
11	Albert Limon	Tasha	No	Tulare	Website Lead	$310,000	Dead for now. Wating till next year or so
12	Brad Vickers	Logan	Yes- HomePlus Mortgage	Visalia	Robyn SOI	$475,000	Canceled & rescheduled for 4/15
13	Daniel Snead	Melissa	No	Visalia	Kari SOI	$850,000	May 3rd appointment
14	Christine Akers	Kari	Cash	Porterville	Website	$500,000	Sellers unsure if moving forward at this point
15	Neil & Paula Brockmeier	Jessica	No	Visalia	Website	$285,000	early to mid May
16	Jake & Winsome Ullman	Logan	No	SW Visalia	Website	$350,000	Dead for now. Wating till next year or so
17	Dan & Debie Cote	Jessica	Yes- CC Mortgage	W Visalia	Website	$425,000	Canceled & rescheduled for 4/15
18	Julian Werts	Kari	Yes- CC Mortgage	Three Rivers	Kari SOI	$400,000	May 3rd appointment
19	Tom & Christy Blue	Melissa	No	Exeter	Open House	$650,000	Actively looking
20	Ryan Atkinson	Jessica	Cash	Visalia	Jessica SOI	$550,000	Meeting Lender this week

Similarly, a *Pending Inventory Pipeline* is simply a list of all of your transactions that are currently pending and under contract. We have also provided blank copies of these two lists for your future use at the end of this chapter.

PENDING INVENTORY PIPELINE

	Client	B or S	Address	City, Zip	Agent	Source	Price	Open	Close Date	Total GCI	Notes
1	William and Erica Pine	Buyer	1600 Palm Dr.	Exeter 93221	Melissa	Melissa SOI	$500,000	12/21/18	4/19/18	$13,500	
2	Luis Guerrero	Buyer	2148 W. Union Ave.	Porterville 93257	Melissa	Website	$255,000	1/9/18	4/11/18	$5,558	
3	Chris and Crystal Smith	Buyer	14663 Avenue 344	Visalia 93292	Melissa	Robyn SOI	$685,000	2/12/18	4/12/18	$12,813	
4	Carly Heinzen-Woods	Seller	813 W. Reese Ct.	Visalia 93277	Robyn	Robyn PC	$224,900	2/15/18	4/13/18	$6,900	Ray Jones (Uncle) 949-555-1243
5	Jennifer De Mascio	Buyer	813 W. Reese Ct.	Visalia 93277	Melissa	Robyn PC	$350,000	2/15/18	4/13/18	$6,900	
6	Henry Hash	Seller	644 W. Loyola Ave.	Visalia 93277	Kari/Robyn	Kari Expired	$249,700	2/22/18	3/23/18	$6,250	
7	Henrique Guerreiro	Seller	1000 Belmont	Porterville 93257	Robyn	Robyn SOI	$205,000	2/23/18	4/9/18	$6,150	
8	Jessica De Mascio	Seller	1025 Princeton Ave.	Visalia 93277	Robyn	Robyn SOI	$219,900	3/1/18	4/13/18	$6,810	
9	Gary Garret	Seller	1331 Laura Ct.	Visalia 93292	Kari	Kari FARM	$389,000	3/15/18	5/21/18	$6,900	Also buying
10	Gary Garret	Buyer	381 S Beverly	Porterville 93257	Kari	Kari FARM	$310,000	3/21/18	5/1/18	$5,125	Also listing/selling
11	Florence Ann Webster	Seller	2400 W Midvalley	Visalia 93277	Kari	Kari PC	$885,500	9/21/18	12/31/19	$14,000	
12	Daniel Snead	Seller	3145 W Ashland	Visalia 93277	Kari	Open House	$249,000	9/22/18	12/31/19	$7,100	
13	Donnie Brandon	Seller	401 N. Powell	Visalia 93291	Robyn	Robyn SOI	$814,900	3/13/18	12/31/19	$16,200	
14	Scott and Kirsten Hyder	Buyer	131 W Putnam	Porterville 93257	Kari	Kari PC	$750,000	3/27/18	5/21/18	$18,400	
15	Samuel Velasquez	Buyer	893 San Ramon	Visalia 93292	Melissa	Website	$350,000	3/28/18	4/26/18	$8,900	Melissa's cousin
16	David & Mel Johnson	Seller	2822 Border Links	Visalia 93291	Robyn	Robyn SOI	$750,000	2/25/18	4/16/18	$14,750	
17	Kimmy Berkley	Seller	236 Feemster Ct	Visalia 93277	Robyn	Open House	$550,000	2/29/18	4/13/18	$9,550	
18	John & Dani Kale	Buyer	145 Beverly Glen	Visalia 93277	Kari	Website	$350,000	3/1/18	4/1/18	$7,525	
19	Mark & Donna Griffel	Seller	856 N. Fairway	Visalia 93291	Robyn	Robyn SOI	$655,500	3/5/18	4/25/18	$11,500	
20	Omar & Katie Vaz	Seller	435 Keogh Dr.	Visalia 93291	Robyn	Website	$450,000	2/15/18	4/6/18	$7,000	
21	Katherine Florentine	Buyer	231 Park Place	Porterville 93257	Kari	Kari SOI	$350,000	3/13/18	5/12/18	$6,250	
21	Larry Burke	Buyer	259 Hyde Way	Tulare 93234	Melissa	Melissa SOI	$250,000	3/18/18	5/2/18	$6,800	Tenant's occupying property
22	Larry Burke	Buyer	1342 Ames Ct.	Exeter 93221	Melissa	Melissa SOI	$259,000	3/26/18	5/14/18	$7,450	

SHARED DRIVES & CRM SYSTEMS

You and your agent can also connect with each other by taking advantage of available technology, like a cloud drive that the two of you share. A shared drive makes it possible to communicate—and access—client and property information anywhere, anytime, and from any device.

You can also implement a shared document program or a Customer Relationship Management (CRM) system. Shared document programs and CRMs help you identify, track and monitor every interaction with your customers.

If you choose a CRM for your client data management, your software should be: (1) uniform across all platforms, (2) keep client data secure, and (3) be easy to use. Speak with your ICC coach for up-to-date information about the best transaction management CRM's for your particular use.

It's possible to use free shared document programs, too, but you will have to customize your spreadsheets. Use the following charts as starting points for finding the system that works best for your office:

BEST FREE SPREADSHEET PROGRAMS AND ONLINE STORAGE SYSTEMS

Program	Benefits	Drawbacks
Google Sheets (Google Drive)	• 15 GB free • Larger storage plan available • Scans stored instantly (PDFs) • Download an app for offline use	• Reliance on Internet connection (unless you have the app).
Microsoft Excel (One Drive)	• 5 GB free • Seamless use with Microsoft Office • Link social media networks • OneDrive for Business encrypts individual files	• Files encrypted in transit only. Syncing may alter files.
Apple Numbers (iCloud)	• 5 GB free • Can locate missing devices	• IOS compatible only
Dropbox	• 2 GB free • Possibility of adding 16GB • Deleted files can be retrieved for up to 30 days	• Use your own spreadsheet
Box	• 10 GB free	• Use your own spreadsheet
Amazon Drive	• 5GB	• Use your own spreadsheet

You and your real estate agent should make it part of your daily routines to log in to the CRM or shared documents to check for updates. One of the best features of using shared storage is that the users on the account will receive an instant email notification whenever a document is modified. That email serves as a reminder to check in.

While we're on the subject of free shared storage, you've probably thought of storing photos on your shared drive. After all, you have quite a few of them. The following chart explores the benefits and drawbacks of three of the most popular online storage systems for photos.

BEST FREE ONLINE STORAGE SYSTEMS FOR PHOTOS

Program	Benefits	Drawbacks
Google Photos (Google Drive)	• Ease of use	• Monthly fees for additional storage
Amazon Drive	• Unlimited for Prime members	• Unable to download multiple images at once • Incompatible with macOS photos without iOS Amazon Photo app
Flickr	• 1TB free • Easy sharing • Easy searching • Easy interfacing	

The best communication takes place face-to-face, but sharing updates in person isn't always possible or practical. You can't remember every detail about every property or every buyer and seller.

Storing your Active Listings and Pending Contracts lists on a shared improves communication and collaboration.

COMMUNICATING WITH THE BUYER/SELLER

As anxious as the buyer is to obtain the property, the seller is often eager to see the sale to close because they may have another property already in mind to purchase and move into.

If your agent represents the sellers, you'll need to keep them aware of important dates, such as when the home inspection will take place. They will want to know that everything is progressing as it should. You can follow up with them by phone, and if you have dates or other critical information, your agent may want you to send a follow-up email like this:

Dear Bob and Jane,

It was great speaking with you on the phone. I could sense how overwhelming the sale must be so, as promised, I'm sending you these dates to put on your calendar:

- *April 6: 10:00 AM   Home inspection*

- *March 3: 2:15 AM   Tentative closing at Apex Title Company*

If these dates change, we will let you know, but I will also check in with you by phone.

Best regards,

If your agent is representing the buyer, you follow up may look like this:

> *Dear Rob and Laine,*
>
> *I could tell how excited you are about purchasing your new home, and we want to make sure you have these dates on your calendar:*
>
> - *April 6: 10:00 AM Home inspection (reports to follow)*
>
> - *March 3: 2:15 AM Tentative closing at Apex Title Company*
>
> *We'll keep you posted on any changes, and you can count on me being in touch again soon.*
>
> *Best regards,*

When communicating with clients, remember that email cannot and does not build rapport with clients. Real estate is a people business, and to connect with people, you must talk to them on the phone and in person. Email serves only as a written reminder of what was discussed. Keep the paragraphs short and use lists or bullets where possible.

Always CC your agent on every email. It is critical to keep your agent current on all communications and occurrences in case your clients reach out to the agent directly, or your agent feels the need to weigh in on a particular matter.

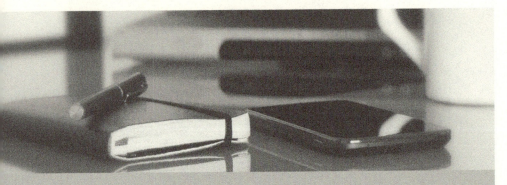

Keeping Up With Critical Deadlines

At this point, you may feel as though you're juggling quite a few balls at one time. You are!

To keep these balls in motion, you must have a system to track each step of the process. That means utilizing a calendar-system to remember the important steps and deadlines listed in your Closing Checklists. Although most real estate teams simply  use free or inexpensive shared calendars like Google Calendar or Apple Calendar, there are a number of other CRMs and shared programs that are also available. Again, please speak with your ICC coach to find out about the latest systems best suited for your particular needs.

Closing with Confidence

If you've been using your Seller and Buyer Closing Checklist for the property sale, you have been methodically ticking off each item on the page, noting progress and date of completion. Now that you're nearing the bottom of the page, you should feel good in knowing that you are helping families realize their goals.

You can close with confidence.

Scheduling Closing

As noted on our sample closing checklists, there are many items to address in the five days leading up to the closing date, and on the closing date itself. The most crucial steps involve the final signing of loan documents and deeds by both the buyer and the sellers.

A closing meeting can take place in a variety of ways, but usually the title company initiates the meeting and offers dates and times based on their availability.

The buyer and seller may arrive at the meeting and sit at the same table or in separate rooms to sign the documents, or they may come in at separate times. If one party lives far away, the process may be done electronically or with a mobile notary.

Your job is to ensure everyone has the correct date and time of the closing meeting, as well as the correct address. Verify that everyone involved in the meeting knows how to get there—not everyone uses GPS to travel. Going to the wrong title company or address allows frustrations to mount quickly during an already stressful time.

Always understand that moving residences is very stressful; now couple that with the purchase or sale of what is typically their largest asset and liability at the same time. Any scheduling mistake at this time can cause severe frustration.

No sale is complete until all monies are transferred and deeds are recorded, but you will have already assisted with the moving schedules for the buyer and seller before the day of closing.

Coordinating Moving Schedules

Find out when the sellers plan to vacate the home.

Before the buyers move in, the seller should be out entirely. There may be a period for painting and other repairs before the buyers move in, but they can take possession of their new home once the money is transferred.

Oftentimes, the exact time of day that keys must be provided and the buyers can take possession is expressly written in the purchase agreement.

Avoid having buyers and sellers schedule their moves on the same day. It will be an emotional day for both parties, and having two moving vans will add to the upheaval.

File Maintenance

With the closing finished and the sale complete, you may be tempted to close out the file folder and move on to your next transaction. The property may have been sold, but you'll still have a few things to take care of.

On your Closing Checklist you will note that there are several items to complete in the few days after closing. These precious few days happen to offer some of the best opportunities for marketing and lead-generation activities to generate more business for your agent. So it is critical to complete all necessary post-closing steps before moving on to the next file.

First of all, check that everything in the folder matches the checklist at the front. Store the client folder with the other completed transaction folders for seven years.

30-Day/90-Day Follow-Ups and Anniversary Date

After you've completed your post-closing items and closed out the file, you should have already calendared to return to this transaction a few more times. On every transaction, you have 30-Day and 90-Day follow-ups and an anniversary date call to conduct.

The best way to conduct these follow-ups is by phone. Understand that the timelines for these follow-up phone calls may vary from agent to agent. Some agents will call a week later, 30 days later, and then again 6 months later. Some call every month for 4 months, and some call quarterly every 3 months.

At 30 days, call to see that all is well with your client. Ask how they thought the transaction went. If your client is the buyer, ask how they are finding their new home. If your client is the seller, ask about their satisfaction with the sale process. You can ask if everything is going well with their home and if they are planning on making any improvements to it. Either way, you can offer to have any of your preferred vendors provide bids to help them out.

When 90 days have passed, call again to see how your clients are doing and if your company can be of any service to them. This also provides another opportunity to ask for positive online reviews, a client testimonial for future use in your agents marketing materials, or possibly even a referral.

It is also common practice to call past clients on the anniversary date of the closing of their home a year later to wish them a "Happy Anniversary". At this point, you might also ask them about the house, offer preferred vendors to help with repairs and improvements, or ask for referrals, online reviews, or client testimonials as well.

Regardless of your particular message, the simple act of checking in a year later is something very few agents do, and it sets your team apart. It shows that your customer-service does not stop at closing, and that you didn't just disappear with your commission check. It helps solidify an ongoing relationship that will bring more business and referrals.

Please note that we cover many of the techniques and scripts for making post-closing contacts to past clients in our next chapter about the *Marketing Director* job duties.

Document each of these contacts on your checklist or in your CRM. Each time you contact them, make a note of it, detailing the date you spoke as well as writing down any concerns that were mentioned and how you followed up with them (by phone/mailer etc.).

With that, you're ready to tackle the next sale, taking it through the process of contract to closing.

SELLER CLOSING CHECKLIST

Property Address: _____

Days After Acceptance	Date Completed	Description	Requested	Complete
0		Upload signed contract, forms & contact info to property file		
0		Calendar all key contract dates & deadlines - see below		
1		Email signed contract & contact info to lender, title & buyers agent		
1		Email signed contract to seller w/ title contact info & next steps		
1		Call seller with next steps, key dates/deadlines & inspection info		
1		All utilities are on, and to be left on?		
1		Change MLS status to pending		
1		Sale pending rider on sign at property		
1		EMD-Earnest Money Deposit received & deposited/logged		
1		Request Preliminary Title Report		
1		Obtain/Order neighborhood contact information for mailers/calls		
1		Submit all documents/forms to broker compliance		
1		Update Team Scoreboard		
1		Listing agent "congratulations" call to seller - ask for referrals		
2		Order all selller-required inspections - see inspection checklist below		
2		Order Home Warranty (if applicable)		
2		Order Natural Hazard Disclosure (if applicable)		
2		Friend request to buyers on Facebook & social media		
2		Send/Request disclosures to/from buyer's agent		
2		"Sale Pending" mailer/flyers to neighborhood ordered		
2		"Sale Pending" Facebook & social media posts		
3		Start agent circle prospecting "sale pending" calls/door knocking		
3		Confirm Earnest Money Deposit (EMD) is deposited		
3		Submit commission disbursement/disbursement authorization		
3		Contact buyer's lender to ensure all docs recvd (tax info, pay stubs, etc)		
3		Has appraisal been ordered? Contact buyer's agent/lender		
7		Call seller with update - what's been done & next steps		
14		Call to check loan status with lender		
14		Call seller with update - what's been done & next steps		
15		Request for inspection repairs received? Remind buyer's agent		
15		Appraisal In? Contact buyer's agent/lender		
17		Home inspection repair request received? Respond to Request?		
17		Appraisal contingency removed?		
17		Agent call seller to congratulate on property appraising		
18		Contact lender - File submitted to underwriter? Still needed?		
19		Request loan contingency removal from buyer's agent		
19		All other inspection reports received? See below		
20		Get clients new address & update SOI database in CRM		
21		Loan contingency removed?		
21		Call seller with update - what's been done & next steps		
22		Contact lender - Underwriter approval? Any conditions?		
23		Are all contingencies of the sale removed? Still needed?		

5 Days Before Closing				
25		Call seller 5 days before closing to explain closing process		
25		Have staging furniture removed		
25		Schedule buyer's final walkthrough inspection		
25		Schedule seller's to sign at closing		
25		Request & review estimated closing statement		
25		Submit any final invoices to to escrow/title/attorney		
25		Loan Documents in and signed by Buyers?		
25		File Housekeeping - contact other agent to ensure file is complete		
25		Order closing gift for sellers		
25		Contact sellers to get utilities list		
26		Signed loan documents sent to lender for loan funding?		
26		Send utilities list to buyer's agent to switch names at close date		
27		Contact escrow/title/attorney - Still needed to close (buyer funds up?)		
28		Buyer walkthrough inspection conducted?		
28		Loan Funded? Has escrow/title/attorney received funds to close?		
29		Request & review final estimated closing statement		
Day of Closing				
30		Confirm Recording		
30		Keys delivered		
30		Agent to call seller w/ "congratulations" - ask for referrals		
30		Receive closing documents from escrow/title/attorney (upload to file)		
30		Change MLS status to "Sold" on MLS		
30		Change Zillow Status to "Sold"		
31		Commission check(s) received/deposited		
30		For sale sign removed from property		
30		Lockbox removed from property		
After Closing				
31		Input "adopted" buyer contact information into CRM database		
31		Update new seller notes in SOI database w/ new address		
31		Start seller on past client email/mailer drip campaign		
31		Send seller congratulations email w/ online review request links		
31		Send seller congratulations letter		
31		Send adopted buyer congratulations letter		
31		Send "Thank You Colleague" letter to co-op agent		
31		Send "Thank You" letter to lender		
31		Update closing on team scoreboard		
32		Calendar Home Anniversary & 30/90 day agent calls (referrals)		
32		Create/save PDFs of all file documents & emails		
32		Start agent "Just Sold" calls to neighborhood		
32		"Just Sold" mailers/flyers to neighborhood & SOI		
32		"Just Sold" - FB & other social media posts		

Key Contract Dates & Deadlines

Description	Dates
7th Day - Disclosures Delivered	
7th Day - Preliminary Report Received	
15th Day - Inspection Repairs Request Received?	
17th Day - Inspection Contingencies Removal Deadline	
17th Day - Appraisal Contingency Removal Deadline	
21st Day - Loan Contingency Removal Deadline	
5 days till close - walkthrough, funding, etc.	
Other:	
Other:	
Closing Date	

Inspection Information Checklist

Type	Company & Contact Info	Date & Time	Report Received?
Termite/Pest			
Home Inspection			
Pool Inspection			
Roof Inspection			
Septic Inspection			
Appraisal			
Well Inspection			
Flood Zone Insp.			
Other Inspection			

BUYER CLOSING CHECKLIST

Property Address: _____

Days After Acceptance	Date Completed	Description	Requested	Received
0		Upload signed contract, forms & contact info to property file		
0		Calendar all key contract dates & deadlines - see below		
1		Email signed contract & contact info to lender, title & sellers agent		
1		Email signed contract to buyer w/ title contact info & next steps		
1		Call buyer with next steps, key dates/deadlines & inspection info		
1		Email seller's agent - all utilities to be left on for inspections		
1		EMD-Earnest Money Deposit delivered		
1		Submit all documents/forms to broker compliance		
1		Update Team Scoreboard		
1		Contact lender to order appraisal		
1		Listing agent "congratulations" call to buyer - ask for referrals		
1		Order all buyer-required inspections - see inspection checklist below		
2		Friend request to buyers on Facebook & social media		
2		Save MLS listing detail as PDF & upload to property file		
2		Request Preliminary Title Report		
2		Send/Request disclosures to/from seller's agent		
2		Obtain/Order neighborhood contact information for mailers/calls		
2		"Sale Pending" mailer/flyers to neighborhood ordered		
2		"Sale Pending" Facebook & social media posts		
3		Start agent circle prospecting "sale pending" calls/door knocking		
3		Submit commission disbursement/disbursement authorization		
3		Contact lender to ensure all buyer docs recvd (tax info, pay stubs, etc)		
4		Appraisal scheduled? Contact lender.		
5		Contact buyers re: help w/ home insurance? (preferred vendors)		
7		Call buyer with update - what's been done & next steps		
12		All inspections conducted & reports received (see list below)		
12		Email inspection reports to buyer & call to go over them		
13		Draft Request for Repairs form		
14		Send Request for Repairs form to seller's agent		
14		Call to check loan status with lender. Still needed from buyer?		
14		Call buyer with update - what's been done & next steps		
15		Appraisal In? Contact Lender		
17		Agent call buyer to congratulate on property appraising		
17		Contact lender - Underwriter approval before loan contingency date		
19		All other inspection reports received? See below		
19		Receive seller's counter to buyer request for repairs?		
20		Get clients new address & update SOI database in CRM		
21		Call buyer with update - what's been done & next steps		
22		Contact lender - Any underwriting conditions? Loan docs when?		
23		Are all contingencies of the sale removed? Still needed?		

5 Days Before Closing				
25		Call buyer 5 days before closing to explain closing process		
25		Schedule buyer's final walkthrough inspection		
25		Request & review estimated closing statement		
25		Submit any final invoices to escrow/title/attorney		
25		Loan Documents in? Schedule buyers to sign & funds to bring		
25		File Housekeeping - contact other agent to ensure file is complete		
25		Order closing gift for buyers		
25		Contact seller's agent to get utilities list		
26		Loan documents signed & sent to lender for loan funding?		
26		Send utilities list to buyers to switch names at close date		
27		Contact escrow/title/attorney - Still needed to close (buyer funds up?)		
28		Buyer final walkthrough inspection conducted?		
28		Loan Funded? Has escrow/title/attorney received funds to close?		
29		Email seller's agent to coordinate keys & garage door controllers		
29		Email seller's agent to ensure proper MLS credit for buyer-side		
29		Request & review final estimated closing statement		
Day of Closing				
30		Confirm Recording		
30		Keys & garage door controllers received by buyers		
30		Agent to call buyer w/ "congratulations" - ask for referrals		
30		Receive closing documents from escrow/title/attorney (upload to file)		
30		Email closing documents w/ congratulations email to buyers		
30		Check MLS listing to ensure buyer-side credit for sale		
31		Commission check(s) received/deposited		
After Closing				
31		Input "adopted" seller contact information into CRM database		
31		Update new buyer notes in SOI database w/ new address		
31		Start buyer on past client email/mailer drip campaign		
31		Send buyer congratulations letter w/ closing statement for taxes		
31		Send buyer congratulations email w/ online review request links		
31		Send adopted seller congratulations letter		
31		Send "Thank You Colleague" letter to co-op agent		
31		Send "Thank You" letter to lender		
31		Update closing on team scoreboard		
32		Calendar Home Anniversary & 30/90 day agent calls (referrals)		
32		Create/save PDFs of all file documents & emails		
32		Start agent "Just Sold" calls to neighborhood		
32		"Just Sold" mailers/flyers to neighborhood & SOI		
32		"Just Sold" - FB & other social media posts		
32		SOLD By sign in yard for 2 weeks		

Key Contract Dates & Deadlines

Description	Dates
7th Day - Disclosures Delivered	
7th Day - Preliminary Report Received	
17th Day - Inspection Repairs Request Deadline	
17th Day - Appraisal Contingency Removal Deadline	
21st Day - Loan Contingency Removal Deadline	
5 days till close - walkthrough, funding, etc.	
Other:	
Other:	
Closing Date	

Inspection Information Checklist

Type	Company & Contact Info	Date & Time	Report Received ?
Termite/Pest			
Home Inspection			
Pool Inspection			
Roof Inspection			
Septic Inspection			
Appraisal			
Well Inspection			
Flood Zone Insp.			
Other Inspection			

ICENHOWER
COACHING & CONSULTING

Buyer Questionnaire & Lead Sheet

Date: _____ Lead Source: _____

Name: _____ Spouse Name: _____

Property Address: _____ City: _____ State: _____ Zip: _____

Phone #s – Mobile: _____ Spouse Mobile: _____ Home: _____ Work: _____

Email: _____ Spouse Email: _____

Family / Children (include ages): _____

1. Have any other agents shown you homes? ☐ Yes ☐ No
   If Yes, do you have a signed agency agreement? ☐ Yes ☐ No
2. Is anyone buying the home with you? _____
3. Are you renting, or do you own a home? ☐ Homeowner ☐ Renter
   a) HOMEOWNER:
      • Do you need to sell your home before you buy? ☐ Yes ☐ No
      • Have you signed a listing agreement to sell your home? ☐ Yes ☐ No   If "No" use Seller Lead Sheet.
   b) RENTER:
      • When does your lease end? _____
4. What date do you want to be moved by? _____
5. Are there any negatives to not moving by then? (suggest lifestyle sacrifices, job, costs, schools, family, etc.)
   _____
6. Tell me all the benefits of buying a new home: (dig deep & find out WHY?)
   _____
7. On a scale of 1 to 10, how would you rank your motivation to move? With 10 meaning you
   must buy as quickly as possible, and 1 meaning you're not sure you'll really buy anything: _____
      • What's missing? What would it take to make you a 10? _____
8. Do you know where you want to move to? _____
9. Will you be paying cash or getting a mortgage? ☐ Cash ☐ Mortgage
10. Have you been pre-approved by a lender? ☐ Yes ☐ No
11. How much will your down payment be? _____
12. What price range are you looking in? _____
13. How many BR: _____ Baths: _____ SqFt: _____ Stories: _____ Other: _____
14. What else are you looking for in a home? _____
15. Will anyone else be involved in your home buying decision? _____
16. "Thank you! I'd love to help you find your perfect home. All that we need to do is to set an appointment so that I
    can help you find the home you're looking for. Does 4:30 tomorrow or 5:00 Wednesday work for you?"

Appointment Date/Time: _____

DISC Behavioral Profile: _____ Why? _____

LISTING INVENTORY

Active Listings

	Client	Buyer too?	Address	City, Zip	Agent	Source	List Price	List Date	DOM	LA Expires	Today
1	Mark Fisher	Yes	1701 S. Crumal St.	Visalia 93292	Robyn	Robyn SOI	$159,900.00	11/14/17	235	11/14/18	7/7/2018
2	Steve Ensslin	Yes	143 Carmelita St.	Pville 93257	Kari	Kari SOI	$329,000.00	11/17/17	232	6/4/18	7/7/2018
3	Dan & Karen Holloway	Maybe	2067 Linda Vista Ave.	Pville 93257	Kari	Open House	$495,000.00	2/26/18	131	6/26/18	7/7/2018
4	Maria Focha	No	1104 S Whitney	Visalia 93277	Robyn	Agent Referral	$225,000.00	3/13/2018	116	6/8/18	7/7/2018
5	Matt Kelly	Yes	763 Park Place Ct	Exeter 93221	Robyn	Robyn SOI	$514,900.00	3/16/2018	113	5/9/18	7/7/2018
6	Ricardo Mora & Sylvia Lopez	No	996 E San Joaquin	Tulare 93274	Kari	Website	$210,000.00	3/22/18	107	9/18/18	7/7/2018
7	Brian and Kara Martinez	Yes	1955 W Wall Ave	Pville 93257	Kari	Kari SOI	$208,000.00	3/28/2018	101	9/21/2018	7/7/2018

Listing Agreement Signed & Waiting to Go Active

	Client	Buyer too?	Address	City, Zip	Agent	Source	LA Signed	LA Expires	Notes
1	Hayley Tashjian	Yes	216 N. Orange Ave.	Exeter 93221	Robyn	Melissa SOI	3/25/18	3/24/19	Active on 4/15
2	April Black	No	2720 W. Caldwell Ave.	Visalia 93277	Kari	Kari SOI	1/31/18	12/31/18	Active on 4/26
3	Barbara (Heaher Saddler)	Yes	3529 W. Howard	Visalia 93277	Robyn	Robyn SOI	3/5/2018	9/4/18	Waiting for yard rennovation
4	Miguel Sanchez	Yes	39 Brook Street	Visalia 93291	Robyn	Rob PC Ref	3/15/2018	12/31/18	Active on 5/1

Listing Leads - No Listing Agreement Signed Yet

	Client	Buyer too?	Address	City, Zip	Agent	Source	Status
1	Andrew Serna	Yes	794 Sheffield Ave.	Exeter 93221	Robyn	Rob SOI Ref	Still can not make contact to reschedule
2	Thomas and Sherry Ferreira	Yes	1704 Cotton Ct.	Visalia 93277	Robyn	Website Lead	Still deciding between us and Uncle who is an agent
3	David & Lindsay Johnson	Yes	2822 W. Border Links	Ivanhoe 93292	Kari	Open House	Still remodeling bathroom. Ready to list when done
4	Susan and Terry Malhman	Yes	15016 Avenue 312	Visalia 93291	Robyn	Robyn SOI	Waiting for summer school break.
5	Bill and Marina Meek	No	5837 W. Stewart Ave.	Visalia 93291	Robyn	Farm	May/June
6	Terra Walker	Maybe	1802 Marroneto Circle	Tulare 93274	Robyn	Zillow Lead	Canceled/Reschedule
7	Jerry Davis	No	24006 Road 224	Lindsay 93247	Kari	Open House	Waiting on tenants to vacate
8	Jerry Davis	No	1825 E Fir St	Lindsay 93247	Kari	Open House	Waiting on tenants to vacate
9	Miguel and Crystal Sanchez	Maybe	2823 W Brooke Ave	Visalia 93291	Robyn	Robyn SOI	Sellers unsure if moving forward at this point
10	Rafael and Sylvia Arzate	No	3613 E. Harvard Ct.	Visalia 93292	Robyn	Robyn SOI	early to mid May
11	Albert Limon	Yes	1032 E. Academy Ave.	Tulare 93274	Robyn	Website Lead	Dead for now. Wating till next year or so
12	Brad Vickers	No	4106 S. Bridge St.	Visalia 93277	Robyn	Robyn SOI	Canceled & rescheduled for 4/15
13	Daniel Snead	No	3145 W. Ashland Ave.	Visalia 93277	Kari	Kari SOI	May 3rd appointment

BUYER INVENTORY

Buyer Agency Agreements (BAA) Signed

	Client	Agent	Pre-Qualified/Lender	City/Area	Source	Price Target	BAA Signed	BAA Expires	Status
1	Mark Fisher	Melissa	Yes- HomePlus Mortgage	NW/SW Visalia	Robyn SOI	$400,000	11/14/17	11/14/18	Actively looking
2	Steve Enaslin	Melissa	No- HomePlus trying to contact	Visalia	Melissa SOI	$550,000	11/17/17	6/4/18	Shown 15 homes. Actively looking
3	Dan & Karen Holloway	Kari	Yes- CC Mortgage	Springville	Open House	$495,000	2/26/18	6/26/18	Actively looking
4	Maria Focha	Melissa	Yes- CC Mortgage	NE Tulare	Agent Referral	$225,000	3/13/2018	6/8/18	Looking for 2 acre lot
5	Matt Kelly	Jessica	Yes- HomePlus Mortgage	Exeter	Robyn SOI	$514,900	3/16/2018	5/9/18	Still can not make contact to reschedule
6	Ricardo Mora & Sylvia Lopez	Kari	No- Trying to connect w/ CC Mortgage	NW Visalia	Website	$210,000	3/22/18	9/16/18	Still deciding between us & agent Uncle
7	Brian and Kara Martinez	Melissa	Cash	Visalia	Melissa SOI	$208,000	3/28/2018	9/21/18	Still remodeling bathroom. List when done
8	Ron & Linda Watts	Melissa	Yes- CC Mortgage	Tulare	Website	$350,000	2/26/18	2/25/19	Waiting for summer school break
9	Don Evans	Kari	Yes- CC Mortgage	W Visalia	Kari SOI	$425,000	3/13/2018	3/12/19	May/June
10	James & Maggie Wilson	Melissa	Yes- CC Mortgage	Visalia	Website	$310,000	3/16/2018	3/15/19	Canceled/Reschedule
11	Debra Mattoon	Melissa	Yes- CC Mortgage	Tulare	Robyn SOI	$475,000	3/22/18	10/21/18	Waiting on tenants to vacate
12	Dan & Abbie Johnson	Kari	Cash	Visalia	Robyn SOI	$850,000	3/28/2018	3/27/19	Waiting on tenants to vacate
13	Jerry Washington	Melissa	Yes- Valley Credit Union	Visalia	Website	$500,000	2/26/18	2/25/19	Sellers unsure if moving forward at this point
14	Jim & Cindy Stephens	Jessica	Yes- HomePlus Mortgage	Porterville	Open House	$285,000	3/13/2018	3/12/19	early to mid May
15	Sarah Watson	Logan	No - Trying to connect w/ HomesPlus	Visalia	Website	$350,000	11/14/17	11/13/19	Dead for now. Wating till next year or so
16	Maggie Henderson	Tasha	Yes- HomePlus Mortgage	SW Visalia	Website	$500,000	11/17/17	11/16/18	Canceled & rescheduled for 4/15
17	Jessica Tulane	Melissa	Yes- HomePlus Mortgage	W Visalia	Open House	$285,000	2/26/18	2/25/19	May 3rd appointment
18	Mike & Angela Fountain	Melissa	Yes- CC Mortgage	Three Rivers	Melissa SOI	$350,000	3/13/2018	3/12/19	Actively looking
19	Terry Wilkenson	Jessica	No - appointment w/ CC mortgage set	Visalia	Website	$425,000	3/16/2018	3/15/19	Meeting Lender this week
20	Brandon Ames	Kari	Yes- CC Mortgage	NW Visalia	Robyn SOI	$400,000	3/22/18	3/21/19	Actively looking

Totals - BAA Signed & Active	
Melissa	10
Kari	5
Jessica	3
Logan	1
Tasha	1
TOTAL	20

Active Buyer Leads - No BAA Signed, But Actively Looking

	Client	Agent	Pre-Qualified/Lender	City/Area	Source	Price Target	Status
1	Andrew Serna	Melissa	No	Exeter	Rob SOI Ref	$375,000	Still can not make contact to reschedule
2	Thomas and Sherry Ferreira	Kari	No	Porterville	Website Lead	$425,000	Still deciding between us and Uncle who is an agent
3	David & Lindsay Johnson	Melissa	Yes- HomePlus Mortgage	NW/SW Visalia	Open House	$400,000	Still remodeling bathroom. Ready to list when done
4	Susan and Terry Mahlman	Melissa	No- HomePlus trying to contact	Visalia	Robyn SOI	$550,000	Waiting for summer school break.
5	Bill and Marina Meek	Kari	Yes- CC Mortgage	Springville	Farm	$495,000	May/June
6	Terra Walker	Melissa	Yes- CC Mortgage	NE Tulare	Zillow Lead	$225,000	Canceled/Reschedule
7	Jerry Davis	Jessica	No	Exeter	Open House	$514,900	Waiting on tenants to vacate
8	Jerry Davis	Kari	Yes- Cousin is a lender	NW Visalia	Open House	$210,000	Waiting on tenants to vacate
9	Miguel and Crystal Sanchez	Melissa	No	Visalia	Robyn SOI	$208,000	Sellers unsure if moving forward at this point
10	Rafael and Sylvia Arzate	Jessica	Yes- CC Mortgage	Visalia	Robyn SOI	$425,000	early to mid May
11	Albert Limon	Tasha	No	Tulare	Website Lead	$310,000	Dead for now. Wating till next year or so
12	Brad Vickers	Logan	Yes- HomePlus Mortgage	Visalia	Robyn SOI	$475,000	Canceled & rescheduled for 4/15
13	Daniel Snead	Melissa	No	Visalia	Kari SOI	$850,000	May 3rd appointment
14	Christine Akers	Kari	Cash	Porterville	Website	$500,000	Sellers unsure if moving forward at this point
15	Neil & Paula Brockmeier	Jessica	No	Visalia	Website	$285,000	early to mid May
16	Jake & Winsome Ullman	Logan	No	SW Visalia	Website	$350,000	Dead for now. Wating till next year or so
17	Dan & Deble Cote	Jessica	Yes- CC Mortgage	W Visalia	Website	$425,000	Canceled & rescheduled for 4/15
18	Julian Werts	Kari	Yes- CC Mortgage	Three Rivers	Kari SOI	$400,000	May 3rd appointment
19	Tom & Christy Blue	Melissa	No	Exeter	Open House	$650,000	Actively looking
20	Ryan Atkinson	Jessica	Cash	Visalia	Jessica SOI	$550,000	Meeting Lender this week

PENDING INVENTORY PIPELINE

	Client	B or S	Address	City, Zip	Agent	Source	Price	Open	Close Date	Total GCI	Notes
1	William and Erica Pine	Buyer	1600 Palm Dr.	Exeter 93221	Melissa	Melissa SOI	$500,000	12/21/18	4/19/18	$13,500	
2	Luis Guerrero	Buyer	2148 W. Union Ave.	Porterville 93257	Melissa	Website	$255,000	1/9/18	4/11/18	$5,558	
3	Chris and Crystal Smith	Buyer	14663 Avenue 344	Visalia 93292	Melissa	Robyn SOI	$685,000	2/12/18	4/12/18	$12,813	
4	Carly Heinzen-Woods	Seller	813 W. Reese Ct.	Visalia 93277	Robyn	Robyn PC	$224,900	2/15/18	4/13/18	$6,900	Ray Jones (Uncle) 949-555-1243
5	Jennifer De Mascio	Buyer	813 W. Reese Ct.	Visalia 93277	Melissa	Robyn PC	$350,000	2/15/18	4/13/18	$6,900	
6	Henry Hash	Seller	644 W. Loyola Ave.	Visalia 93277	Kari/Robyn	Kari Expired	$249,700	2/22/18	3/23/18	$6,250	
7	Henrique Guerreiro	Seller	1000 Belmont	Porterville 93257	Robyn	Robyn SOI	$205,000	2/23/18	4/9/18	$6,150	
8	Jessica De Mascio	Seller	1025 Princeton Ave.	Visalia 93277	Robyn	Robyn SOI	$219,900	3/1/18	4/13/18	$6,810	
9	Gary Garret	Seller	1331 Laura Ct	Visalia 93292	Kari	Kari FARM	$389,000	3/15/18	5/21/18	$6,900	Also buying
10	Gary Garret	Buyer	381 S Beverly	Porterville 93257	Kari	Kari FARM	$310,000	3/21/18	5/1/18	$5,125	Also listing/selling
11	Florence Ann Webster	Seller	2400 W Micvalley	Visalia 93277	Kari	Kari PC	$885,500	9/21/18	12/31/19	$14,000	
12	Daniel Snead	Seller	3145 W Ashland	Visalia 93277	Kari	Open House	$249,000	9/22/18	12/31/19	$7,100	
13	Donnie Brandon	Seller	401 N. Powell	Visalia 93291	Robyn	Robyn SOI	$814,900	3/13/18	12/31/19	$16,200	
14	Scott and Kirsten Hyder	Buyer	131 W Putnam	Porterville 93257	Kari	Kari PC	$750,000	3/27/18	5/21/18	$18,400	
15	Samuel Velasquez	Buyer	893 San Ramon	Visalia 93292	Melissa	Website	$350,000	3/28/18	4/26/18	$8,900	Melissa's cousin
16	David & Mel Johnson	Seller	2822 Border Links	Visalia 93291	Robyn	Robyn SOI	$750,000	2/25/18	4/16/18	$14,750	
17	Kimmy Berkley	Seller	236 Feemster Ct	Visalia 93277	Robyn	Open House	$550,000	2/29/18	4/13/18	$9,550	
18	John & Dani Kale	Buyer	145 Beverly Glen	Visalia 93277	Kari	Website	$350,000	3/1/18	4/1/18	$7,525	
19	Mark & Donna Griffel	Seller	856 N. Fairway	Visalia 93291	Robyn	Robyn SOI	$665,500	3/5/18	4/25/18	$11,500	
20	Omar & Katie Vaz	Seller	435 Keogh Dr.	Visalia 93291	Robyn	Website	$450,000	2/15/18	4/6/18	$7,000	
21	Katherine Florentine	Buyer	231 Park Place	Porterville 93257	Kari	Kari SOI	$350,000	3/13/18	5/12/18	$6,250	
22	Larry Burke	Buyer	259 Hyde Way	Tulare 93234	Melissa	Melissa SOI	$250,000	3/18/18	5/2/18	$6,800	Tenant's occupying property
	Larry Burke	Buyer	1342 Ames Ct.	Exeter 93221	Melissa	Melissa SOI	$259,000	3/26/18	5/14/18	$7,450	

ACTIVE LISTING INVENTORY

Active Listings

	Client	Buyer too?	Address	City, Zip	Agent	Source	List Price	List Date	DOM	LA Expires	Today
1											
2											
3											
4											
5											
6											
7											

Listing Agreement Signed & Waiting to Go Active

	Client	Buyer too?	Address	City, Zip	Agent	Source	LA Signed	LA Expires	Notes
1									
2									
3									
4									

Coming Soon - No Listing Agreement Signed Yet

	Client	Buyer too?	Address	City, Zip	Agent	Source	Status
1							
2							
3							
4							
5							
6							
7							
8							
9							
10							
11							
12							
13							

PENDING CONTRACTS

Client	B or S	Address	City, Zip	Agent	Source	Price	Open	Close Date	Total GCI	Notes
1										
2										
3										
4										
5										
6										
7										
8										
9										
10										
11										
12										
13										
14										
15										
16										
17										
18										
19										
20										
21										
21										
22										

CHAPTER 6:

THE MARKETING DIRECTOR: BUILDING YOUR REAL ESTATE BUSINESS

LEARNING OBJECTIVES

- Leverage transactions with Listing to Closing Marketing
- Assemble Buyer and Seller packages
- Manage Social Media
- Organize events, from Client Appreciation to Open Houses
- Create and manage a Marketing Funnel
- Obtain amazing Online Reviews and Client Testimonials

I. **THE MARKETING DIRECTOR: BUILDING YOUR REAL ESTATE BUSINESS**

II. **LISTING TO CLOSING MARKETING**

III. **BUYER AND SELLER PACKAGES**

IV. **MANAGING SOCIAL MEDIA**
   A. Creating Fresh Web Content (profiles, blogs, etc.)
   B. Social Media Platforms
   C. Online Listings
      1. Writing Property Descriptions
      2. Taking Pictures

V. **CREATING MANAGING A MARKETING FUNNEL**
   A. Creating Your Funnel
   B. Narrowing the Funnel
   C. Determining Your Niche

VI. **CLIENT & VENDOR APPRECIATION EVENTS**
   A. Appreciation Events
   B. Your Client Event Contact Plan
   C. Invited guests
   D. Event costs

VII. **HOW TO HOLD AN OPEN HOUSE**
   A. Who else should come to the Open House?
   B. Location
   C. Scheduling
   D. Staging
   E. Signage and Promotions
   F. Registration
   G. Follow Up
   H. Getting Feedback

VIII. **GETTING ONLINE REVIEWS**
   A. Where Are Your Online Reviews?
   B. Get the Reviews You Want and Deserve
      1. Existing Clients
      2. Past Clients
      3. Client Appreciation Events
   C. The Data You Need

IX. **CLIENT TESTIMONIALS**

X. **NEXT STEPS**

XI. **APPENDIX**

THE MARKETING DIRECTOR: BUILDING YOUR REAL ESTATE BUSINESS

So far, you've uncovered what it means to wear the first three hats of a real estate administrator's role. Whether you're a solo agent or a real estate assistant, you are your company's administrative manager, listing manager, and transaction coordinator, and the fourth hat in your job description is the *Marketing Director*. This role is critical for building the real estate business you (or you and your agent) hope to have, and it's also the most fun!

Building a business is about creating connections with people, regardless of what you're selling. In the case of selling real estate, you're selling a property, but so much more goes into the sale. Real estate is about creating rapport, building trust, inspiring hope. You are asking people to trust you with one of the biggest—and possibly most stressful—decisions of their lives: buying or selling a home.

If your client is selling their home, they will be saying goodbye to neighbors and friends as well as memories of the time spent in their home. Those who are buying a property may feel a mixture of anticipation and trepidation as they look forward to a new stage in their lives.

You and the real estate agent make their dreams happen.

When you sell real estate, you do more than sell property. You're building neighborhoods and bringing dreams to life. You are selling connections, and as you'll see, connections are your most valuable asset in real estate.

The first thing you will need to do is to let people know you exist. As Marketing Director, you'll handle specific tasks like these:

- Manage client database management programs & systems.
- Create and regularly prepare all buyer & seller consultation packages.
- Coordinate the preparation of all listing and open house flyers, graphics, signage and all other marketing materials.
- Manage and update agent website(s), blog(s) and online listings.
- Regularly assist agent to manage and enhance agent's social media presence.
- Track and coordinate all inbound leads from websites, social media and other online sources.
- Coordinate all client and vendor appreciation events.
- Regularly obtain client testimonials for websites, social media and other marketing materials.
- Coordinate and implement agent marketing videos and property videos on website(s), blog(s), social media and client database email campaigns.

In Chapter 6 you'll devote your attention to handling multiple aspects of business building, beginning with preparing print materials for the agent and organizing social media campaigns. Specifically, you'll learn how to:

- Leverage transactions with Listing to Closing marketing.
- Assemble Buyer and Seller packages.
- Manage Social Media.
- Organize events, from Client Appreciation to Open Houses.
- Create and manage a Marketing Funnel.
- Obtain amazing Online Reviews and Client Testimonials.

LISTING TO CLOSING MARKETING

After thoroughly reviewing our Pre-Listing, Listing, and Closing Checklists, you have likely noticed that there are a significant number of marketing activities amongst the many procedural items necessary to properly service clients. We have again provided copies of these checklists at the end of this chapter for your further inspection. Note that they contain a variety of tasks designed to generate more business, such as:

- Asking for client referrals
- Requesting online reviews
- Obtaining client testimonials
- Just Listed, Sale Pending, and Just Sold marketing
- Open House Marketing
- Coordinating agent prospecting calls around properties

Most marketing activity is done for two reasons: (1) to generate business and branding for the agent and the real estate company, and (2) to appease and please our seller clients who want to see us doing everything we can to market their home. When we market a listing for sale, we're not only marketing the property, we're also marketing ourselves.

We're marketing to clients that we want to impress but we're also *marketing to other agents*. When agents are representing a buyer who is looking for a home, the first thing they do is look in the Multiple Listing Service (MLS). To be honest, buyer's agents very rarely look anywhere else. They don't look in magazines and they certainly aren't looking on Facebook or waiting for a postcard to arrive through their door.

The main purpose of those marketing strategies is creating general brand awareness and, particularly, pleasing the sellers and providing excellent customer-service. These strategies are definitely important for building trust and rapport with clients. However, these things are rarely instrumental in actually selling the home. Instead, our most impactful marketing is done through the MLS and marketing the property to other agents.

In Listing to Closing, every status-change presents a marketing opportunity that should be leveraged. For example, if you have a property that's going to be listed soon, you can market "Coming Soon", if that's permissible in your area. You can also advertise when the property is "Just Listed" or "Under Contract" as well as marketing "Open House" events (or multiple open house events). Every change along the way presents a marketing opportunity, all the way through to "Sale Pending" and "Just Sold". You can even market the property after it's been sold, as a comparable in a Comparative Market Analysis mailer to the entire neighborhood.

At every stage in Listing to Closing, the marketing director should find a way to advertise and talk about both the property and your company's success. Not only are you *seeking* business, but you are also telling people that you have business and are *sought after*. Whether it involves an email, a newsletter, social media, or a flyer, all the marketing steps up to sale-pending are about trying to sell the home, and all of the marketing steps after that are about evidencing your success. That is: showing and telling people, *look what we did* and, more importantly, that *it worked.*

BUYER AND SELLER PACKAGES

Buyer and seller packages can help you turn your listings from cold to sold. Seller packages, also known as listing consultation packets, are used at the agent's in-person listing appointment, typically at the sellers home. Buyer packages, or buyer consultation packets, are usually utilized at the initial buyer consultation appointment.

A well-thought-out package inspires confidence in the client and establishes you as a professional in the real estate industry. When a potential client reviews the information you've collected, they realize that you are an expert in your field. A thoughtful, detailed package can alleviate their worries by helping them to understand the process. We have included sample templates of our Buyer and Seller packages to help you get started in customizing your own.

Another benefit of buyer and seller packages is that they can save you valuable time. Many of the most frequently asked questions are answered in the packet, and provide sellers with an opportunity to obtain any information the agent will need before the listing appointment or buyer consultation.

What goes into the packets?

- The real estate agent's Bio. Think of this insert as your first chance to build rapport and create a powerful impression with a potential client. Agents need a professional headshot and a well-written description.

- Checklists. A checklist is a useful tool, whether a seller is preparing a house for the market or the buyer would benefit from a 'moving checklist'. A Listing Consultation Checklist informs sellers what they need to have in place so that you can list their property. This valuable list saves time for everyone.

- An overview of what to expect from the real estate agent. Purchasing real estate can be overwhelming, whether it's your first home or your fifth. Provide a document that explains the process, *without using real estate jargon*.

- Useful information, such as: market valuations, how many homes are for sale in the area, and the average number of days a house typically stays on the market. Other necessary information might include school ratings, the nearest emergency medical clinic, and which local restaurants deliver to the neighborhood.

- A page of testimonials from satisfied clients.

- A blank real estate contract.

A Seller Package can also be used as a Pre-Listing Presentation Packet that is delivered to potential seller clients via email and/or personal delivery prior to the agent's listing consultation appointment at their home. This truly helps set your agent apart from the competition when potential clients are interviewing multiple agents to list their home for sale.

MANAGING SOCIAL MEDIA

Social media provides you with
a platform to not only advertise
yourself and your brand, but
also promote the properties you
have listed for sale. Your website
and social media networks are
dynamic places for gathering
information and discovering
what users find interesting and
relevant.

CREATING FRESH WEB CONTENT (PROFILES, BLOGS, ETC.)

Search engines measure the efficacy of your webpage by the
relevance and value of your content. That means using keywords
that pertain to your industry so that prospects can discover you
online.

Building a website is fairly easy, and almost anyone can create an
attractive landing-page. A professionally designed site, however,
will speak volumes about your business. It will cost more for a site
like this, but you will attract more business.

As well as a landing page, your website should also have: an
About Us page, agent's Bios, a page about the neighborhood,
and home valuations.

Your website should also be current and provide value. Add new
content—whether in the form of a blog, newsletter or checklist—
every week. Blogs can be further promoted on a variety of social
media platforms. You can also provide checklists that potential
clients can download (in exchange for their email address).

Incorporate SEO keywords to make your site easy to find. If
you're not sure of the real estate keywords you need, try one of
the free keyword search sites like WordStream to compile a list of
the keywords that will help prospects find you.

Social Media Platforms

Don't ignore the power of social media.

While buyer's agents are busy looking on the MLS, the buyers themselves are browsing their Facebook and Instagram. These social media platforms can be useful in showcasing homes when you post a picture and a hash-tag or a comment.

If one of your listings has a gourmet kitchen, post a picture of the professional gas range with a caption that asks a question, like, "Cook a holiday meal at home or make reservations?" After the question, insert the link in case someone wants to see the rest of the pictures, which they always will.

Social media is also a great way to stay connected with people in your Sphere of Influence or your agent's Sphere of Influence. We'll discuss this in more detail in the next chapter but, essentially, your SOI refers to everyone you know and everyone who knows you by name. Encourage, friends, family and followers to like and comment on your social media posts.

Post often in social media to remain relevant and in people's minds. Over time, you'll generate enough data to tell you when most of your viewers are online, and you'll want to post during those peak times.

ONLINE LISTINGS

Online listings are often shared on social media and are a key component of your online marketing strategy. Most people who are looking for a home turn to their computers first. It's more time-efficient not to mention cost-efficient and convenient to look at homes online before setting out in a vehicle to see the property in person. That's why your online listings must showcase your best work in presenting a property.

Understand that online listings are typically syndicated. When you post a listing in the Multiple Listing Service, it's automatically syndicated to other secondary sites where people tend to search for homes—Trulia and Zillow are well-known examples, but there are many more, and there are also ways to syndicate a listing to your company website too.

An online listing has two main components: Words and Pictures.

WRITING PROPERTY DESCRIPTIONS

Property descriptions get used in several different places, so it's essential that they be perfectly and precisely composed.

Typically, online sites like the MLS impose a character limit for writing property descriptions. Too, when advertising a home in a small flyer, postcard or social media, it's best if the property description is as short and sweet as possible. You will need to be precise but pack a lot of punch.

Always include the most important information in the first sentence. When the listing is syndicated to other sites, oftentimes these secondary sites don't allow as many characters for descriptions, so you want that first sentence to contain essential information that captivates and informs in the same sentence.

At larger companies, the marketing director may have a degree in communications or marketing and is likely to have excellent writing skills. Administrative assistants or solo agents that perform marketing duties may need to hone this skill through practice. Alternatively, you can hire the services of a freelancer to write specifications. Regardless of who writes the description, it is essential that you are putting your best foot forward as you step out online.

Using preformatted templates will help you improve your writing skills while also saving you time. Writing property descriptions is simply another task to be completed as carefully and efficiently as possible. Don't overly agonize or labor over it. Think of it like a Mad Lib with blank spaces that can be completed in various ways and combinations using different verbs, nouns, and adjectives.

For example:

The following template can produce an endless variety of property-descriptions.

This _____ ___ bedroom, ___ bathroom, _____ square foot home, listed at $_____ is located in the _____ _____ neighborhood.

This stunning 4-bedroom, 3-bathroom, 3200 square foot home, listed at $450,000 is located in the beautiful St. John's neighborhood.

This immaculate 2-bedroom, 1.5 bathroom, 2300 square foot condominium, listed at $850,000 is located in the desirable Nob Hill neighborhood.

You get the idea.

Words paint a verbal picture of a property, making prospects eager to see the listing in person. You never want to lie when writing a description, but you should do everything you can to make it sound attractive. Using hot keywords like these can create a sense of urgency among clients looking for a home.

- Sought-after
- Tasteful
- Breathtaking
- Luxurious
- Exclusive
- Unparalleled

- Impressive
- Pristine
- Custom
- Elegant
- Beautiful

Conversely, words like these can turn prospects away from the listing:

- Foreclosed
- Needs work, updating, etc.
- Rebuilt
- As-is

Having said all this, don't get carried away when writing property descriptions and never lie. After all, when buyers visit the property in person they'll soon discover the truth behind any hyperbolic embellishment. And, of course, the property's pictures are telling a story too.

TAKING PICTURES

While words paint a verbal picture of a property, prospective buyers want to see actual photographs! In a survey by the National Association of Realtors, homebuyers rated photos as the feature they use most when searching for homes online.

Take fabulous pictures, and you'll create the kind of interest and buzz that sells homes. Take dark and blurry pictures of messy, cluttered homes, and potential clients will remember the home for all the wrong reasons.

Imagine that you have a $500,000 property for sale. The current owners are anxious to get it sold, and the home is perfect for the right kind of buyer—someone who wants a move-in ready place. You arrive on the scheduled date and time to take the pictures, but the homeowners began packing earlier that day. As a result, there are boxes everywhere. The pizza box from their dinner is hanging out of the trashcan, and the husband is napping on the sofa!

In desperation to get home to your own family, you begin snapping pictures with your phone. Your only idea is to capture what pictures of the house that you can and get them posted online.

If those pictures include the overflowing trash can, scattered boxes, or a sleeping family member on the bed or sofa, no amount of explaining or wordsmithery will ever convince a potential buyer that the home is move-in ready, not when everything is in such disarray.

Do this:

- Showcase the house and property, not the furnishings
- Take pictures of interesting features
- Remove shower curtains before taking a picture of the tub/ shower
- Use a flash, or a lot of natural light
- Capture plenty of enticing pictures
- Use a professional digital camera, not your phone
- Stay out of the mirror shot
- Review your photos before leaving the shoot

Not that:

- Fish-eye distortions
- Laundry rooms with dirty clothes
- Kitchens with dirty dishes
- Unmade beds
- Anything that is soiled or in need of repair
- Overflowing trashcans
- Bright flashes in bathroom mirrors
- Overgrown lawns
- Pet feeding areas in the house
- Clutter
- Tilted objects
- Taking pictures of the home's interior from the outside
- Pictures of the property taken from your vehicle

If you feel as though your photos might not measure up, hire a professional real estate photographer to get you the pictures and videos you need. Many real estate professionals also use drones to capture properties at their very best. Most real estate commissions will more than pay for the work of a professional—it truly is a worthwhile investment.

Always post your best pictures first. When MLS listings are syndicated, oftentimes only the first few pictures in the MLS listing appear on secondary sites. Showcase the home's best features first rather than dot them throughout a 50-picture step-by-step walkthrough.

Save the best pictures for mail-outs to neighbors when a house in their area has sold. Chances are that they know the home, and they'll be impressed that you made the house look so good in the picture. Neighbors will keep you in mind when they're ready to sell their properties too.

CREATING AND MANAGING A MARKETING FUNNEL

A marketing funnel is a metaphor for visualizing the process of converting raw leads into actual clients or customers. As with a real funnel that has a wide mouth and a narrow stem, marketers advertise to a wide audience and capture as many leads as possible before narrowing down potential clients in each stage of the funnel.

As your company's marketing director, you will need to cast a wide net, creating broad brand awareness and cultivating interest with your marketing strategy before narrowing the focus and targeting precisely the right clients whom you can serve best.

Obviously, your marketing funnel goal is to create as many lead conversions as you can. Ideally, your marketing funnel would more resemble a cylinder with as many potential clients making it through as possible!

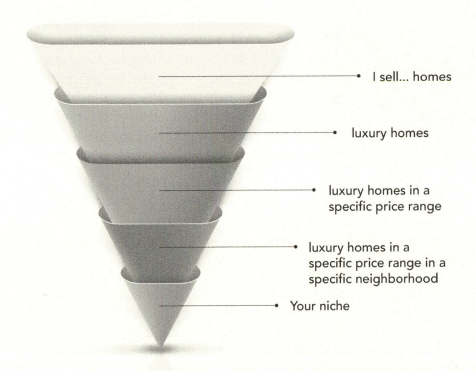

I sell... homes

luxury homes

luxury homes in a specific price range

luxury homes in a specific price range in a specific neighborhood

Your niche

CREATING YOUR FUNNEL

There are many types of marketing funnel models and ways to apply the concept. Increasingly, a funnel refers to online marketing strategies that convert viewers, visitors, web-traffic, and social media followers into leads. Generally, capturing a lead involves strategies for obtaining people's email address or other contact information, so that you can then market to that lead in a variety of other ways, nurturing it to the point of conversion.

It doesn't matter if your aesthetically-pleasing website has a million viewers a day, or you have thousands of Instagram followers. If you're not obtaining their contact information, your leaky funnel is simply allowing leads to browse and pass through rather than convert. When creating your funnel, provide as many ways for people to contact, sign up and subscribe to you as possible. Your online content and social media posts should constantly guide them towards those opt-in points.

An effective marketing funnel connects to every other type of marketing you do; it doesn't operate in isolation.

- Sparkling client testimonials and glowing online reviews capture the attention and trust of your audience, making them more likely to sign up to you.

- Showcasing your listings with excellent property descriptions and beautiful, high-quality photographs encourages people to contact you or sign up for a viewing.

- Every ad you create, from the mailers you send to the pictures and videos you post on social media, should not only inform and entertain, but it should guide them closer to you—and you to them.

NARROWING THE FUNNEL

Your funnel works like the car ad where a buyer says, "I'd like to purchase a car." Suddenly, hundreds of cars begin whizzing past him until he says, "I'd like it to be a used car." The funnel narrows and fewer cars drive by, but a lot of them are really old and beaten up. "With only one previous owner," he adds. The funnel narrows again, and there are even fewer cars, but they're in significantly better condition. As he continues to add descriptors, the number of cars dwindles further, until there are only a couple of vehicles left that meet his description.

You'll be doing the same thing with your marketing funnel. Simply saying, "I sell houses" is too broad of a statement. While you want to attract as wide an audience as possible, narrowing down quality leads and attracting serious buyers/sellers involves having an ideal audience or target niche in mind ahead of time.

DETERMINING YOUR NICHE

Your target niche should be narrow but flexible. For example, your company may focus on selling houses in the $950,000 to $2 million range, but obviously most agents wouldn't have an issue selling a home that listed for $925,000 or $3.2 million, even though both prices are clearly outside the identified niche. If the target area is between $250,000 and $400,000, most agents will assist with property transactions below or above the niche.

However, it's important to identify the niche so that you know how to craft your marketing funnel and attract the right buyers. Like the man wanting to purchase a car, you'll create your funnel by identifying these characteristics in a potential client:

- Optimum price-range?
    - Do you want to work in specific neighborhoods or geographic locations?
    - Luxury clients or investment properties?
- Are you seeking to work primarily with sellers or buyers?
- Do you prefer first-time buyers? Empty nesters? Are families your thing?
- Must the buyer be prequalified for a loan?
- What kind of problems do your potential clients face?
- Are they harried two-career professionals, or do they work from home?

The most important part of this exercise is to figure out where *you* fit in this picture. What unique or specialized service do you provide clients with? When you know how to ease their pain points, you have discovered your niche, and all of your marketing efforts can drive the right clients to your business.

If you haven't done it yet, speak with your agent to determine who the ideal client is for your real estate business. Answer the above questions, or develop some of your own to create a picture or profile of your ideal client.

When you have your list, write a client bio. Go ahead and name the client(s), list their ages, income, and anything else that will give you insight into their purchasing habits. Where do they work? How do they spend their free time? By putting the imaginary biography in writing, you are creating a solid identity for your client, and this avatar will help you fine-tune all of your various marketing strategies.

You can further narrow the funnel by marketing directly to your target buyers. Perhaps you may want to attract clients seeking to buy a home in the next twelve months, or those families whose jobs have required that they make a location change. Providing comparatives of schools in the area or moving expenses could be of interest to your potential clients.

Remember, they have a problem, and you are trying to solve it. When potential customers see that you are meeting every one of their needs, they will be more likely to use your services when purchasing or selling a home.

An effective marketing funnel begins with creating awareness and letting them know you exist in the first place. From there, it's up to you to provide value and interest by educating, informing, and even entertaining them. Once you've captured their interest, you're more likely to capture their contact information, which is crucial for following-up and nurturing that lead all the way to conversion.

CLIENT AND VENDOR APPRECIATION EVENTS

No one can sell real estate without connections. In the next chapter, we'll explore Sphere of Influence (SOI) connections in more details. These are the people *we* know that we hope do business with us and/or refer us to the people that *they* know.

While we want to stay first in mind and in constant contact with people in our Sphere of Influence, we don't want to feel as though we're hassling them. Constantly asking for business will turn off your SOI and have the opposite effect we wish for. Client Appreciation events are one of the best ways to turn on our SOI and provide something of value to them. Everyone loves a party or to at least be invited to one!

Holding an appreciation event for your clients and vendors can be a tremendous way to brand your real estate business and get referrals. Most people have two questions:

- What kind of event should I hold?
- Who do I invite?
- How much will it cost?

APPRECIATION EVENTS

There are all kinds of appreciation events. The possibilities are, essentially, limitless. Consider the few events on this list:

- Christmas photos with Santa Claus (with eggnog and hot chocolate)
- Seats at a local sporting event (with beer and hotdogs)
- A dinner buffet at a local restaurant
- Hold a BBQ at a nearby park
- Offer a Sundae on Sunday party with ice cream and toppings
- Sponsor a 5k race or a 'wine walk' through a neighborhood

The event you host may depend on your location. For example, if you have an outstanding community theatre, you might see if the organization would let you purchase discounted tickets for one of their dress rehearsals as a sneak preview. You are creating a win-win opportunity by offering to pay for a rehearsal that is usually closed to the public, and the theatre can make some extra money. Your guests get to preview a play. Serve wine and cheese or coffee and desserts, and your event will be a success.

If you're a new company starting out and you're worried about enough people showing up, casual open-house style events, where people come and go throughout the evening, can make an event appear successful even if numbers are low overall.

While you want your event to be creative and successful, the contacts leading up to the event are more important than the event itself, so don't spend too much time agonizing over event ideas. Your overall purpose is to maintain contact with your invitees and stay top of mind leading up to the event itself.

YOUR CLIENT EVENT CONTACT PLAN

To get people to attend your event, you have to be in front of your prospects regularly and often. You have to make contact and connect with them on a systematic basis. These contacts, or touches, are made in a variety of ways, from 'Save the Date' emails, to formal mailed invitations, social media posts and reminders, and personal invitation phone calls from your agent.

We have attached our sample Client Event Contact Plan that illustrates how to make up to 15 contacts, or touches, to members of an agent's Sphere of Influence through the promotion of an event.

The more touches you can make before an appreciation event, the better your event turnout will be.

As the old proverb says, "Out of sight, Out of mind."

Those six words are particularly true in real estate. If people don't immediately think of your business when they think of real estate, you haven't created enough touches to stay ahead of the other real estate agents in town. You have to find ways to stay in front of every prospect, and you do it through multiple touches.

Play the game of touches to stay at the forefront and ensure that your appreciation event is the one that people attend.

INVITED GUESTS

This section is called "client and vendor appreciation," so many people think about the clients they've had and the vendors they work with.

In reality, though, everyone is a client—even your vendors. Everyone needs a place to live, so you ought to be the company that connects your vendors with their new homes. This kind of thinking will expand your client list in no time.

You'll also benefit from their referrals.

EVENT COSTS

"How much will all of this cost," you might ask?

Hosting an appreciation event can be as inexpensive or as costly as you'd like, depending on the funds and ingenuity you have on hand. You could host coffee and donuts at the office or rent out a nightclub. Anything is possible.

You'll want your event to be memorable. Clients may not be looking for a new home right now, but a great appreciation event can be huge in paying it forward for building your brand. Whether it takes months or years for a client to turn to you for real estate help, the event may be what drives that contact.

Sound expensive? Your vendors may be interested in underwriting a portion of the event costs in exchange for advertising and adding your clients to their databases.

How to Hold an Open Houses

An Open House is a tremendous marketing opportunity.

Not only does it appease our sellers that we're showcasing their property and getting valuable feedback from viewers, but it's also a fantastic way to meet both buyer and seller leads. Obviously, buyers who are actively looking at properties are live leads, but open houses also attract potential sellers who are thinking of listing their property and are there to check out the neighborhood competition.

People in the neighborhood will likely be curious. They may even want to recommend the property to friends they'd like to have as neighbors. While they might swing by of their own accord, they might be hesitant and assume the event is exclusively for interested buyers.

It's a great idea, then, to create a flyer and personally invite people in the neighborhood to the open house. An open house has two purposes: showing the property and showing your agent's skills. Ask neighbors to come and get to know each other and talk about the benefits of living in the community. Create a memorable experience. The neighbors who come to the open house will remember you when they are ready to list their homes.

Who else should come to the Open House?

Ideally, all of your contacts, but you won't get them there unless you spend time on marketing. That's where the game of touches comes in. What can you do to create market buzz and interest in attending the event? Utilize heavy promotion strategies, the kind that generates multiple touches, and comes from a variety of outreach efforts, including:

- Emails
- Social media posts and invitations
- Phone calls in the neighborhood
- Newspaper ads
- MLS listings online
- Knocking on doors nearby
- Well-placed signs throughout the neighborhood

You'll meet plenty of leads at the event because you took the time create at least seven touches.

While it can be a lot of fun to meet new people at an open house and add to your database of contacts, an open house event can also advance your brand, show the seller how motivated you are to sell this home, and help you obtain more listings.

And ultimately, you'll also sell the property.

Not every home is a contender for an open house, and every open house will be a little different based on location and size, but some characteristics will be the same.

LOCATION

If you've listed a home in a highly visible location with plenty of parking, you might consider presenting an open house, especially if the home has been vacated or has been professionally staged. It's much harder to hold an open house if the owner has housecats or the home sits in a dangerous neighborhood.

SCHEDULING

Take advantage of community events that draw people to an area. Market days, antiquing events, and sporting events may present the perfect time for holding an open house. The more people in the area, the more likely you are to have visitors for your showing. Coordinating multiple open houses at once is also a great way to increase traffic.

STAGING

Before holding an open house, or showing any property for that matter, have the seller de-clutter and depersonalize the property. That means removing personal artifacts, photographs, or other small objects, leaving out only the necessities such as a coffee pot and two pretty cups, or setting the table as though expecting company.

Most people have too much stuff, including furniture, so out it goes. The seller can put it in storage if need be.

It may be appropriate to hire a professional staging company to help you present the listed home at its finest. Think of it as renting a luxurious evening gown for a gala.

SIGNAGE AND PROMOTIONS

No one will come to your open house if they can't find it.

Although many buyers use GPS, it's helpful to have signs pointing the way at every turn, and an 'Open House' sign in the front yard confirms that they have found the right place.

Also remember to place signage throughout the neighborhood of the subject property as well. Neighbors that show up often have homes to sell soon themselves. Plus they often know friends and family members looking to move into the neighborhood.

Be sure to promote the open house well in advance of the event. A few hours before the open house is scheduled to start, turn to social media to remind people they won't want to miss this opportunity!

REGISTRATION

A sign-in is a must, for several reasons. First, the mandatory sign-in list will help you keep track of who has visited. Knowing that you'll want contact information may be enough to keep burglars away from the event.

That sign-in will also reveal valuable information, like how people found out about the event and when in the future they may want to purchase a home.

Finally, a sign-in helps you expand your Sphere of Influence. Those names and contact information are a valuable source of potential leads. Remember the marketing funnel—success is not about the number of visitors who come to your website or your open house, it's about capturing contact information so that you can follow up and nurture your leads.

FOLLOW UP

Take that sign-in list and contact the people who came to the open house. Thank them for their time, and ask a specific open-ended question about the home, or use one of the ICC scripts to talk to the prospect about their timeline for purchasing a home.

GETTING FEEDBACK

Be sure to get feedback from the people who have come to the open house. You can ask for feedback during your follow-up phone calls, but there's another way to gather it more efficiently.

 Have pre-printed questionnaire cards and a few pens lying next to a pretty basket or container at the open house. Fill out a couple of cards in advance and toss them in the basket so people will know what to do. The cards should ask, "What do you think about this home?" At the bottom of the card, ask for the responder's name and contact information, and add a box that says, "May we use your comment in our advertising?

Not only will an open house generate excitement among potential buyers, the homeowner will appreciate knowing that you are actively marketing the property for sale. When done right, an open house will help you expand your Sphere of Influence, which we'll explore soon in Chapter 7.

GETTING ONLINE REVIEWS

There was a time that real estate agents could confidently rely on neighborhood word-of-mouth recommendations from satisfied customers. People in the neighborhood talked to each other about who provided the best services.

 Comments made on social media platforms are examples of some of the new word-of-mouth strategies. Online reviews are incredibly powerful because the Internet extends your reach, allowing prospects to find out who you are, what you do, and how well you do it.

Online reviews are becoming increasingly important. Asking for feedback is hard to do.

After all, you're making yourself vulnerable and open for attack. Getting online reviews can be especially nerve-wracking because they are immediately public.

You should embrace online reviews because they are one of the best marketing tools you have available to you. That's where your potential clients are.

If your reviews are good, kudos to you and your team! That means you've provided a superior customer experience, one that people want to share and brag about. They are the comments you hope will go viral.

Bad reviews aren't the end of the world, but they can feel like it. If you can embrace negative comments for their honesty, these uncomplimentary reviews will show you exactly what to do to improve your consumer experience.

The good news is that you can use all of your online reviews to help you improve your real estate services. You can also help your clients write better reviews.

WHERE ARE YOUR ONLINE REVIEWS?

Most people today have a digital footprint.

Four out of five people in the market for a new home will turn to the Internet for their searches. In doing so, they'll read about listings and the real estate companies offering these properties for sale. They'll also learn who the best buyers agents are.

Your goal is to be one of those top real estate providers, and you can do it with Internet platforms that allow customers to leave a review.

Zillow is the most popular home search site in the United States so it's essential to get good Zillow reviews. When asking clients for online reviews, it's important to make it a quick and easy process for them. Send them a link to your Zillow page. Don't expect them to know where to go—guide them there.

Other digital review platforms include:

- Trulia
- Google
- Realtor.com
- Facebook reviews
- Hotpads

- Glassdoor
- TripAdvisor
- YellowPages
- Yelp
- Angie's List

Determine the platforms most prevalent in and relevant to your geographic location and target markets, and focus on those.

GET THE REVIEWS YOU WANT AND DESERVE

If you want a five-star review, you'll need to show and tell your clients what a five-star experience looks like. Getting great online reviews can often be as simple as asking for one. However, by setting an expectation of what a five-star experience looks like, you are also helping the client hold you accountable for superior service.

Envision what a five-star experience looks like for your client, then create a checklist of everything that experience might entail and include (and that you do), so clients know exactly what they are looking for.

Getting online reviews begins with setting expectations for a referral or a review, and you do it by using the right terminology and teaching it to your clients.

Make sure you'll ace the review. Ask what you can do to make the five-star review a certainty, and continue to ask throughout the process of buying or selling a property.

Don't stop there.

Ask clients and vendors to find out what they'd like to see more of. Maybe they want more interesting articles in your newsletter, or they have an idea for your next open house. Encourage discussion and then implement the recommendations.

You can ask questions that have yes/no answers, but the best insight will come from open-ended questions like these:

- What was the easiest part of the process?
- How would you rate your customer experience?
- On a scale of 1-10, with 10 being the highest, what number would you use to describe our presentation package? Why?

When transactions close, ask clients to provide you with reviews. Most consumers do this anyway; you are simply asking for something they've already provided.

You may be surprised at how often your clients will agree to a review when you say, "Your insight is something others would benefit from. May I share what you thought about our services?"

Don't stop there.

If you notice they've posted something positive on social media or other real estate sites, reference the comment and ask to use it in your client testimonials. They're not just helping you; they will be assisting other like-minded consumers who want a five-star real estate experience.

As you've seen, scattered throughout our Listing and Closing checklists are numerous items calling for both the administrative assistant and the agent to contact clients to ask for referrals, online reviews and client testimonials. To effectively weave lead-generation in with customer service activities, these crucial tasks must never be neglected.

Although it can seem daunting to pick up the phone and ask the clients for something, this is a discipline that has been perfected by top real-estate administrative managers. At the end of this chapter, you will find some of our scripts that will help you reach out to existing and previous clients and complete this essential activity.

EXISTING CLIENTS

Top administrative assistants ask for reviews and referrals early and often in a systematic fashion throughout transactions. Note that many of these tasks are placed on the Listing and Closing Checklists immediately after positive or celebratory events occur. For example, it's much easier to reach out and ask for referrals right after a successful open house, when multiple offers are received, when an offer is accepted above asking price, when property appraises for full valve, when inspection repairs are negotiated in favor of the client, or right after the transaction closes.

PAST CLIENTS

Most agents take their commission check and run. Very few agents take the time to follow up and ask how the home is coming along, offer help with vendors to make repairs or improvements, or offer congratulations after the one-year anniversary of their home purchase.

Reaching out to see how you can help sets you apart and helps establish a relationship beyond a single transaction. Clients appreciate and become more comfortable with referring your services to others because of it.

CLIENT APPRECIATION EVENTS

Another great place to ask for online reviews is at Client Appreciation events. Simply set up a laptop and ask your clients if they would mind giving you a glowing 5-star online review. Most people will be more than happy to do this for you and, of course, it's hard to refuse when they're attending an event you're throwing for them!

THE DATA YOU NEED

Social media platforms like Facebook, Pinterest, YouTube, LinkedIn, and Instagram also generate valuable data you can use in refining your real estate strategy. Many platforms provide you with weekly analytics that show you which posts performed well and received the most audience engagement.

You also can determine *when* most of your prospects are online, so that you know the best times and days for posting and boosting your content. This data is instrumental in understanding what your clients need and want from you and when they're most likely to see it.

And, of course, prospects always turn to Google for their searches, so if you've done your homework and kept up with SEO words and phrases in your blog and website, they will also find you there. At that point, you can analyze their engagement and generate metrics to help you improve in recommended areas.

Review your data weekly to analyze trends and make adjustments to your online review marketing strategy. You'll quickly come to see which sites offer the best value, and then you should tend those sites as carefully as you would tend to heritage flowers in a garden.

Tending to your online marketing strategy requires consistent effort as you nurture clients and develop the kinds of relationships that result in five-star reviews.

CLIENT TESTIMONIALS

What your clients say about you matters. Real estate is a competitive industry, so it's important to set yourself apart from the competition by obtaining trust from people before they become your clients. Putting time and effort into obtaining client testimonials helps to make the decision of which agent to use an easier one. This is why it's a frequently included task on your Listing and Closing checklists.

Not everyone will know exactly what to say, however. They may genuinely love your work, but they might not know where to begin expressing it in a testimonial, so you may need to give them some pointers about what a typical testimonial looks like.

Essentially, there are three main things people want in a realtor. People want you to:

1. Sell your home for the highest price possible.
2. Sell your home in the quickest amount of time.
3. Sell your home with the least amount of hassle.

Ideally, client testimonials should touch upon one or all of those items, whether it's testifying to your amazing customer-service and how easy you made the entire process, or whether it's raving about the great price you got for their home and how quickly it sold.

A client testimonial can come in various shapes and sizes. It might be a statement made by your clients about your amazing marketing efforts with their family photo in your Listing Consultation packet. It could also be included in a video interview with your clients that is used on your website, Facebook page or attached to a pre-listing appointment email. A simple statement about your amazing customer-service can be shown in quotes in a meme posted on social media networks. You might even have a dedicated page on your website for a long list of client testimonial statements.

Whatever form they take, you should ask for—and use—client testimonials often and in as many ways possible.

NEXT STEPS

As you can see, as your company's Marketing Director you're promoting your business in innumerable ways and employing many different and overlapping public relations and advertising strategies. This role is so important to the success and growth of your business that we cannot say everything we'd like to in a single chapter. For that reason, in the next chapter we'll continue the discussion by exploring your pivotal Sphere of Influence in more detail. See you there!

PRE-LISTING CHECKLIST

Property Address: _____

Days Prior to Listing Appt	Date Completed	Description	Requested	Complete
3		Create new listing file with all forms & templates		
3		Schedule listing appointment in agent's calendar		
3		Locate & save old MLS listings for subject property		
2		Obtain property profile, assessments & taxes		
2		Call title & request legal description & deed		
2		Obtain parcel map & survey info		
2		Print agent's pre-listing presentation materials for consultation		
2		Prepare seller net sheet(s)		
2		Prepare CMA for agent's review		
2		Prepare map & directions to property		
2		Fill out & print seller's disclosures for listing consultation		
1		Prepare listing packet		
1		Fill out MLS input sheet w/ missing info still needed		
1		Input client into CRM database		
1		Pre-listing packet hand delivered to client		
1		Prelisting packet & video emailed to client		
0		If listing is NOT signed, schedule a follow-up call for agent		
0		If listing IS signed, start "Listing to Contract Checklist"		

LISTING TO CONTRACT CHECKLIST

Property Address: _____

Days After Listing Agmt	Date Completed	Description	Requested	Complete
0		Admin intro call to sellers - immediately after listing signed		
0		Receive signed listing agreement		
0		Did Agent ask for referrals at listing appointment?		
1		Schedule Open House(s) with Sellers/Agent		
1		Create property file and/or upload all pre-listing documents		
1		Obtain all signed & completed sellers disclosures		
1		Obtain showing instructions from agent/sellers		
1		Obtain seller mortgage statement or loan info		
1		Put seller on MLS listing auto-alert email drip for home(s) to buy		
1		Put seller on MLS listing auto-alert drip- MLS status changes in neighborhood		
1		Get seller pre-qualified for loan to purchase next home		
1		Order preliminary title report, HOA Documents & CCRs		
1		Call stager to schedule staging consultation		
1		Call photographer to schedule photo shoot		
1		Order & schedule yard sign		
1		Add sellers to admin weekly update call list		
1		Add sellers to agent's weekly update call list		
1		Enter listing into MLS as incomplete for agent to proof		
1		Assign lock box to MLS listing		
1		Add client to CRM database		
1		Add new listing to Team Scoreboard		
1		Turn listing contract/disclosures in to brokerage compliance		
2		Get MLS listing edits/approval from Agent		
2		Upload MLS Client Detail Report to property file		
2		Email MLS Client Detail Report to all team members		
2		Add/Enhance Listing on all other websites		
2		Add listing to broker tour/caravan		
2		Calendar Listing Expiration Date		
2		Prepare property flyer template (& Open House flyer)		
2		Create "Just Listed" Facebook & social media posts		
2		Obtain Neighborhood Contact Information		
2		Get 2 sets of keys made - for lockbox & office		
2		"Just Listed" mailers/flyers created & ordered		
2		"Open House" mailers/flyers created		
2		First Open House day/time scheduled with sellers/agents?		
2		Add clients as friends on Facebook/Social Media		
2		Order Seller Coverage Warranty		
3		Claim listing on Zillow/Trulia & set up reporting		
4		Sign up at property		
4		Lockbox on at property		
4		Flyers delivered to property		

5		LISTING GOES ACTIVE on MLS		
5		Send Thank You/Gift Card to Person who Referred Listing		
5		Start agent prospecting calls around new listing		
5		"Just Listed" email to neighborhood & SOI		
5		"Just Listed" posted on Facebook & social media		
7		Email Activity Report to sellers		
7		Weekly Activity Report Call to sellers		
7		Agent ask for referrals on weekly call?		
8		Order "Open House" Mailers/Flyers for neighborhood		
8		"Open House" email to neighborhood & SOI		
8		"Open House" posted on Facebook & social media		
14		Email Activity Report to sellers		
14		Weekly Activity Report Call to sellers		
15		Schedule 2nd Open House?		
21		Email Activity Report to sellers		
21		Weekly Activity Report Call to sellers		
28		Email Activity Report to sellers		
28		Weekly Activity Report Call to sellers		
35		Email Activity Report to sellers		
35		Call to sellers for PRICE REDUCTION APPOINTMENT?		
42		Email Activity Report to sellers		
42		Weekly Activity Report Call to sellers		
49		Email Activity Report to sellers		
49		Weekly Activity Report Call to sellers		
56		Email Activity Report to sellers		
56		Weekly Activity Report Call to sellers		
63		Email Activity Report to sellers		
63		Weekly Activity Report Call to sellers		
70		Email Activity Report to sellers		
70		Call sellers for RE-LISTING APPOINTMENT? Price Reduction?		
		Once Offer(s) Received		
71		Prepare summary(s) of key offer terms to present to sellers		
71		Prepare net sheet(s) for offer(s) to present to sellers		
72		Draft response(s) to offers for sellers to sign- acceptance/counter offer		
72		Send counter offer (or acceptance) to buyer's agent		
		Once Offer Accepted - Start Seller Closing Checklist		

SELLER CLOSING CHECKLIST

Property Address: _____

Days After Acceptance	Date Completed	Description	Requested	Complete
0		Upload signed contract, forms & contact info to property file		
0		Calendar all key contract dates & deadlines - see below		
1		Email signed contract & contact info to lender, title & buyers agent		
1		Email signed contract to seller w/ title contact info & next steps		
1		Call seller with next steps, key dates/deadlines & inspection info		
1		All utilities are on, and to be left on?		
1		Change MLS status to pending		
1		Sale pending rider on sign at property		
1		EMD-Earnest Money Deposit received & deposited/logged		
1		Request Preliminary Title Report		
1		Obtain/Order neighborhood contact information for mailers/calls		
1		Submit all documents/forms to broker compliance		
1		Update Team Scoreboard		
1		Listing agent "congratulations" call to seller - ask for referrals		
2		Order all selller-required inspections - see inspection checklist below		
2		Order Home Warranty (if applicable)		
2		Order Natural Hazard Disclosure (if applicable)		
2		Friend request to buyers on Facebook & social media		
2		Send/Request disclosures to/from buyer's agent		
2		"Sale Pending" mailer/flyers to neighborhood ordered		
2		"Sale Pending" Facebook & social media posts		
3		Start agent circle prospecting "sale pending" calls/door knocking		
3		Confirm Earnest Money Deposit (EMD) is deposited		
3		Submit commission disbursement/disbursement authorization		
3		Contact buyer's lender to ensure all docs recvd (tax info, pay stubs, etc)		
3		Has appraisal been ordered? Contact buyer's agent/lender		
7		Call seller with update - what's been done & next steps		
14		Call to check loan status with lender		
14		Call seller with update - what's been done & next steps		
15		Request for inspection repairs received? Remind buyer's agent		
15		Appraisal In? Contact buyer's agent/lender		
17		Home inspection repair request received? Respond to Request?		
17		Appraisal contingency removed?		
17		Agent call seller to congratulate on property appraising		
18		Contact lender - File submitted to underwriter? Still needed?		
19		Request loan contingency removal from buyer's agent		
19		All other inspection reports received? See below		
20		Get clients new address & update SOI database in CRM		
21		Loan contingency removed?		
21		Call seller with update - what's been done & next steps		
22		Contact lender - Underwriter approval? Any conditions?		
23		Are all contingencies of the sale removed? Still needed?		

5 Days Before Closing				
25		Call seller 5 days before closing to explain closing process		
25		Have staging furniture removed		
25		Schedule buyer's final walkthrough inspection		
25		Schedule seller's to sign at closing		
25		Request & review estimated closing statement		
25		Submit any final invoices to to escrow/title/attorney		
25		Loan Documents in and signed by Buyers?		
25		File Housekeeping - contact other agent to ensure file is complete		
25		Order closing gift for sellers		
25		Contact sellers to get utilities list		
26		Signed loan documents sent to lender for loan funding?		
26		Send utilities list to buyer's agent to switch names at close date		
27		Contact escrow/title/attorney - Still needed to close (buyer funds up?)		
28		Buyer walkthrough inspection conducted?		
28		Loan Funded? Has escrow/title/attorney received funds to close?		
29		Request & review final estimated closing statement		
Day of Closing				
30		Confirm Recording		
30		Keys delivered		
30		Agent to call seller w/ "congratulations" - ask for referrals		
30		Receive closing documents from escrow/title/attorney (upload to file)		
30		Change MLS status to "Sold" on MLS		
30		Change Zillow Status to "Sold"		
31		Commission check(s) received/deposited		
30		For sale sign removed from property		
30		Lockbox removed from property		
After Closing				
31		Input "adopted" buyer contact information into CRM database		
31		Update new seller notes in SOI database w/ new address		
31		Start seller on past client email/mailer drip campaign		
31		Send seller congratulations email w/ online review request links		
31		Send seller congratulations letter		
31		Send adopted buyer congratulations letter		
31		Send "Thank You Colleague" letter to co-op agent		
31		Send "Thank You" letter to lender		
31		Update closing on team scoreboard		
32		Calendar Home Anniversary & 30/90 day agent calls (referrals)		
32		Create/save PDFs of all file documents & emails		
32		Start agent "Just Sold" calls to neighborhood		
32		"Just Sold" mailers/flyers to neighborhood & SOI		
32		"Just Sold" - FB & other social media posts		

Key Contract Dates & Deadlines

Description	Dates
7th Day - Disclosures Delivered	
7th Day - Preliminary Report Received	
15th Day - Inspection Repairs Request Received?	
17th Day - Inspection Contingencies Removal Deadline	
17th Day - Appraisal Contingency Removal Deadline	
21st Day - Loan Contingency Removal Deadline	
5 days till close - walkthrough, funding, etc.	
Other:	
Other:	
Closing Date	

Inspection Information Checklist

Type	Company & Contact Info	Date & Time	Report Received?
Termite/Pest			
Home Inspection			
Pool Inspection			
Roof Inspection			
Septic Inspection			
Appraisal			
Well Inspection			
Flood Zone Insp.			
Other Inspection			

MARKETING LISTING
CONSULTATION

Prepared by:
Enter Name Here
Seller Specialist

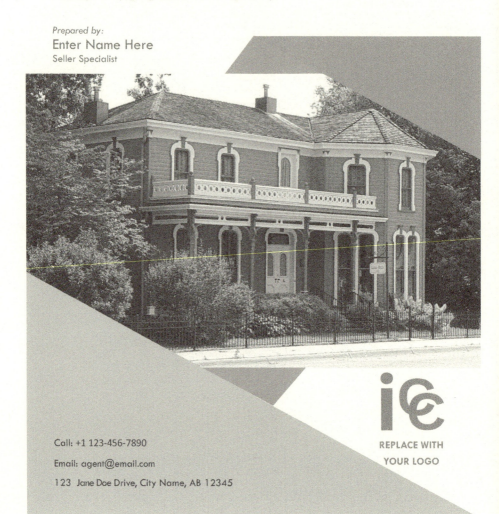

Call: +1 123-456-7890

Email: agent@email.com

123 Jane Doe Drive, City Name, AB 12345

REPLACE WITH
YOUR LOGO

THANK YOU FOR THE OPPORTUNITY
TO MEET WITH YOU TODAY

Studies show only 22% of home sellers were satisfied with their agent. We do everything it takes to make sure you are satisfied with our services. Our quality customer service has given us a trusted name with a five-star client satisfaction rating. Our team is here to serve your real estate needs in every way possible.

ADVICE TO SELL YOUR HOME QUICKLY

You'll get suggestions on how to prepare your home so that it will show its best and make a positive impression on buyers.

CONTRACT PROPOSALS – PROS & CONS

When we bring the contract proposals to you for your consideration, we will explain them, and include an estimated-closing-cost statement so that you can make an educated decision. We will use our negotiating skills to help you get top dollar.

THE HOME SELLING PROCESS

We'll explain the entire selling process so there won't be any surprises along the way.

If you hear of anyone who would benefit from our services, we'd greatly appreciate you passing along one of our business cards.

THANK YOU!
TEAM NAME HERE

YOUR TEAM NAME   2

MEET THE TEAM

Brian Icenhower

Real estate executive, speaker and coach Brian Icenhower is the creator of TheRealEstateTrainer.com, the world's leading production training website for real estate agents. Mr. Icenhower is also the Founder & President of Icenhower Coaching & Consulting, which offers structured real estate coaching programs designed to fit the specific needs of real estate agents and brokers seeking to increase their business income while maintaining balanced lives.

Name Here

Lorem ipsum dolor sit amet, consectetuer adipiscing elit. Nam cursus. Morbi ut mi. Nullam enim leo, egestas id, condimentum at, l aoreet mattis, massa. Sed eleifend nonummy diam. Praesent mauris ante, elementum et, bibendum at, posuere sit amet, nibh. Duis tincidunt lectus quis dui viverra vestibulum. Suspendisse vulputate aliquam dui. Nulla elementum dui ut augue. Aliquam vehicula mi at mauris. Maecenas senectus et netus et malesuada fames ac turpis egestas. In posuere felis nec tortor. Pellentesque faucibus ut accumsan ultricies.

Another Name

Lorem ipsum dolor sit amet, consectetuer adipiscing elit. Nam cursus. Morbi ut mi. Nullam enim leo, egestas id, condimentum at, l aoreet mattis, massa. Sed eleifend nonummy diam. Praesent mauris ante, elementum et, bibendum at, posuere sit amet, nibh. Duis tincidunt lectus quis dui viverra vestibulum. Suspendisse vulputate aliquam dui. Nulla elementum dui ut augue. Aliquam vehicula mi at mauris. Maecenas senectus et netus et malesuada fames ac turpis egestas. In posuere felis nec tortor. Pellentesque faucibus ut accumsan ultricies.

TEAM NAME HERE

YOUR TEAM NAME

3

NEW AGE MARKETING

FOR A NEW DEMOGRAPHIC

WE DO MORE THAN THE AVERAGE AGENT

YOUR TEAM NAME

4

MARKETING CHECKLIST

☐ Lorem ipsum dolor sit amet, conse ctetur adipiscing elit, sed do eius mod tempor incididunt

☐ Gut labore et dolore magna aliqua. Ut enim ad minim veniam, quis nostrud

☐ Exercitation ullamco laboris nisi ut aliquip ex ea commodo consequat. Duis aute irure dolor

☐ In reprehenderit in voluptate velit esse cillum dolore eu fugiat nulla pariatur. Excepteur sint

☐ Occaecat cupidatat non pro ident, sunt in culpa qui officia deserunt mollit anim id est

☐ Lorem ipsum dolor sit amet, conse ctetur adipiscing elit, sed do eius mod tempor incididunt

☐ Put labore et dolore magna aliqua. Ut enim ad minim veniam, quis nostrud

☐ Exercitation ullamco laboris nisi ut aliquip ex ea commodo consequat. Duis aute irure dolor

☐ In reprehenderit in voluptate velit esse cillum dolore eu fugiat nulla pariatur. Excepteur sint

☐ Occaecat cupidatat non pro ident, sunt in culpa qui officia deserunt mollit anim id est

☐ Occaecat cupidatat non pro ident, sunt in culpa qui officia deserunt mollit anim id est

☐ Lorem ipsum dolor sit amet, conse ctetur adipiscing elit, sed do eius mod tempor incididunt

☐ Lorem ipsum dolor sit amet, conse ctetur adipiscing elit, sed do eius mod tempor incididunt

☐ Gut labore et dolore magna aliqua. Ut enim ad minim veniam, quis nostrud

☐ Exercitation ullamco laboris nisi ut aliquip ex ea commodo consequat.Duis aute irure dolor

☐ In reprehenderit in voluptate velit esse cillum dolore eu fugiat nulla pariatur. Excepteur sint

☐ Occaecat cupidatat non pro ident, sunt in culpa qui officia deserunt mollit anim id est

☐ Lorem ipsum dolor sit amet, conse ctetur adipiscing elit, sed do eius mod tempor incididunt

☐ Put labore et dolore magna aliqua. Ut enim ad minim veniam, quis nostrud

☐ Exercitation ullamco laboris nisi ut aliquip ex ea commodo consequat.Duis aute irure dolor

☐ In reprehenderit in voluptate velit esse cillum dolore eu fugiat nulla pariatur. Excepteur sint

☐ Occaecat cupidatat non pro ident, sunt in culpa qui officia deserunt mollit anim id est

☐ Occaecat cupidatat non pro ident, sunt in culpa qui officia deserunt mollit anim id est

☐ Lorem ipsum dolor sit amet, conse ctetur adipiscing elit, sed do eius mod tempor incididunt

YOUR TEAM NAME

5

THE 5P's OF REAL ESTATE

MOST AGENTS DO: THE FIRST 3 "P's"

1. Place Sign in your yard

2. Put in MLS

3. Pray someone else sells it

WE DO THE 4TH AND 5TH "P"

4. Price Watch – Consistently and systematically

Watch what listings come on the market, which ones go into escrow, and what has sold most recently both on and off the MLS. Our system gives us real time information providing you with the details so that you can make an intelligent pricing decision.

5. Prospecting – a potential or likely customer, client, etc.

We are in "the field" daily talking to buyers and sellers via the phone, and knocking on doors. We are always pro-actively searching for the buyer that wants your home instead of waiting for them to find us.

TEAM NAME HERE i℮ REPLACE WITH YOUR LOGO

YOUR TEAM NAME   6

i℮

MARKETING PLAN

OPTIMIZE your home's potential through recommending STAGING changes proven to provide greater financial returns and a quicker sale.

PRICE your home strategically considering current market conditions and trends.

DIVERSIFY your home's exposure by layering different types of media to attract as many people as possible.

- Print Media Mailers Flyers
- Open houses
- Technology driven marketing
- Video
- Phone calls
- Neighborhood door knocking
- Yard signs
- MLS
- Websites
- Social media platforms

POSITION your home to show off its best qualities through PROFESSIONAL PHOTOGRAPHS and compelling descriptions utilized in collateral materials given to agents and buyers.

LOCAL & INTERNATIONAL EXPOSURE when your home is advertised to over 118,000 **Company Name** located in over 700 market centers across the globe.

PROMOTE your home to top agents in the area.

RESPOND quickly and effectively to all inquires regarding your home.

QUALIFY prospective buyers of your home prior to presenting any offers.

FOLLOW UP and encourage feedback from agents that have shown your home, potential buyers we have shown it to, and open house visitors.

COMMUNICATE with you frequently regarding interest in your home, recent activity, potential buyers, agent feedback, recommended changes, pending and accepted offers.

NEGOTIATE the best price and terms for you - proven by our 99% **LIST** to **CLOSE** ratio and holding the number 3 spot of ALL agents in the MLS for Listing Volume SOLD.

SATISFACTION GUARANTEE if you are not 100% satisfied with our services, you may cancel at anytime.

RESULTS DELIVERED the MAIN THING that sets us apart is we absolutely get it done! Validated by our "Raving Fans" and valued relationships!

YOUR TEAM NAME   7

PRINT
MEDIA

I will strategically advertise in several publications. Our display advertising appears in local, regional and national/ international publications, which target specific audiences for unique or estate properties. I will select the publications appropriate for the marketing of your property.

Your Ad SAMPLE Here

Your Ad SAMPLE Here

Your Ad SAMPLE Here

Your Ad SAMPLE Here

Your Ad SAMPLE Here

iℰℰ

REPLACE WITH YOUR LOGO

YOUR TEAM NAME

8

iℰℰ

BUYER
CONSULTATION

Prepared by:
Enter Name Here
Buyer Specialist

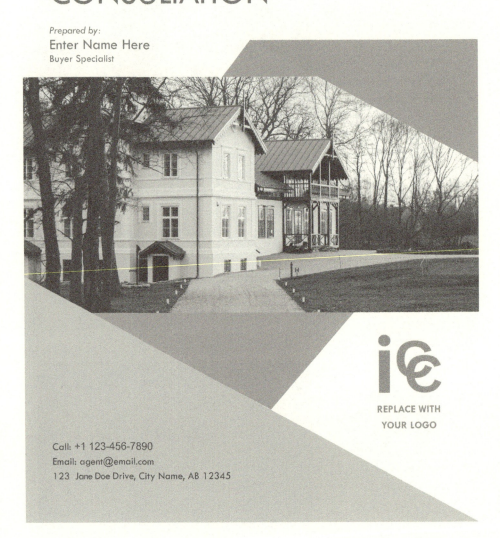

REPLACE WITH
YOUR LOGO

Call: +1 123-456-7890
Email: agent@email.com
123 Jane Doe Drive, City Name, AB 12345

PRINT MEDIA

I will strategically advertise in several publications. Our display advertising appears in local, regional and national/ international publications, which target specific audiences for unique or estate properties. I will select the publications appropriate for the marketing of your property.

REPLACE WITH YOUR LOGO

YOUR TEAM NAME

8

EXECUTIVE
SUMMARY

CONGRATULATIONS!

You've made a wise decision! You've chosen
to interview one of the best real estate teams in ABC County.

COMPANY NAME is recognized for the high quality service we offer our clients. You have the opportunity to experience that service. Our top-notch team has streamlined and systematized every detail of the home buying and selling process to make it enjoyable and stress-free for you. We handle everything with the utmost care and concern.

GOALS

COMPANY NAME has put together a team of dedicated professional specialists. We go above and beyond the normal activities required to buy a property. Our goal is to satisfy clients' wants and needs so well they'll be happy to refer us to others. We work diligently to help you buy your new home at the best price in the shortest amount of time so you can fulfill your vision and get on with your life.

PURPOSE

The purpose of this consultation is to provide the information you need to help you select the best person and company that will best represent you in buying your home. We hope after reviewing this material, you'll have a clearer understanding of how much we value your business.

REFERRALS

We appreciate the opportunity to show you our superior marketing and ultimate service. Please take the time to check the comments from our past clients and find out why most of our business comes from referrals. A referral is the highest compliment we can receive. That's why we perform outstanding, exceptional work during each and every transaction to earn them. Working together, we will achieve your goal and ours. We truly appreciate the opportunity to interview for the position of your Realtor. We consider it an honor and take it very seriously. This is our career, not a part-time hobby. We will strive to serve you beyond your expectations. We look forward to working with you!

YOUR TEAM NAME

3

MEET THE TEAM

REPLACE WITH
YOUR LOGO

SERVICE

When you hire **TEAM NAME**, you get more than one agent who is trying to be all things to all people. You will have a dedicated buyer specialist - your own personal shopper! Their job is to make sure you are educated throughout the process. If your agent goes on vacation or is tied up elsewhere, fear not! We cover each other, so you will never feel neglected. Need utility information? Need to schedule the home inspector? Our client care manager will dot every i and cross every t. We are ALL here working for YOU!

Experience

Your **COMPANY NAME HERE** has a combined total of over **14** years of experience, with over **368** homes sold!

Expertise

Specializing: Having lived and worked in this community for many years, there is no better expert on the local real estate market.

Communication

Our TEAM MEMBER AND TITLE, has extensive communication experience. Our team believes in sharing what's next" before clients even formulate the question.

Clients for Life

The majority of our business is referral based. We've experienced such fulfillment helping our clients over the years and have found that exceptional people tend to befriend exceptional people. We'd love to work with your friends too!

Awards/Recognition

COMPANY NAME HERE regularly receives awards and recognition leading in units sold, volume sold, and commendable transaction coordination.

Our Commitment To You

To provide unsurpassed service to help you buy your home at a fair market price, in the shortest time with the least inconvenience to you.

YOUR TEAM NAME   4

READY
TO BUY?

Answer these four questions.

If you answer yes to all of them,
you are probably ready to buy a home.

01

Do you have a steady, reliable income?

In other words, have you been employed on a regular basis for the last two years, and do you expect to maintain your employment?

02

Do you have a good record of paying your bills?

Have you made regular, on-time payments? If not, read on; there is still hope.

03

Do you have money saved up for a down payment and closing costs?

Many home buyers think that a down payment of 20% is needed. It's not. Many loans exist today that allow buyers to put down 10% to as little as 3.5% on the purchase of a home. So don't give up just because you can't come up with a 20% down payment.

04

Can you pay the mortgage each month

as well as additional costs that go along with homeownership, such as taxes, insurance, and maintenance?

YOUR TEAM NAME

5

CLIENT EVENT CONTACT PLAN
for 15 total SOI contacts leading up to the event

Week 12 - 12 weeks prior to event
- Save the Date email (1)
- Save the Date mailer (2)

Week 11
- Start SOI Invitation Phone Calls - 5 per day until complete (3)

Week 10
- Save the Date sent to SOI w/ Direct/Personal Messages on FB (4)
- Continue SOI invitation calls

Week 9
- Formal Invitation mailed (5)
- Continue SOI invitation calls

Week 8
- Formal Invitation email (6)
- Continue SOI invitation calls

Week 7
- Formal Invitation to SOI w/ Direct/Personal Messages on FB (7)
- Continue SOI invitation calls

Week 6
- Post Event Invitation on FB Business Page (8)
- Continue SOI invitation calls

Week 5
- Share Event Invitation on FB Business Page on personal FB pages
- Continue SOI invitation calls

Week 4
- Event Reminder Email (9)
- Continue SOI invitation calls

Week 3
- Continue SOI invitation calls
- Bulk Text event reminder (10)

Week 2
- Event Reminder Email (11)
- Sly Dial/Sly Broadcast event reminder bulk voice message to SOI (12)

Week 1
- Re-Post Event Invitation on FB Business Page & Personal Pages
- Event Reminder Email (13)

Post Event
- Thank you email (14)
- Thank you letter (15)
- FB Post w/ event photos – tag all attendees in post.

Past Client Follow Up Script

The script below can be used 2 or 3 times annually to continuously attempt to provide customer service beyond normal expectations. Additionally, this script can be used interchangeably to ask for 3 different items at the end: 1. Referrals; 2. Online Reviews; or 3. Client Testimonials.

1. Hi _____ , with ABC is is _____ with the _____ real estate team. I'm just calling as a customer service to check in with you to check in to see how you're doing in your new home. How has it been treating you?

2. What have you done to it?

3. Are you planning on doing any work or improvements to it in the future?

4. Would it help if I gave you the contact information of some professionals that we trust and regularly recommend that could help you get that done at a reasonable cost?

5. You see, we want you to think of us as your total home resource. Like your own personal Angie's List. So you can save yourself some time & frustration by letting us refer you to a tested & trusted professional for any homeownership needs that may come up. Would that benefit you?

6. *(Now Choose 1 of the 3 scripts below)*

    - REFERRALS
    Oh and by the way, we prefer to run our business by word of mouth. We like to work with the people that know who we know. So with that said, do you happen to know anyone else looking to move in the near future?

    - ONLINE REVIEWS
    Oh and by the way, what our clients think of us is of the utmost importance to us and our business. So would you mind taking a few quick minutes to give us a 5-Star review on (Google, Zillow, etc.) if I emailed you the link(s) right now?

    - CLIENT TESTIMONIALS
    Oh and by the way, what our clients think of us is of the utmost importance to us and our business. So would you mind taking a few quick minutes to reply to an email with your thoughts about our marketing and customer service efforts so that we can use it in our marketing materials as a client testimonial quote?

Existing Client Referral Scripts

Top administrative assistants will ask for client referrals early and often in a systematic fashion throughout each transaction. They always bring up the topic just after listing consultations, after successful open houses, after offers are accepted, after inspection repairs are completed, after homes appraise, at closings, and after other successful steps in the transaction are completed. So, use any one of the 5 scripts below as much as you can:

1. We want to work with more clients like you, and we find that people looking to move know others in the same position. How would you feel about referring our services to them?

2. It's been really great working with you thus far, and we feel really grateful to Jane for introducing us to you. So I just wanted to take the time to be sure to ask you if you happen to know anyone else that is looking to buy or sell a home soon, and if you would feel comfortable referring them to us?

3. Who else do you know that needs to move right now?

4. You are so great to work with, and we find that people typically have relationships with similar people. Since we would love to work with more people like you, who do you know that might be looking to move in the near future?

5. Because you are in the process of moving right now, you will overhear a lot of conversations from different people looking to move when you are out and about. When you do, would you mind giving them our phone number and ask them to call us?

CHAPTER 7:

YOUR SPHERE OF INFLUENCE (SOI)

ICENHOWER
COACHING & CONSULTING

LEARNING OBJECTIVES

- Identify the people in your Sphere of Influence (SOI)
- Formulate strategies to grow your SOI

I. YOUR SPHERE OF INFLUENCE

II. THE CENTER OF THE GLOBE

III. CUSTOMER-BASED OR BUSINESS-BASED

IV. IDENTIFYING YOUR SPHERE OF INFLUENCE

A. Inner Circles
B. Outer Circles

V. HOW TO GROW YOUR SPHERE

A. Emails
B. Mailers
C. Telephone Calls
D. Social Media

VI. DEVELOPING YOUR SOI DATABASE CONTACT PLAN

A. Lucky Number 7
B. 40 Annual Contacts
   1. The Basic Plan
   2. Value-Based Contact Plan (or Giving to Get)
   3. The Efficient Plan

VII. ACCOUNTABILITY IS KEY

VIII. APPENDIX

YOUR SPHERE OF INFLUENCE

Do you remember the classic Christmas movie, *It's a Wonderful Life*? Beset with serious troubles, George Bailey feels as though he has nobody to turn to. As he thinks about ending it all, his guardian angel appears and shows him all the lives he has touched and how different life in his community would be if he had never been born. As it turns out, George Bailey has a lot more friends than he ever realized.

You do, too. Most people vastly underestimate the number of people they know but, today, there are far more possibilities for creating connections than in George Bailey's time.

Every minute of every day presents a possibility to create connections, whether you're at the grocery store, getting a manicure, or cheering on your children at a swim meet or soccer match. Too, social media platforms like Facebook, Instagram, LinkedIn, and Pinterest can potentially connect us to hundreds if not thousands of people through our mutual connections and acquaintances.

All of these acquaintances and associations are what's known as your *Sphere of Influence* (SOI), a dynamic database of current connections and potential clients.

Your college friends who live thousands of miles from you may not be interested in buying a home in your town, but they may know someone who is. It's only natural to refer them to your business because you are someone they *know*. The same is true for your local connections. They would prefer to work with someone with whom they've built a relationship.

Relationships keep our connections alive.

We're all connected somehow, through family and friends and through our neighborhoods and communities. The Six Degrees of Separation theory says that any person on the planet can be connected to another person on the planet through a chain of six or fewer friends or acquaintances. What we *do* with those associations can drive our business.

Chapter 7 teaches you how to develop and nurture your Sphere of Influence and put these strategies to immediate use.

Specifically, you'll learn how to:

- Identify the people in your Sphere of Influence (SOI)
- Formulate strategies to grow your SOI

THE CENTER OF THE GLOBE

While there are many ways to generate business, from prospecting to farming and online lead-generation, most top-producing teams generate more than 50% of their business from the SOI's of their team members. Consequently, SOI database management is one of your chief priorities.

Whether you're a solo agent or an administrative assistant, a successful Sphere of Influence revolves around you. No matter how big or small your team, you're responsible for ensuring that everyone on the team consistently grows, maintains and stays in contact with their SOI database.

However, please note that this chapter does not only pertain to developing your agent's SOI database. It is very common for administrative assistants and managers to also be responsible for growing, contacting and cultivating their own SOI referral databases to generate business for the company as well. So pay close attention since SOI development is important for all members of a real estate team.

CUSTOMER-BASED OR BUSINESS-BASED

If your real estate office is business-based, your services are about you and the business at hand: helping people buy and sell houses. While there's nothing wrong with being business-based, you'll eventually reach a plateau. The business will never reach its true potential.

Think of it this way: the business does not exist for the sake of being a business. Your real estate office exists to provide a consumer service, which happens to be selling a property.

A customer-based service, on the other hand, is a dynamic opportunity to serve others by creating connections among them. Real estate professionals are a valuable resource for people who need a property question answered or want recommendations for the best landscapers or remodelers in town.

Because you have connections with these service-providers, the people you associate with and help along the way will come to you when they are ready to sell and buy their homes. You build a customer-based business by solving problems for people, and they'll remember you when they require professional real estate services.

A customer-based business is one that is built to last. Take care of customers, and they'll help you grow your business. By assisting the connections in your SOI, they come to regard you as the expert you are. For those of you who are an administrative assistant, you will be working in two Spheres of Influence, merging them into one: yours and your agent's.

You have to reach out to these connections, just like your real estate agent will be doing. Let's get started.

IDENTIFYING YOUR SPHERE OF INFLUENCE

Everyone has a Sphere of Influence. By definition, your SOI is *everyone you know that knows you are by name*. Your SOI should never include people that you haven't met or who wouldn't recognize you by name. Staying in constant contact with members of your SOI database can cost you precious time and money, so you don't want to waste your efforts on people who don't know who you are.

Think of your SOI as a globe with several layers, much like our planet. There is an inner core, an outer core, the mantle, and crust.

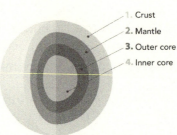

1. Crust
2. Mantle
3. Outer core
4. Inner core

You are the inner core, the center of the sphere. Around you is your outer core, the circle of family and close friends that enfold you. These are the people who love you and support you no matter what. Beyond them are those acquaintances that make up the mantle, which is like a cloak surrounding your friends and family. Although your acquaintances may not be as familiar as your close friends, you enjoy meeting with them and they know who you are. On the outermost layer, or the crust, are your professional contacts—the people you do business with.

We can group these categories into two circles: the inner and the outer.

Inner Circles

Your inner circle consists of your loved ones, your allies and your advocates. These are the people who want you to be successful in your real estate business, and they'll do whatever they can to help you out.

Typically, your strongest advocates can be found in the following categories (and, by extension, the network of each of these people):

- Spouse and immediate family members
- Close friends
- Extended family members
- Neighbors
- Past co-workers

Reaching out to these key people to obtain or update their contact information (physical address, email address, and phone number) will kick-start your SOI database.

As a collective group, these connections will help spread the word that you are in the real estate business. They can hand out your contact information and provide important testimonials about who you are as a person. These people are easy to contact because you know them the best, and they genuinely want you to do well.

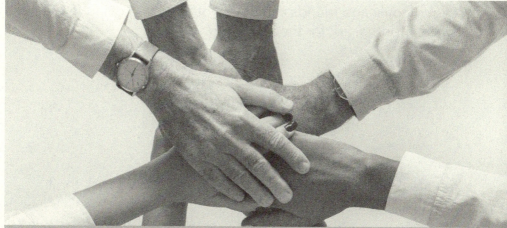

You have to ask your inner-circle for help, however. While they care about you and want you to do well, don't assume that they will automatically champion your cause. Your friends and family won't provide the assistance you need unless you're vulnerable enough to ask for it. What's more is that you will need to tell them precisely what you're looking for.

It's not enough to say, "Hey, I'm in real estate now, helping out an agent, so spread the word."

A better approach is to ask a direct question, one with a yes or no answer, like this:

"Do you know anyone thinking about moving this year?"

If they say yes, ask your friend or family member to forward your contact information to those who are thinking about moving. Better yet, ask for their contact information so that you can follow up with them.

If your family and friends can't think of anyone moving in the next twelve months, ask for their support:

"If you do run into someone thinking about moving, can I count on you to recommend me and get their phone number for me?"

You are more likely to get the help you need if you ask for it directly.

OUTER CIRCLES

When you have tapped into the assistance of your inner-circle, you are ready to engage the acquaintances in your outer-circle and expand your SOI.

Work the acquaintances in the mantle first. These are the people in your community that you know well because you routinely do business with them. Ask yourself:

Who do I know?

Like we said, you know a lot more people than you think you do. Here are some of the more common categories in our outer-circle to get you started, but think of other contact names you can add to this network:

- Accountants
- Appraisers
- Builders
- Babysitters
- Church Community
- Cleaning Services
- Dentists
- Doctors
- Hairdressers
- Home Inspectors
- Insurance Agents
- Mortgage Lenders
- Teachers
- Wedding Planners

You know these people, and they each have their own spheres of influence. Even if they are not going to be in the market for a new home in the next year, you can still ask them to forward your contact information to someone they may know who will be house-hunting.

Once this part of your outer circle is complete, it's time to think of the outermost layer. These are people you know too, but not as well as those in the first layer of your outer-circle. The list might include:

- The manager at your favorite restaurant
- An artist whose work you admire
- A store director
- The person who sold you your last vehicle

 There's a caution to keep in mind, however. Each contact you include must be someone you know personally. Culling the name of every hairdresser or carpet cleaner in town and inserting them into your database won't help you build a successful Sphere of Influence. They may fatten your list, but there's no real muscle backing it up.

Treat the list honestly, and you'll see it become a powerful networking tool.

How to Grow Your Sphere

An SOI is not a collection, like coins or stamps that sit on a shelf or in a drawer until you want to take them out and look at them. Like any living and growing thing, you'll have to treat your Sphere of Influence with care, continually working on ways to nurture and expand it.

For administrative assistants, you have the additional tasks of creating a unified SOI that represents the entire community you and your real estate agent share with each other.

Whether you're a solo agent or an assistant, your company will need to systematically stay in contact with everyone in your sphere over the course of the year. Communication with your SOI referral database must be consistent in order to generate predictable results.

What's more, *you will need to make 40 connections—or contacts—per year with each SOI member* using a variety of communication tactics.

There are predominantly four ways to make contact with people in your Sphere of Influence: Email, Mailers, Telephone Calls, and Social Media. Understand that this chapter simply provides a basic overview of these strategies. At ICC, we teach an entire SOI course that goes into a lot more detail about building a real estate agent's sphere of influence.

Employing a variety of contact strategies ensures that you are not contacting or targeting them too frequently through one method of communication. These are people that we have relationships with and that we want to refer business to us, so it's important that you don't offend or constantly bombard them with a single type of contact.

EMAILS

One of the first ways to reach out and connect with people in your SOI is through email. Email is cost-efficient and takes minimal time and effort to manage. They can also be automated to increase efficiency. After being written and scheduled, emails can be sent to your SOI automatically throughout the year. What's not to like?

Plenty, as it turns out.

Emails, especially when used in isolation of any other strategy, have some of the lowest conversion rates of any marketing strategy. Although an SOI Contact Plan composed of 40 emails a year may seem both inexpensive and efficient, it is also relatively ineffective. No more than 65% of the contacts made in your SOI Contact Plan should be through email. We'll cover that more in just a moment. For now, understand that email campaigns only work well when used with other marketing strategies. You will have to engage in additional ways to market the business.

You may wonder why you should bother at all with an email campaign?

Emails are used to generate awareness, not to collect business. Their purpose is to get your brand in front of your audience on a frequent and consistent basis. Email gives you an immediate and regular presence in people's minds, or what marketers call 'mind share'.

Effective mind share marketing establishes you as the first person people think of when they think of a real estate agent or real estate company. Even if people in your SOI don't open and read every single one of your emails, simply seeing your name in their Inbox will create mind share. When someone asks them if they know a good real estate agent, your name will be first on the tip of their tongue.

MAILERS

Mailers are any printed material that arrives in your mailbox. Mailers reach potential customers directly. The beautiful thing about a mailer is that it has a longer life than an email.

Most people who receive a mailer will pick it up and look at both sides. They may even hang on to it for a while, *especially if it's useful*, such as a conversion chart for kitchen measurements, a holiday recipe, or essential community phone numbers. Even a photo of a recently sold property in the neighborhood can be cause for taking a good look at a mailer. If a homeowner likes the way you presented the property, he or she may contact you when they are ready to list their home.

Most real estate CRMs (Customer Relationship Management systems) come with pre-made mailing templates for agents. Some CRMs even contract directly with a mailing service to send scheduled mailers to your entire database throughout the year. So, as with email, physical mailers take very little of your time once they are set up and managed efficiently.

Obviously, however, mailers are not free. Printing and postage will cost as much as $1.25 per mailer, and they will quickly eat up a marketing budget. As a rule, any agent's marketing costs should not exceed 10% of the Gross Commission Income (GCI), and mailers should never be more than 5% of the GCI.

In an agent's first year of business, mailers may have to be used on a limited basis if there is not much commission income coming in yet.

TELEPHONE CALLS

The best marketing strategy is to talk to someone. You won't be able to make it door to door to talk to your contacts on a daily basis, but you can pick up the phone and check in with them.

Remember, these are people you already know, so this is not a cold call—it's a warm reconnection. A few minutes spent on the phone can help you foster the connections you have with your SOI, and they may help you generate some leads, especially if you ask if they know of anyone planning to sell their home in the next twelve months.

As easy as the phone call is to make in theory, finding the time or the nerve to do it can be difficult. Agents come up with all kinds of excuses for avoiding making SOI calls. Both you and your agent will have full days, but the ten minutes it takes to make the calls can help you expand your sphere and grow your business.

This is where accountability is necessary. Solo agents must hold themselves accountable, and administrative assistants are responsible for holding agents accountable to the rainmaking activities they've committed to do.

SOCIAL MEDIA

Social media platforms make reaching out to those in your SOI easy and inexpensive. All it takes is a little creativity and regular effort to make your posts. Your posts should *add value* to your followers' feeds.

What to post:

- A single picture from a listed home, along with the link to view more.
- Useful homeowner information (reminders to protect pipes during freezes, how to create holiday door appeal, potted plants that ward off pests or are deer-resistant)
- Pictures of you and your agent at work (your workspace, your favorite coffee mug, a plant in the office that you'd like some advice about).
- Sharing other useful posts (community swap meet, where to get coupons, etc.)
- Shout Out & Thank You posts to a vendor, a client, or someone who helped you with something.

Facebook posts are less about self-promotion and more about engagement among your community of followers. Get them talking and commenting on your posts. Ask questions and post replies to keep the conversation going. And be sure to comment on other people's posts too. This keeps you top of mind with your personal SOI and also gets your name and face out there among the people that they know.

Post daily on Facebook and other social media platforms to stay present in people's minds. As with email, this can also be automated and scheduled in advance to increase efficiency. As with any other aspect of your job description, social media is a task to be completed and checked off as quickly as possible. Don't get caught up in spending hours per week reading and recreationally posting (as opposed to strategically posting) on social media.

For added impact, transfer your Facebook friends to your CRM or other SOI database, along with their known email addresses, telephone numbers, and physical addresses. They then become part of your broader SOI Database Contact Plan.

DEVELOPING YOUR SOI DATABASE CONTACT PLAN

Before technology, people relied on a Rolodex, a spinning wheel of client business cards.

Today's savvy agents or assistants enter the contact information from business cards and other sources into a database contained by a Customer Relationship Management (CRM) System.

This is the first step in developing your SOI Database Contact Plan.

Each contact in your CRM should include the person's name, telephone number, email address and physical address.

Even simple spreadsheet programs like Microsoft Excel are an efficient way to manage large numbers of contacts and, unlike the old-fashioned Rolodex, there's no limit to the size of your SOI. Contacts in your database can be sorted according to whatever parameters you establish and you can also make important notes about them.

Best of all, you can also document and keep track of contacts made to each SOI member, identifying who received emails, mailers, and phone calls.

As you'll see, a Database Contact Plan is a *systematic* process of staying in contact with the members of your SOI, and an effective plan with a solid conversion rate involves making *40 contacts per year with each individual SOI member.*

LUCKY NUMBER 7

Based upon decades of coaching, training, and tracking the results of real estate agents, we know that a Database Contact Plan with 40 annual contacts (using a variety of contact methods) will result in 1 closed transaction for every 7 people in your SOI database.

That is, if you have 300 SOI members in your database, a 7:1 conversion rate results in 43 closed transactions a year from your SOI database alone.

New agents might expect to close 20 closed transactions from a 'starter' SOI database, but that's still an impressive result. Imagine your conversion numbers if you can continually and systematically expand your Sphere of Influence year after year!

All you have to do is develop a plan of action for contacting each member of your SOI 40 times per year using a variety of contact strategies.

40 Annual Contacts

An effective Database Contact Plan involves making a *minimum* of 40 contacts per year with each SOI member. Certain contact methods have more or less value or effectiveness than others, however, and each strategy should make up a specific amount or percentage of your 40 contacts. For example, emails should make up no more than 65% of your contact plan.

At ICC, we have three plans to choose from: the Basic Plan, the Value-Based Contact Plan, and the Efficient Plan.

The Basic Plan

Just starting out? Start with the Basic plan.

With the Basic plan, your SOI contact goals look something like this:

- 40 Annual Contacts
- 26 emails (once every 2 weeks)
- 12 mailers (sent once a month)
- 2 phone calls (made once every 6 months)
- Post regularly on social media

Over the course of a year, you will build your mind share, gather a following, and see a 7:1 conversion rate if you put in the effort and do your work.

Value-Based Contact Plan (or Giving to Get)

It's been said that people don't care how much you know until they know how much you care. The same is true in real estate, or in any service-based industry for that matter. To show that you care, you'll need to give away a little something and provide value to your SOI members, whether it's giving away a small gift or some of the knowledge you have.

Giving gifts can quickly become expensive, and involves many more than 40 contacts. We recommend this plan only be used on smaller SOI databases or just those SOI members that you can count on the most. Administrative Assistants should help their agents identify which SOI contacts will most likely help you with referrals. Then develop a monthly give away.

With the Value-Based Contact Plan, our SOI contact goals look something like this and can be adapted and modified according to the size and complexity of your company and your SOI:

- 18 Emails (automated in CRM to send every 3 weeks)
- 3 Phone Calls
- 1 Drop-By (for example, pumpkins delivered to doorsteps in October)
- 1 Client Appreciation Event
- 4 Invitations to Client Appreciation Event: 2 emails, 1 mailer, and 1 phone call
- 1 Post-Event Email showing photos of event highlights and announcing event contest winners
- 12 Value-Based Mailers (sent once a month)

For Value-Based Mailers, try the following or come up with your own ideas!

- January: Happy New Year "*Thank You for Making it a Great Year*" postcard w/ photo of team
- February: Flyers/Coupons for local area Home, Garden & Patio Show
- March: Local College & Pro Sports Schedules
- April: Local & National Market Update
- May: Flower & Garden Seed Packets
- June: Summer Local Events Update (Graduations, Water Park Coupons, Summer Camps, etc.)

- July: Local & National Mid-Year Market Update
- August: Back to School Shopping Coupons & Sales
- September: Flyers/Coupons for local area Home, Garden & Patio Show
- October: Local & National Market Update
- November: Canned Food Drive (leave bags on doorstep to pickup) & include Holiday Recipe
- December: Happy Holidays Cards

THE EFFICIENT PLAN

The Efficient Plan combines the strategies of the Basic and the Value-Based Contact plans but is much more efficient and less costly. This plan puts less emphasis on gifts and mailers and more emphasis on agent activities like phone calls.

The Efficient Plan looks something like this:

- 4 Quarterly Newsletters (mailed out every 3 months)
- 26 Emails (automated in CRM and sent every 2 weeks)
- 1 Client Appreciation Event
- 4 Invitations to Client Appreciation Event: 2 emails, 1 mailer, and 1 phone call
- 3 Phone Calls to SOI
- 1 Facebook direct message (to update database contact information)
- 1 Drop-By Visit (with treats)

Those of you who are assistants should have a meeting with your real estate agent and map out which plan you'll be implementing. Schedule each task and activity on your calendar, especially large events that will need to be broken down into smaller tasks and planned far in advance.

ACCOUNTABILITY IS KEY

Everyone plays a part in implementing a systematic Database Contact Plan. Emails and mailers are usually created, managed, and automated by the administrative assistant or marketing director at larger companies. The agent, of course, makes phone calls, and they may also handle their social media. However, the administrative assistant is responsible for holding the agent accountable to all agreed-upon goals and activities.

To stay on track with your contact goals, your and your agent will need to work according to a system. While it's easy to automate emails, mailers, and even social media, agents will need to maintain a systematic phone call schedule in order to contact everyone in their SOI twice a year.

The larger the SOI database, the more phone calls they will need to make each day and week. For example, if you have 300 SOI members that you need to call twice a year, that's 600 annual phone calls, which works out at 12 phone calls a week or 2-3 phone calls per day. While 600 sounds like a daunting number, agents should easily be held accountable for making a couple of phone calls a day.

It is critical that all sales agents and administrative staff members are held accountable to (1) adding people to their SOI and (2) maintaining regular and consistent contact with their SOI. (Administrative team-members might be expected to add 1 or 2 SOI members a week. This is very normal.)

Top real estate teams track their "SOI Contacts" and "SOI Growth" activities on a scoreboard to hold everyone accountable to these tasks. An example of this section of a team scoreboard is shown below.

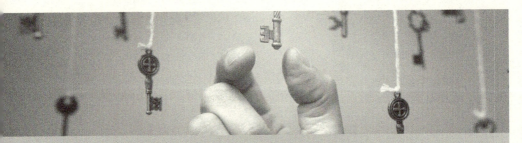

TEAM SCOREBOARD

Team Member	Weekly Actual 6/27-7/3	Weekly Actual 7/4-7/10	Weekly Actual 7/11-7/17	Weekly Actual 7/18-7/27	Weekly Goal	Monthly Actual	Monthly Goal	Yearly Actual	Yearly Goal	Notes
LEAD MEASURES										
SOI CONTACTS										
Robyn					15		60		1200	
Melissa					25		100		1200	
Karl					25		100		1200	
Logan					5		20		240	
Jessica					5		20		240	
Tasha					25		100		480	
SOI GROWTH - Members Added										
Robyn					3		13		150	
Melissa					3		13		150	
Karl					2		9		100	
Logan					1		4		48	
Jessica					5		20		240	
Adrianna					5		20		240	
Tasha					5		20		240	

Your Sphere of Influence is a critical part of developing a thriving real estate business. The larger your database, the more sales your real estate office will see. Your goal is to help make that happen.

TEAM SCOREBOARD

Team Member	Weekly Actual 6/27-7/3	Weekly Actual 7/4-7/10	Weekly Actual 7/11-7/17	Weekly Actual 7/18-7/27	Weekly Goal	Monthly Actual	Monthly Goal	Yearly Actual	Yearly Goal	Notes
LEAD MEASURES										
SOI CONTACTS										
Robyn					15		60		1200	
Melissa					25		100		1200	
Kari					25		100		1200	
Logan					5		20		240	
Jessica					5		20		240	
Tasha					25		100		480	
SOI GROWTH – Members Added										
Robyn					3		13		150	
Melissa					3		13		150	
Kari					2		9		100	
Logan					1		4		48	
Jessica					5		20		240	
Adrianna					5		20		240	
Tasha					5		20		240	

CHAPTER 8:
CREATING THE ULTIMATE USER EXPERIENCE

LEARNING OBJECTIVES

- Distinguish between assumptions and perceptions
- Evaluate contacts and associates
- Select ways to nurture your Sphere of Influence
- Assemble your Business Operations Manual

I. CREATING THE ULTIMATE USER EXPERIENCE

II. WORKING WITH ASSUMPTIONS AND PERCEPTIONS

A. Buyers & Sellers
B. Your Agent
C. Cooperating Agents

III. SCRIPTS TO HELP YOU

IV. NURTURING YOUR SPHERE OF INFLUENCE

A. Security and Safety
B. Who to include in your SOI, who to leave out
C. Physical Safety
D. Personal Information Security

V. YOU'RE THE BOSS

VI. REVIEW OF YOUR BUSINESS OPERATIONS MANUAL

A. Policy and Procedures Manual

VII. YOU'RE THE BOSS

VIII. APPENDIX

CREATING THE ULTIMATE USER EXPERIENCE

Now that you've identified your Sphere of Influence, it's time to create the ultimate User Experience.

User Experience is a marketing term for how people experience and ultimately feel about your business. If your clients, colleagues or SOI contacts have a negative experience with your company, all the marketing in the world will not make them endorse or refer you business.

Creating the ultimate user experience includes providing value to your clients and making their experience as easy and pleasant as possible. And, as you'll see later in the chapter, the people who use and experience your company includes your team members as well as your clients and customers. It's just as important to create a great user experience for them too.

Creating an amazing experience begins with understanding that everyone is different and not everyone will feel the same way about something as the next person. As you will soon see, people's experience is influenced by their perceptions and the assumptions they make based on those perceptions. It's important, therefore, that we take assumptions and perceptions into account when communicating and working with the different people we interact with each day. Our assumptions and perceptions are not always accurate, factual, or true, but it's important that we don't offend or alienate our clients by dismissing their perceptions or challenging their assumptions.

Your learning objectives for this chapter include these goals:

- Distinguish between assumptions and perceptions
- Select ways to provide value and positive experience for your Sphere of Influence
- Assemble your Business Operations Manual

WORKING WITH ASSUMPTIONS AND PERCEPTIONS

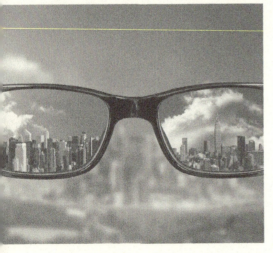

People make decisions based on assumptions and perceptions.

A perception is how a prospect uses his or her senses to interpret something. An assumption is a judgment or evaluation that he or she makes as a result of that perception.

The client may want to see a home, for example, based on its online description. It's the right size, the right price, and in a coveted neighborhood. When pulling into the driveway, however, it's apparent that there's a lot of construction going on in the area because of the hammering and pounding. The noise is distracting, but the client goes into the home anyway.

There's a clean smell, and the light scent of freshly baked bread or cookies wafts throughout the house. The client's senses are heightened and engaged. Obviously, this home has been well cared for, they assume. Their assumption is based on perception. In this case, the client has concluded, rightly or wrongly, that a clean home where people have time to bake is one that is well cared for, and people like to purchase well cared for homes.

But what if the client walked into the home, and it was in desperate need of cleaning? Imagine if there were chips in the paint on the wall, and the cracked window had duct tape keeping it in its frame. And the smell? Pets.

The potential buyer might assume, based on perceptions, that this home would require considerable TLC, which may or may not be true, but that's what they believe.

In your role as the administrative assistant, you'll be working with clients who have distinctly different perceptions and make assumptions based on them. The agent you work for and other cooperating agents will have perceptions and assumptions as well.

Indeed, you will too.

BUYERS & SELLERS

One of the most common assumptions among those selling a home is that it is worth far more than its actual value.

That's because of the perceptions surrounding the home. The sellers are likely to have a lot of memories surrounding their home, like when they measured the growth of their children by marking their height each year with a penciled line on the kitchen door jamb. The homeowners cooked their first holiday meal in this house, or they learned how to grow stunning roses. Every moment of their lives up to now is embedded in the home they are about to sell, so of course, to them, it's worth quite a lot.

It's understandable, then, that sellers want the buyers to have the same feelings about the home—they want them to value it as much as the sellers do.

Naturally, the buyer will want to get the most value for his or her investment but, often, buyers will view the same home—and its value—in a very different way to the sellers. Every buyer brings his or her own perceptions and assumptions to the table, too.

Some buyers may have already made assumptions that:

- An older home has less value and more repairs that will have to be made.
- Red front doors are best.
- Landscaping is expensive.
- Swimming pools are bothersome to care for
- Every backyard needs a swing set.
- Remodeling is too much work
- Any crack in a wall is dangerous.

Our assumptions and perceptions are not always accurate, factual, or true, but it's important that we don't offend or alienate our clients by dismissing their perceptions or challenging their assumptions.

Telling your sellers that buyers don't think their home is worth that much will be incredibly hurtful and offensive to them. You have to be extremely careful when communicating with your clients. It's very important to stay neutral. Don't insert too much personal or emotional opinion, and don't impose your own perceptions and assumptions on the client.

You can help clients with their perceptions by being as factual and transparent as possible. You won't be able to change their perceptions, but you can provide honest answers and objective data in a professional and steady way. Don't be hyperbolic. Don't downplay concerns but, equally, don't give excessive importance or value to things based on your own perceptions, assumptions, or opinions.

If they ask you a question about the property or purchasing process, and you aren't sure of the correct answer, say so. Never tell them something based on a hunch or presumption. Follow up by stating that you will find out and provide a factual and judgment-neutral answer within a specific amount of time.

Following through on our promises is one of the best ways to create a reassuring and predictable user experience.

Your Agent

Perceptions and assumptions are not limited to buyers and sellers, however. Everyone in the real estate office makes assumptions based on perceptions, including the real estate agent.

Agents also need facts and concrete information to do their work. Assumptions serve only to muddy the waters and make sales more difficult.

Assistants can help their agents avoid making assumptions and reacting emotionally to situations by providing accurate and real-time proof and information. For solo agents, the task is to remember that you are not immune to making assumptions and develop an ability to recognize when you are being falsely influenced by your perceptions and assumptions.

This may mean going the extra mile to get precise comparables or property descriptions. Accurate, data-driven decision-making can drive the business forward in a compelling way. It also helps you to be a steady and calming presence when presenting information to your clients, which is crucial in creating a wonderful client experience for them.

Facts and data are critical to every aspect of your business-operations. Every action you take should be based on facts instead of perceptions and assumptions. There should never be any assumptions about what's working and what's not working at the company.

Remember that a great company user experience applies to your coworkers and team members as well as your client. For those of you who are administrative assistants, your agent should never need to assume that SOI contact-quotas are being met or that you've scheduled the necessary appointments. Regular and frequent communication, as well as accurate and data-driven documentation, will add proof to their perceptions and help to avoid surprises.

COOPERATING AGENTS

A cooperating agent represents the other party (either the buyer or seller) in a transaction. They too will bring their own assumptions based on their perceptions.

Ultimately, one of the best ways to handle perceptions and assumptions is to use what you learned about the DISC behavior in the first chapter. Remember that, every day, you will be dealing with different people who display the following tendencies and traits:

- D: dominant and are direct
- I: influencers who are full of ideas and energy
- S: people who are steady and supportive
- C: those who adore compliance and want to analyze data and facts

As you work with your real estate agent, cooperating agents and buyers/sellers, you'll be able to identify behavior types and provide each of them with what they need, in the way that they need it, to make accurate decisions rather than rely on assumptions.

Just remember that your loyalty must be to the agent you work with and the clients you represent.

SCRIPTS TO HELP YOU

Knowing what to say in different situations can be tricky, especially if you are new to real estate.

For this reason, we have provided various scripts for you to use, whether you are reaching out to the contacts in your Sphere of Influence or you are following up with a buyer. Don't be afraid to refer to them and use them frequently until you become comfortable with them. Our scripts have been tested and proven with some of the highest performing teams, agents and administrators in the industry, and they'll work just as well for you.

A script can help you communicate, and using a script regularly ensures understanding in these ways:

- You know you are making the points that need to be made.
- You are less likely to forget a point.
- The script helps you sound more fluent and knowledgeable.

Some people hate the idea of using a script because it can sound like you're reading from a paper. In essence, you are! The trick is to rehearse the script so well that it sounds natural. You may even find that you can adapt parts of it to fit your own voice and style. Don't be alarmed if it feels extremely uncomfortable the first time you use a script. That's normal. It can take some time to feel confident and comfortable with them.

You will have mastered this form of communication when you can deliver the message in the script in a way that flows smoothly, and the person on the other end of the phone can't even tell that you're using a script.

Nurturing Your Sphere of Influence

It's okay to be yourself, too. Not everything you say has to be scripted. You'll have plenty of impromptu opportunities to engage with clients and contacts as you nurture your Sphere of Influence.

Our SOI is a significant component in creating the ultimate user experience. Remember that user experience is about how people experience and ultimately feel about your business. Not everyone in your SOI will have personally done business with you, but they experience who you are as a company every time you make contact with them and seek their referrals.

When nurturing your SOI, you always need to create a positive perception of your company. You also need to provide value to your SOI members. They may not have done business with you yet, but they will in the future if you create a wonderful user experience for them too. And, when seeking their referrals you need to create a strong sense of how wonderful your company is so that they can refer you to their friends and family with confidence and trust.

 As we've covered in previous chapters, there are many ways to provide value to your SOI and create positive feelings about your company. For example, you may want to pick one community need and focus on that. Maybe you adopt the tradition of giving new homeowners symbolic gifts of desserts. You also organize canned food drives, and people in the community know they can count on you for helping at the food pantry.

Continue to nurture your SOI with small remembrances like these:

- **Birthday & Anniversary Cards:** Develop a tickler system for special dates. Send cards in the mail.

- **Grow Your Network:** Mail (or drop off) packets of seeds according to the season. Give away wildflower seeds in the fall or vegetable seeds in the spring.

- **Holiday Cards:** Send cards for Thanksgiving, Christmas, or other holidays widely celebrated in your community.

- **Social Media Posts:** Be present. Like, share, and comment, but always focus on the positive.

Regardless of the mementos and warm fuzzy comments you provide, the best way to nurture your SOI is to build trust and reliability with regular and consistent communication.

Security and Safety

Creating the ultimate user experience isn't just about gifts and exciting events.

When clients do business with you, you need to create a sense of security, trust and reassurance in every way.

Who to include in your SOI, who to leave out

When growing your SOI database, it's crucial that you understand who belongs in it and who doesn't. The only people in your SOI should be people you and the members of your team know, period. These are the people you call by name, and you know something. They recognize you by name as well. By sticking to the people you know in your SOI, you are limiting your risk and exposure to strangers.

Physical Safety

The real estate agent is responsible for maintaining safety and security when showing a property, but you'll be stepping up and helping out with open houses and client appreciation events.

People have the best of intentions, but it wise to plan with personal safety in mind. Your agent may want to initiate a check-in system with you, especially when showing a property. The two of you will want to keep secure the properties you show.

Personal Information Security

The personal information you have for clients is sensitive information that must be maintained securely. No one should have access to client folders except you and the real estate agent. The same is true of the information you retain.

Avoid using your personal mobile phone to look up specific client data. In the event you were to lose your phone, someone else could gain access to private files and secure information.

You're the Boss

Remember that you are also in charge of hiring, training, and overseeing the onboarding of any future hire. This is another opportunity for you to provide the ultimate user experience but, in this case, the user is not a client or SOI member, they are your new employee or team member.

In marketing, an important aspect of creating a great user experience is the ease with which customers can find, access, review, and buy products and services. Likewise, when onboarding new team members, you can create a great user experience for them by making it an easy and seamless process. The key to managing the chaos associated with the training and onboarding of new team members is to systematize the process.

To help you do this, we have provided a copy of our sample "1st Day Welcome Checklist" that will help create an impactful first day on the job for new hires. Customize this sheet to include all essential information at your particular company, as well as any materials and tasks that need to be accomplished and provided on the first day on the job.

We have also attached our 'First Quarter Training Checklist' to help create a training schedule for your new hire's first three months on the job. Both of these checklists should be filed in the Administrative Manager section of your Business Operations manual.

Training will include watching various ICC video courses, or reading specific ICC books that will benefit them in their new role. Certainly, any new administrative hire should be required to read *ADMIN* and watch our video material on how to systematize administrative processes. Administrative training could also include online classes about MLS forms, or videos to watch about your company's CRM system, as well as shadowing other team members.

Sales agents will do a lot of 'on the job' training, but they will benefit enormously from ICC's courses such as *SOI – Building a Real Estate Agent's Sphere of Influence* and *BEHAVIOR – Improve Communication & Sales Performance in Real Estate*, both of which provide a higher level of detail about SOI and DISC behavior than we could detail in this book.

Starting out in a new role in the real estate industry can be extremely disorienting, so providing this much-needed structure for new hires creates a straightforward, reassuring and empowering user experience for them.

And for you, creating structure and self-managed training will result in a smooth and efficient onboarding process that doesn't steal too much time from your busy schedule. When onboarding and training new administrative hires, it's especially important to lead by example and embody the efficiency, organization and professionalism that you want them to emulate in their administrative role.

A key component in creating a great user experience for your team is by providing them with a robust and comprehensive Business Operations manual.

REVIEW OF YOUR BUSINESS OPERATIONS MANUAL

By now you should have a clear idea about how to create, categorize, and customize your Business Operations manual according to your company's actual structure, needs, and functions.

As we mentioned in Chapter 1, your operations manual should include detailed job descriptions for each role as well as the various checklists, forms, and scripts that will assist employees in performing their tasks and duties. This manual is the backbone of your business, and the last step is to compare the checklists found in the appendices of each chapter to the documents you have customized and assembled.

Original documents should live in this binder, and this is your go-to book when you need to make copies of forms, checklist or scripts. Avoid using the original document, or it will quickly become worn and ragged.

Your manual should also include your company's policies and procedures.

To assist you, we have attached a sample of our 'Real Estate Team Policy and Procedures Handbook' for your review. This sample document should help you develop and codify considerations about dress code, hours of operation, holidays, confidentiality, conduct

and performance, as well as your company's mission and core values. It also contains a significant number of legal policies, disclaimers and procedures, so we strongly recommend having your attorney review them since different state laws and practices can change their impact greatly.

Though you or your employees may be the only people who ever lay eyes on this document, its effects reach far beyond you and will impact clients, colleagues, and your company in ways you'll never think of. A good operations manual that is clearly organized and well written will ensure that you provide an amazing user experience for *everyone* who interacts and engages with your business.

[REPLACE WITH YOUR TEAM LOGO]

TEAM POLICY & PROCEDURES
HANDBOOK

Effective Date: October 15th, 2017

NOTE: Before using this sample Team Policy Handbook, be sure to have your attorney review it for many issues that are state specific.

Table of Contents

WELCOME STATEMENT

Welcome! On behalf of [ENTER TEAM NAME], I welcome you to our team, and wish you a fulfilling and rewarding experience as we strive to be a leader in the industry and one of the best real estate teams in the [ENTER STATE]. We hope that you will be challenged, find success, and that your work here will be enjoyable.

Sincerely,

[ENTER NAME]

TEAM MEMBER STATUS

The purpose of this handbook is to establish a uniform system of daily conduct by and between us when dealing with each other, other members of the team, our clients, and members of the public. You are responsible to read and review this handbook and to comply with its policies and procedures.   If you have any questions, please ask our Director of Operations.

When you review these polices, please keep in mind that they should be regarded as guidelines only, which, in a business like ours will require changing from time to time. The team leader or, the team's director of operations, retains the right to make decisions involving policy changes as needed to conduct work in a manner that is beneficial to agents, employees, and customers of the team. This handbook replaces any and all prior handbooks, policies, procedures and practices of the team.

INDEPENDENT CONTRACTORS

The team has an independent contractor relationship with its sales agents. Agents are not employees of the team, and are not entitled to any employee benefits. Sales agents must abide by the office policies and must strictly adhere to the professional and ethical standards. Failure to comply with the team policies or procedures may result in the end of the contractual relationship.

Nothing in these office policies is intended to alter or amend the terms and conditions of the independent contractor agreement for those on the team who operate as independent contractors. In particular, nothing in this handbook is intended to alter the right of either party to terminate the independent contractor agreement, with or without cause, as set forth in the independent contractor agreement. Neither the policies contained in this handbook, nor any other written or verbal communication by any member of the team, are intended to create a contract of employment or a warranty of benefits. The policies contained herein may be added to, deleted, or changed by the team in its sole discretion.

3

EMPLOYEES

Licensed and non-licensed assistants, administrative staff, and any other individuals who are compensated by the team by a means other than commissions (ex. - hourly or salaried pay) resulting from their own efforts are considered employees of the team.

ASSISTANTS

Sales agents who wish to hire an assistant(s) must first seek and obtain approval of Management. The agent will be the employer of the assistant, and the agent shall bear responsibility for assuring compliance with all issues relative thereto, including tax withholding, Social Security and Medicare taxes, and state workers compensation and unemployment taxes, etc. Agents and assistants must execute the appropriate forms and addendum to modify the agent's independent contractor agreement(s).

VALUE PROPOSITION & CORE VALUES

VALUE PROPOSITION

As its value proposition, the team offers: [MODIFY WITH YOUR VALUE PROPOSITION BELOW]

- A growth environment that makes your development a priority through one-on-one consulting, training, accountability and mentoring.

- A guarantee that all systems are in place and working for you, so you spend less time servicing transactions and more time selling properties

- A positive work environment that allows individuals to "fail forward" and learn in their respective roles.

[REPLACE WITH YOUR TEAM LOGO]

CORE VALUES   [MODIFY WITH YOUR CORE VALUES BELOW]

At the core of the team is a conviction that who you are in business with matters. We believe that the company we keep can contribute to our lives in untold ways. To help cement this understanding, we've formalized the following core values to outline how we do business:

4

MISSION: Our Mission is to be an industry leader, the team of choice for our agent partners, employees and clients.

BELIEFS: We believe that when you take care of other's needs, your needs are automatically taken care of. We believe that people don't care how much we know until they know how much we care. We also believe that no one succeeds alone, and through our passion we help those around us fulfill their dreams.

PERSPECTIVE: A training, consulting and systems based organization that also provides front end and back end services that lead to productivity and profitability. Our team thinks like a top producer while acting like a consultant, and focuses all its activities on service, productivity, profitability and a positive culture.

EXPECTATIONS: It's all about our customers and their needs. We provide service that exceeds their expectations. If we can master their needs, success will come without effort. It's all about them.

INTEGRITY: As a member of the team, you will be responsible for setting new standards for the real estate industry. We want our peers to continue to look to us for integrity and as people with whom they would like to do business. As we create these new standards, we will create a great experience not only for our clients, but with cooperating agents and their clients as well.

WOW EXPERIENCE: We want individuals we come in contact with to be "wowed" when they work with us. We hope that they will want to not only work with the team again, but also tell others about their amazing customer service experience with our team.

EXPECTATIONS & CONDUCT

ACCOUNTABILITY EXPECTATIONS

Each week, a re-cap of the previous week's accomplishments and a plan for the following week will be either discussed with or e-mailed to the Team Leader or Director of Operations. Accountability expectations will be discussed between you and the Team Leader and modified when needed.

TRAINING

The performance of each team member within the team is an integral part of achieving all team goals. Team members are expected to attend all team training sessions and weekly meetings. No cell phones are permitted during team training sessions and meetings.

TIME OFF

When you are off work, be completely off and unplug from the job! You have several team members that are able to handle your business. If the team does not know the details of a transaction, someone from the office will try to reach you to find out the answers._If you are going to be out of town, you are encouraged to always have a team member answer your voicemail, and cell phone. Forward email along with an automated response to your clients that you're out of town through your email system. Forwards can be done through the same system.

The team strongly encourages you to schedule one day off each week. If this means forwarding your calls to another team member, or even giving a team member your cell phone to enjoy a guilt-free day off, please do it.

PHONES

The team's goal is that every client that calls will speak with a live person. The team business telephones (including forwarding to personal cell phones) shall be answered between 8:00 a.m. – 8:00 p.m. Answer the telephone with the following greeting: "[ENTER TEAM NAME], this is _____ (your name)." The only exception to this greeting is if Caller I.D. identifies the incoming call as an immediate family member.

Remember that your schedule is *very* flexible as an agent in real estate, but for that privilege, agents are expected by their clients to be on call 8:00 a.m. – 8:00 pm seven days a week. Return all calls as promptly as possible. The team standard is to **return all calls within 15 minutes**. If you can return a call within 5 to 10 minutes, your odds of earning that person's trust will increase dramatically. We understand that sometimes you are in a meeting or showing a house. Therefore, you should be able to return a call within 15 to 30 minutes.

Please call *everyone* back (agents, lenders, title companies, prospects, and clients), even if you do not have the answer to a question or concern. If, after 15 to 30 minutes you cannot get an answer, then please call the client and inform them that you are diligently working on it for them. If you cannot return a call that is waiting for a response within 15 - 30 minutes, let your Team Leader know so that someone from the team's offices can return the call.

APPEARANCE & ATTIRE

Professional dress and appearance is required at all times when in the offices. Team Members may dress as they like when working out of the office, but must always remember to dress professionally when dealing with clients. Business casual "plus" is generally acceptable. Many people are sensitive to colognes and perfumes in the event you choose to wear a cologne or perfume please be advised that a little goes a long way in a small work environment. The team in its sole discretion will determine what constitutes professional dress and appearance.

SERVICE EXPECTATIONS

Team members are to service our clients, both buyers and sellers, each and every week. Always stay positive and deal courteously with all parties at all times. Customers expect and we intend to deliver the "FOUR A's":

6

1. Accuracy
2. Availability (they can reach us in person as much as possible)
3. Ability to be listened to and understood
4. Advise from an professional expert

As a best practice, team members should **pick one business day during the week to service all active clients** (both buyers and sellers included). Active clients include home buyers not yet under contract for the purchase of a home, listings not yet active on the market, and all clients under contract for the purchase of a home.

Team members understand the value of communication and the down sides of the lack of communication with their clients and what that does for the brand reputation as well as the client experience. It is understood that of the home buyers and sellers interviewed by the NAR, 74% of those who were unhappy with their agent's performance were unhappy due to the lack of communication. Team members understand that communication should occur via a phone call at least once a week. It is understood that text messages and emails are only a supplement to this primary form of communication, voice to voice.

ATTENDANCE & PUNCTUALITY

To maintain a safe and productive work environment, team members are expected to be reliable, to be punctual in reporting for scheduled work and to work all of their scheduled hours. Absenteeism, tardiness and leaving early places a burden on other members of the team. In the rare instance when a team member cannot avoid being late to work or is unable to work as scheduled, he or she must notify his or her supervisor of the anticipated tardiness or absence as soon as possible and in no event later than the team member's scheduled start time. Poor attendance and excessive tardiness are disruptive, and may lead to disciplinary action or termination.

The team's general Office hours are from 8:00 am to 5:00 pm with a one-hour lunch break unless otherwise scheduled in advance. Exempt team members are expected to work whatever hours are required to satisfactorily perform his/her job.

FAIR HOUSING

The team has zero tolerance for violations of the Fair Housing laws and prohibits any client, customer, agent or employee from discriminating in the provision of any of the team's services on the basis of age, sex, race, color, religion, physical or mental disability, familial status, marital status, national origin, genetic information, sexual orientation, or any other protected category.

Prohibited practices may include, but are not limited to the following behaviors:

1. Refusing to show, sell or rent based on a person being a member of a protected class.

7

2. Different treatment/disparate treatment to persons of a protected class.

3. Steering or guiding potential homebuyers to selected areas based on where you think they need to live.

4. Discriminatory advertising that "expresses" a preference for buyers of a particular protected category.

5. Harassment (i.e., coercion, intimidation, threats, or interference with a person's fair housing rights or because a party is abiding by fair housing law).

6. Applying more burdensome criteria to applicants of protected classes.

7. Blockbusting, which is defined as any illegal, discriminatory practice whereby an agent induces a property owner to list his or her property by representing that the neighborhood may change as a result of race, color, sex, religion, sexual orientation, marital status, national origin, genetic information, disability or any other protected category.

Any violation of fair housing laws or this policy must be reported to the team's Director of Operations or the team leader acting principal broker immediately. Independent contractors are prohibited from engaging in any conduct in violation of this policy and are subject to removal from their duties or activities with the team for violations of this policy.

EQUAL EMPLOYMENT OPPORTUNITIES AND ANTI-HARASSMENT POLICY

The team is an equal employment opportunity employer. The team prohibits any discrimination based on race, gender, pregnancy, color, national origin, religion, age, disability, or any other status or characteristic protected by law. Discrimination is prohibited throughout all phases of your employment – including being interviewed, hired, promoted, compensated, and provided benefits.

The team forbids retaliation against anyone who reports prohibited discrimination and/or harassment. The team's policy is to investigate any complaints of unlawful discrimination and/or harassment and to take any necessary corrective action, up to and including termination. It is also the team's policy to ensure against and to take corrective action against any Employees who harass, embarrass, or retaliate in any respect against anyone who has made a complaint regarding unlawful discrimination. Any complaints concerning unlawful discrimination and/or harassment or retaliation for having raised a complaint should be immediately directed to the team leader or the team's Director of Operations.

It is the policy of the team that all employees, customers and clients be free of discrimination and harassment on the basis of an individual's race, color, sex, pregnancy, sexual orientation, national origin, genetic information, religion, marital status, veteran status, physical or mental disability, age or any other protected category under federal or state law. The team will not tolerate sexual or other unlawful discrimination or harassment in the workplace or in other settings in which employees, customers and clients may find themselves in connection with their employment or agent-related business. The team also will not tolerate any retaliation against anyone complaining of harassment or anyone who has cooperated in an investigation of harassment in accordance with this policy.

The team takes allegations of violations of this policy seriously, and will respond promptly to complaints of harassment. Where the team determines that inappropriate conduct has occurred, the team will act promptly to eliminate the conduct and take any necessary corrective action, including disciplinary action where appropriate.

While this policy sets forth the team's goals of promoting a workplace that is free of unlawful harassment, the policy is not designed or intended to limit the team leader's or the team's Director of Operations authority to discipline or take other remedial action for any workplace conduct that is deemed unacceptable, regardless of whether the conduct satisfies the legal definition of harassment. Employees are prohibited from engaging in any conduct in violation of this policy and are subject to removal from their duties or activities with the team for violations of this policy.

Definition of Sexual Harassment

The team believes that all its employees, customers, and clients have the right to a work and business environment free from all forms of unlawful discrimination and harassment. The team will not tolerate the harassment of any employee, customer, client or other covered third party on any legally protected basis, including sex. Sexual harassment is defined as unwelcome sexual advances, requests for sexual favors, and other verbal, physical, and nonphysical conduct of a sexual nature when:

- Submission to such conduct is made explicitly or implicitly a term or condition of employment;

- Submission to or rejection of such conduct by an individual is used as the basis for employment decisions affecting that individual; or

- Such conduct has the purpose or effect of unreasonably interfering with an individual's performance at work, or creates an intimidating, hostile, or offensive work environment.

Under this definition, direct or implied requests by someone in a supervisory position for sexual favors in exchange for actual or promised job benefits such as favorable performance reviews, salary increases, promotions, increased benefits, or continued employment constitutes sexual harassment.

The legal definition of sexual harassment is broad and, in addition to the above examples, other unwelcome sexually oriented conduct, whether it is intended or not, that has the effect of creating a workplace that is hostile, offensive, intimidating, or humiliating to male or female

9

employees, customers, and clients may also constitute sexual harassment. Sexual harassment also includes non-sexual comments and conduct that are directed at an individual because of his or her gender or otherwise motivated by gender discrimination.

Consequences for Violating this Policy.

Harassment may be indirect or even unintentional. Violations of this policy, whether intended or not, will not be permitted. If it is determined that one of the team's employees or agents has engaged in inappropriate conduct, the team will take such action as is appropriate under the circumstances. Such action may range from counseling to immediate termination of employment, affiliation or contract, and may include other forms of disciplinary action, as is deemed appropriate under the circumstances.

Retaliation is Prohibited

All employees and agents should take special note that, as stated above, retaliation against an individual who has complained about harassment under this policy or participated in an investigation of harassment will not be tolerated, and will be treated as another form of harassment in accordance with this policy. All incidents of retaliation must be immediately reported in accordance with the reporting procedure described below.

Reporting Procedure for Discrimination and Harassment

If you observe unlawful discrimination or harassment, you must follow this reporting procedure to notify the team of the problem so that the company can promptly and thoroughly investigate this matter and take appropriate action. Do not allow an inappropriate situation to continue by not reporting it, regardless of who is creating the problem. No employee or agent of the team is exempt from its policies prohibiting harassment or discrimination. All complaints will be considered confidential, and disclosure will be limited to those with a need to know in order to investigate the complaint and/or take corrective action. The investigation will include a private interview with the person filing the complaint and, where appropriate, the witnesses. A private interview will be conducted with the person alleged to have committed harassment. In circumstances where it is appropriate to do so, the person who filed the complaint and the person alleged to have committed the conduct will be informed of the results of the investigation.

If the team determines that inappropriate conduct has occurred, the team will act promptly to eliminate the offending conduct and, where appropriate, to impose disciplinary action up to and including immediate termination of employment, affiliation or contract. the team will also take other corrective or remedial actions, when appropriate.

The team encourages the reporting of complaints so that it may appropriately address and correct any problems. An employee or agent who participates in good faith in any investigation under this policy has the team's assurance that it will not tolerate any retaliation against him or her as a result of bringing the complaint or otherwise participating in the process. All employees and agents are expected to be truthful, forthcoming, and cooperative in connection with a complaint.

LEGAL COMPLIANCE

In addition to any obligations set forth in this handbook, you are required to comply with all federal and state laws. If you have any questions or concerns, you should promptly consult the team's Director of Operations or the team leader.

Agents are responsible for maintaining strict compliance with license law for all of the states in which they are operating. Examples of compliance include, but are not limited to: meeting ongoing education requirements, maintaining license renewal, and having a working knowledge of all regulations and staying abreast of changes to the current rules and regulations which can be obtained from the licensing authority of each state through their respective websites.

All team members are required to maintain compliance with all local Multiple Listing Service (MLS) and Association of REALTORS® (AOR) rules and regulations.

SOCIAL NETWORKING AND BLOG POSTINGS

Postings on social networking sites including, but not limited to, Twitter, Facebook, LinkedIn and Instagram, as well as on blogs has become increasingly common. The team prohibits agents from any such postings, viewing or in any way participating in such sites while using any of the resources or equipment of the company. The team's internet resources are only to be used in accordance with the office rules and policies on confidentiality, harassment, use of the internet and use of office equipment.

The team neither encourages nor discourages any of its agents from posting on social networking sites or blogging using their own equipment. However, agents should be aware that these postings are public; even if access to them is restricted they may be forwarded out of the restricted group by those who have rightful access, and live on virtually forever. And, even if a posting is taken down, it never truly disappears but rather continues to exist somewhere in cyberspace. As a result, agents need to be mindful that Internet postings (whether images or comments), even though done on your own time and using personal equipment, can cause damage to not only your own reputation and interests, but also the reputation and interests of the team employees of the team, the principal broker, clients, and the public serviced.

Should you choose to blog or participate in any social networking site on your own time, using your own resources and equipment, you are required to follow these guidelines:

1. Confidential information of the team or any information whatsoever about our employees or clients must never be disclosed.

11

2. Postings must not violate any laws or policies of the team, including but not limited to harassment, or confidentiality of the team's employees or clients.

3. Postings must comply with the REALTOR® Code of Ethics and the statutes and regulations governing advertising by real estate licensees. In particular, current license law requires you to comply with all advertising requirements when you post information on such sites. This means that posts must include all the information required to be provided when you produce traditional advertising.

4. Postings must be respectful to the team, employees, clients, and competitors.

5. For non-real estate transactions, views, opinions, ideas, or information expressed are yours and yours alone and are not in any way attributable to the team.

Agents should report violations of this policy to the team leader, Director of Operations for the team. It is the responsibility of all agents and employees to help the team ensure compliance with the policy. Violation of any aspect of this policy is subject to disciplinary action, up to and including termination of the agency relationship, regardless of whether such conduct occurred away from work or on non-work time.

ONLINE SALES CREDIT

It is understood that when an agent working with the team records a sale with the team, that sale is then posted on multiple online sources as the sale for the team leader/ team. This sale credit belongs to the team and the team leader. In the event an agent chooses to leave the team, then the agent will not have any rights to take control of these recorded sales or any transferring of the credit of the recorded sale. These sales and the credit of these sales are the property of the team and the team leader.

CONFIDENTIALITY POLICY

All agents are expected to use extreme caution to ensure that the team's confidential information and the confidential information of our clients remains confidential, and does not become available to anyone inside or outside of the team who is not entitled to know it.

Definition of Confidential Information

- Due to the nature of the team business, agents have access to a broad range of confidential information that must be protected. By way of example and not limitation, confidential information includes:

- Non-public information about our clients, including motivation and all financial information.

- Marketing plans and strategies;

- Costs, funding, and the methods used to determine the price of listings, etc.;

- Internal initiatives, strategies, processes, and methods; and
- Confidential information which agents may obtain concerning our employees, including personnel files, personnel evaluations, and the like.

General Restrictions

Confidential information may not be used or disclosed by agents unless such use or disclosure is required by their job responsibilities on behalf of the team. Confidential information as described in this policy is the exclusive property of the team with all proprietary rights and under no circumstances whatsoever shall agents have any rights to use, disclose, or publish to others such confidential information during or after their affiliation with the team.

Maintain Confidentiality at All Times and Take Precautions in Public Spaces

To maintain all confidential information in strict confidence, all agents must avoid:

- Discussing confidential information with anyone other than those who have an authorized, legitimate need to know to carry out their job responsibilities;
- Disclosing confidential information to unauthorized the team personnel.
- Discussing specific transactions, or any other confidential information in a public place (including restaurants, etc.) where you may be overheard. Lower your voice or move to a private area when speaking on a cell phone for business.
- Talking unnecessarily about confidential information anywhere, including in your own office or home.

Physically Maintain Confidential Information in a Manner Designed to Preserve Confidentiality

Information must be maintained in the office (and elsewhere, if you are permitted to bring work home or to other locations) in a manner to protect confidentiality.

- Desks, credenzas, and other workspaces should be cleared at the end of each day. Anything remaining on the desk that contains confidential information should be in a folder or envelope or otherwise similarly protected from view.
- You may remove from our filing system only the client files currently being worked on at your workspace. All other files should be continually maintained in a secure location.
- Agents may not take transaction files home or otherwise out of the office without specific prior authorization from the team leader.
- If you are permitted to travel with confidential information, whether bringing the information home or on business travel, be mindful at all times about protecting the information. Do not leave confidential documents face up or otherwise in view in your vehicle. Keep sensitive information in a briefcase, closed folder, or use similar means to

protect it. Keep your vehicle locked when you are not in it. Keep your briefcase, folders, personal digital assistants, etc. with you at all times when traveling. Do not leave anything containing confidential information unattended. Be careful to preserve confidentiality if you choose to create or review confidential documents while traveling. It is very easy for other passengers to view your work, so make good decisions about whether you should take documents out on a plane, train, etc., and whether you should work on your laptop in such public settings. Similarly, if working at home, keep any confidential information in your home office or other private setting, and not in view of other individuals in the home.

Confidential Information In Electronic Form Must Also be Protected

Take steps to maintain confidentiality when sending or receiving information electronically, and when storing information on the computer.

When sending e-mail messages concerning confidential and/or proprietary information, agents must exercise significant caution. Questions regarding what level of security is needed for particular information to be sent or received over email should be directed to the team leader.

Agents must also exercise caution in saving information while working on their computers. For example, confidential or proprietary information should be stored on the team network, which provides safeguards for protecting information, and should not be stored on a local hard drive, desk top, disk, or portable drive. Highly confidential information may need to be password protected or other measures may need to be taken to safeguard it from unauthorized internal or external access.

Reasonable precautions must also be taken in regards to the physical security the team's information technology that may contain confidential information. Disks, drives, and other devices containing sensitive information should be contained in a locked drawer wherever possible. Computers should be turned off when not in use for an extended period of time or when an agent is out of his/her office. Agents are also encouraged to use screen savers so that any sensitive information that is displayed on an agent's screen will be covered if the agent is away from his/her desk. Screen savers provide an additional safeguard and are not intended to replace the expectation that agents minimize or close documents containing sensitive information when they walk away from their computers.

Visitor Access Must be Limited to Avoid Providing Access to Confidential Information

To protect confidentiality and avoid access to confidential information that could be viewed or overheard in the team offices, visitors, including agent's families and friends, should visit in the reception/lobby areas or in conference rooms and not in individual offices or workspaces. All visitors should enter the offices at the reception/lobby areas.

14

Procedures Upon Separation from Agency Relationship to Protect Confidential Information

Upon separation from affiliation with the team, agents must deliver to the team any and all confidential information in their possession, including all copies of all available forms. All confidential information must be returned regardless of whether the information was made or compiled by the agent or furnished to the agent during his or her affiliation.

An exit interview process should be implemented to insure compliance with return of confidential information.

CONFLICTS OF INTEREST

If you or a family member have a personal interest in either selling or purchasing a property, you must disclose this interest in writing to all parties involved in the transaction. All parties to the transaction must acknowledge in writing the existence of this interest **prior** to any offer being made.

For any other potential conflict of interest, you are required to bring the issue to the immediate attention of the team leader.

SAFE DRIVING & VEHICLE USAGE

The team recommends that you use your cell phone only when your car is stopped safely on the side of the road. You are expected to keep your automobile in a clean, properly maintained, and safe operating condition at all times. It is your obligation to drive in a safe, responsible and alert manner. This is especially true if you have clients in your car.

Each team member, whether and employee or independent contractor, will maintain automobile insurance with liability coverage of at least $1,000,000; and name [TEAM NAME] as an additionally name insured party on the policy.

SAFETY

To assist in providing a safe and healthy working environment for employees, agents, customers, and visitors, the team has established a workplace safety program. The team provides information to agents about workplace safety and health issues through regular internal communication such as meetings, bulletin board postings, memos, or other written communication. Some of the best safety improvement ideas come from individuals in the workplace. Those with ideas, concerns, or suggestions for improved safety in the workplace are encouraged to raise them with the team leader. Reports and concerns about safety in the team's workplace may be made anonymously. All reports can be made without fear of reprisal.

  15

Each agent is expected to obey safety rules and to exercise caution in all work activities. Agents must immediately report any unsafe condition to the appropriate supervisor. Agents who violate safety standards, who cause hazardous or dangerous situations, or who fail to report, or where appropriate, remedy such situation, may be subject to termination of the contractual relationship.

In the case of accidents that result in injury, regardless of how insignificant the injury may appear, agents should immediately notify the team leader.

USE OF FIRM-OWNED PROPERTY, INCLUDING COMPUTERS AND OTHER COMMUNICATIONS EQUIPMENT

E-mail, Voicemail, Internet and Computer Network, Software, and Hardware:

Voicemail, Internet, e-mail, and all other computer and communications resources (all collectively referred to in this policy as "IT resources") are business tools, provided to you at significant cost to the team. Thus, the expectation is that you will use the IT resources for business-related purposes and not for personal purposes unless specifically authorized by the team leader. Some examples of business related purposes include, but are not limited to, communicating with clients and researching information for the benefit of the team. The team requires that you conduct yourself honestly and appropriately on the Internet and in using other IT resources and respect copyrights, software licensing rules, property rights and privacy of others, just as you would in any other business dealing. To be absolutely clear, all existing the team office policies and governing laws and regulations apply to your conduct in using all IT resources, especially (but not exclusively) those that deal with intellectual property resources, sexual and other harassment, data security and confidentiality. Also, the systems as provided to you are the team property. The messages sent, retrieved, deleted and/or stored via the team systems are at all times the property of the team.

All agents should be aware that the team has the right, but not the obligation, to monitor all agents' use of any the team resources. For this reason, agents cannot and should not expect privacy in their use of the team IT resources, and should instead expect that their e-mail messages, voicemail messages, computer and Internet use, and other use of the team's IT resources is not confidential and may be monitored/reviewed.

Inappropriate Use of IT Equipment:

Inappropriate use of the IT resources is prohibited and subject to termination of the agency relationship. Examples of inappropriate use include, but are not limited to, the following:

- the creation, display, viewing, or sending of any kind of sexually explicit image or document on any the team system is a violation of our policy on sexual harassment. In addition, sexually explicit material may not be stored, distributed, edited, or recorded using the team's network, voicemail or computing resources.

16

- the use of the team e-mail, voicemail, Internet, or other IT resources for personal gain, political, religious, or charitable campaigning, soliciting for non- the team outside organizations or commercial ventures, selling Internet or other carrier access time, unless authorized by the team leader.

- the creation and/or forwarding of any disruptive or potentially offensive messages and/or pictures which may cause offense to any person or group, including those protected by the team's harassment policy.

- frequenting websites on the Internet unrelated to your agent responsibilities and/or the team business.

- having or using network passwords on the team's computer which are not known to the team.

The ultimate responsibility for assuring correct use of the team Group e-mail and Internet systems and other IT resources belongs with every user.

Unauthorized Access:

Unauthorized access of the team IT resources is prohibited. Agents are not permitted to use a code, access a file, or retrieve any stored communication unless authorized to do so or unless they have received prior clearance from an authorized the team representative. The team computers and IT resources are for business use by the team's personnel and authorized agents. Non-employees may not use the team IT resources without permission from the team leader.

Use of the team employee's or agent's account, user name, or password, or accessing another's files without their consent (by anyone other than authorized representatives of the principal or managing broker) is strictly prohibited. Obtaining, or trying to obtain, other users' passwords, or using programs that compromise security in any way is prohibited.

Passwords are required for many of the applications of the team IT resources, and users may be required to change passwords periodically for security purposes. All passcodes and passwords are the property of the team. No agent may use a passcode, password, or voice mail access code that has not been issued to that agent by the team or that is unknown to the team. Users of the team computers, network, and other IT resources must take reasonable precautions to prevent unauthorized access to the team IT resources. Passwords should not be divulged to unauthorized persons, and should not be written down or sent over the Internet, e-mail, dial-up modem, or any other communication line.

Snooping:

Probing or "snooping" into the team IT resources is prohibited. Accessing the team files or any other files on the network or the system that you did not create is prohibited unless you have prior authorization from your manager or another appropriate management representative. Observations of probing or "snooping" should be reported to the IT Department.

     17

Sabotage:

Destruction, theft, alteration, or any other form of sabotage of the team information technology and/or IT resources, including, but not limited to, computers, programs, networks, web-sites, files, and data is prohibited and will be investigated and prosecuted to the fullest extent of the law.

Hacking:

Hacking, the breaking into and corrupting of information technology, is prohibited. Hacking into third party computer systems using the team IT resources is prohibited, and may be reported to the local authorities. Vulnerability in the team IT resources should be reported to the team leader.

Viruses:

Use of virus, worm, or Trojan horse programs is prohibited. If a virus, worm or Trojan horse is identified, it should be immediately reported to the team leader.

Confidential Information:

All the team data and information (including customer information) is considered confidential unless the team has granted permission for a user to use it. Specific examples of confidential information include, but is not limited to, personnel and payroll records of present or past employees, information concerning transactions with clients, financial records of the team, records of purchases from vendors and suppliers, and any other information regarding the business affairs or operating practices or procedures of the team. Accessing or attempting to access confidential data is strictly prohibited.

Confidential information should be used only for its intended purpose. Agents' responsibility for confidentiality continues outside of work, therefore agents should use special care when using home computers and other portable devices.

When sending **e-mail messages** concerning confidential and/or proprietary information, agents are expected to exercise significant caution because of the ability of others to "crack" the system. Questions regarding what level of security is needed for particular information should be directed to the team leader.

Safeguarding the Physical Security of Communications System:

Reasonable precautions should be taken in regard to the physical security of the team IT resources. Disks, drives, and other devices containing sensitive information should be contained in a locked drawer, wherever possible. Computers should be turned off when not in use for an extended period or when an agent is out of his/her office.

18

All software installed on workstations, whether for business or personal use, must be approved by the team leader. In no way should personal computer hardware (thumb drives, MP3 players, etal) be installed at the team unless authorized by the team leader.

Agents should not install the team software on home computers without the prior approval of the team leader.

Agents are not allowed to introduce to the team network, Internet, computers, or other IT resources media from any external sources, including, but not limited to, CDs, disks, zip drives, personal digital assistants (including, but not limited to, BlackBerries and palm pilots), USB portable drives, and other removable drive devices. Agents also may not copy, transmit, or otherwise remove any information from our network, Internet, computers, or other IT resources to CDs, disks, zip drives, personal digital assistants, USB portable drives, or other removable drive devices without prior authorization from the team leader.

Agents may not download anything from the Internet to the team's computer without prior authorization. This includes, but is not limited to, screensavers, music, e-mail stationary, and other images.

Copyright Infringement/Unauthorized Copying:

The team strictly prohibits the illegal duplication of software. Copyright laws are clear. The copyright holder is given certain exclusive rights, including the right to make and distribute copies. Title 17 of the U.S. Code states that "it is illegal to make or distribute copies of copyrighted material without authorization" (Section 106). The only exception is the users' right to make a backup copy for archival purposes (Section 117).

Even the users of unlawful copies suffer from their own illegal actions. They receive no documentation, no customer support and no information about product updates. According to the U.S. Copyright Law, illegal reproduction of software can be subject to civil damages and criminal penalties.

19

RECEIPT AND ACKNOWLEDGMENT OF HANDBOOK FOR INDEPENDENT CONTRACTORS

This Handbook is an important document intended to help you become acquainted with the team. This Handbook will serve as a guide; it is not the final word in all cases. Individual circumstances may call for individual attention.

Please read the following statements and sign below to indicate your receipt and acknowledgment of the Handbook.

- I have received a copy and understand that it is my obligation to read the Office Policies and Procedures Handbook. I understand that the policies described in the Handbook are subject to change at the team sole discretion at any time. It will be my responsibility to update my personal copy as additions or revisions are provided to me. I understand that this Handbook supersedes and replaces all other previous manuals and personnel policies for the team.

- I understand that I am an independent contractor, subject to an express written contract and that I am not an employee of the team. My association with the team may be terminated at any time for any reason not prohibited by law, with written notice by me or the team leader.

- I am aware that this Handbook does not create an express or implied contract for any rights or benefits, and that the Handbook is intended as a set of guidelines only. I will consult with the team leader regarding any questions I may have regarding any of the team's policies.

- I am aware that during the course of my affiliation with the team, confidential information may be made available to me. I understand that this confidential information must not be given out or used outside of the team with non-team employees or agents, except as required by law or in accordance with the governing rules of ethics.

- I understand that my signature below indicates that I have read and understand the above statements and have received a copy of the Office Policies and Procedures Handbook.

_____
Printed Name

_____   _____
Signature   Date

© Enter Company Name Here. All rights reserved.   20

PHOTO, IMAGE & VIDEO RELEASE

I consent to the use of my name, portrait, picture, video or photograph as part of any endorsement for the team. This pertains to all future and current collection of images of team employees and licensed agents, in work situations, intended to showcase the team's activities.

The images in this collection may be used on the team's websites as well as in departmental communications or promotional products, such as publications, CR-ROMs, DVDs, displays, video emails, television commercials, pamphlets and presentations. Uses include:

- engaging current employees and clients (internal and external communications)
- attracting prospective employees and clients (recruitment)
- enhancing Sphere of Influence relations (marketing and outreach)
- informing local, National and International audiences (external communications)

I understand that my name, portrait, picture or photograph may be included in this image bank for a maximum of 7 years. Further, I understand that if I leave the team within this seven-year period, any image in this collection bearing my likeness may still be considered for use.

In addition, should I wish to have my name, portrait, picture or photograph removed from the team's image bank, I am to contact the team leader directly.

I agree that I shall have no claim against the team or against anyone accessing or using images form this or future the team collections that you've agreed to have taken.

I confirm that I am over 19 years of age and that I have not given anyone the exclusive right to use my name, portrait, picture or photograph.

_____
Printed Name

_____   _____
Signature   Date

ICENHOWER
COACHING & CONSULTING

1st Day Welcome Orientation Checklist

- ☐ Add Organization on FB/LinkedIn page as new place of employment. Make a post about your first day.
- ☐ Confirm Calendar Shared with rest of team/appropriate members/clients
- ☐ Finalize Employment / Independent Contractor Agreement, non-compete/disclose & onboarding paperwork
- ☐ Find Copy Center/Printer Area
- ☐ Find Workspace
- ☐ Find Manager/Staff Desks
- ☐ Get set up on CRM, dialer, technology
- ☐ Give Map of Facility and Parking Area
- ☐ Give Map of Local Transportation, Lunch, Child Care, etc.
- ☐ Introduce to team – attend organization team meeting
- ☐ Like Organization Business Page on FB / Twitter / Pinterest / LinkedIn
- ☐ Meet All staff, exchange contact information where appropriate
- ☐ Office tour with manager
- ☐ Order/Receive Keys, key card, Business Cards
- ☐ Review Company Mission Statement/Story/Traditions
- ☐ Review Dress Code
- ☐ Review Emergency Procedures
- ☐ Review Guest & Visitor Policy
- ☐ Review Holidays & Leave of Absences
- ☐ Set up wireless access to Wi-Fi and copier/printer
- ☐ Review Internet Usage Policy

- ☐ Review Organization Online Resources for Training, Accountability
- ☐ Review Parking & Transportation options
- ☐ Review Restrooms, Lunchroom, Discuss local delivery places & restaurants
- ☐ Review Sick Day Policies & Procedures
- ☐ Review Where to Get Supplies
- ☐ Review & Explain the "First Quarter Checkmark"
- ☐ Review & Explain the "Leverage Training Curve"
- ☐ Schedule 60 mins with manager to go over client greeting & Expectations
- ☐ Schedule 60 mins with manager to go over Presentation templates
- ☐ Schedule CRM Training
- ☐ Schedule Daily Script Test Review Talk and Daily Review Meeting for first week/month
- ☐ Schedule Photo Shoot for headshot
- ☐ Schedule Team Lunch
- ☐ Schedule technology training with manager/trainer to debrief what you will be using
- ☐ Schedule Tracking Training with Staff: regarding CRM, Script Review, etc.
- ☐ Schedule Weekly Coaching / Accountability Session
- ☐ Send Bio/Photo to Administrative staff to add to Websites
- ☐ Set up cell phone voicemail with Organization approved greeting
- ☐ Set up e-mail; sync with cell phone
- ☐ Sign off on Expectations paperwork

ICENHOWER
COACHING & CONSULTING

ADMINISTRATIVE
First Quarter Checklist

Week 1

	Task	Assigned To	Date Completed
Day 1	Complete First Day Welcome Checklist		
	Complete Employee Information Card		
Day 2	Set up Payroll / Direct Deposit		
	Assign keys to office		
	Assign mailbox		
	Setup Business Phone Extension		
	Record Voice Mail Greeting		
Day 3	Update Employee Directory and Send Out Update Email to Team		
	Prepare & Deliver W4 & I9 Form		
Day 4	Receive W4 & I9 Form from Employee		
	Introduce to ALL Team Members		
	Order Business Cards		
	Verify Set up Voice Mail		
	Set up Email Account		
	Set up Email Signature		
	Set up Electronic Stationery		
	Add to Employee to Appropriate Team Internal Email Lists		
Day 5	Overview of CRM		
	Overview of MLS System		
	Overview of In-office Phone System		
	Overview of Any Other Office Software Used		
	Practice Adding/Updating 10 Practice CRM Entries		
	Review Vendor List		
	Review Team Mission Statement		
	Take Ownership Office Supplies		

ICENHOWER
COACHING & CONSULTING

ADMINISTRATIVE
First Quarter Checklist

Week 2

Task	Assigned To	Date Completed
Review Pre-list Package if Applicable		
Explain Daily Activity Record		
Review Buyer Agent Worksheet and Report		
Practice Filling out Buyer Information Sheet		
Practice filling out Seller Information Sheet		
Review Buyer Presentation + Process		
Review Listing Presentation + Process		
Review Lead Management A-B-C Buyers and Sellers		
Review Buyer Lead Sheet		
Review Seller Lead Sheet		
Review Ideal Weekly Schedule		
Read through Support Staff Scripts		

ICENHOWER
COACHING & CONSULTING

ADMINISTRATIVE
First Quarter Checklist

Week 3

Task	Assigned To	Date Completed
Review and Practice Support Staff Scripts		
Sit in on Several Phone Calls to See Preferred Phone Etiquette		
Set up Role Playing Sessions for Answering the Phone and Talking w/ Potential Buyers and Sellers		
Sit through Initial Buyer Consultation		
Draft Introduction Letter to Support Staff's past clients or sphere		
Sit in on One Coaching Call		
Have New Hire Create Daily CRM Task List Based on First Exposure (This list will evolve as they learn more)		
Review 3 Submitted Contracts (if applicable)		
Review Previous Training and Practice Tasks w/o supervision		
Attend 1 Closing (if applicable)		
Overview of Tracking and Reporting		
Review a & Take Ownership of Monitoring Website		

After week three the task training list will begin to dwindle because the new hire will begin to take ownership of different responsibilities. Their day will be filled with these new responsibilities and they will begin to add more challenging and complex tasks or responsibilities at a slower rate.

ADMINISTRATIVE
First Quarter Checklist

Week 4

Task	Assigned To	Date Completed
Take Ownership of Daily CRM/ Data Entry Tasks		
Shadow Track & Reporting Activities		
Meet with Primary Vendors		
Tour of Market Area		
Review Schools for primary selling communities		
Guided Practice of Track & Reporting Activities		
Review 3 Pending Buyer Files (if applicable)		
Review 3 Completed, (Closed) Buyer Files (if applicable)		
Set Goals for First Quarter		
Review Session to Discover Pain Points in Training Process		

Week 5

Task	Assigned To	Date Completed
Revisiting Any Training as a Result of Review Session		
Transaction Cycle Review		
Transaction Cycle Shadowing		
Take Ownership of Tracking and Reporting Process		
Take Ownership of ALL incoming Calls		

ADMINISTRATIVE
First Quarter Checklist

Week 6

Task	Assigned To	Date Completed
Intro to Basic Prospecting		
Shadow Prospecting Calls		
Making 5 Prospecting Calls on Their Own		
Guided Script & Role Play with real Clients		
Take Ownership of Files Going into Transaction Cycle		

Week 7

Task	Assigned To	Date Completed
Set Prospecting Goals Based on Previous Weeks Progress		
Take Ownership of ALL Packages Pre-List, Listing,		
Review Farming Practices		
Take Ownership of Farming Marketing Activities		

Week 8

Task	Assigned To	Date Completed
Review of Financial Responsibilities Admin is to Take Ownership		
Review Offer Received Process & Take Ownership		
Review Session to Discover Pain Points in Training Process		
Revisiting Any Training as a Result of Review Session		

ADMINISTRATIVE
First Quarter Checklist

Week 9

Task	Assigned To	Date Completed
Review After Closing Procedure & Take Ownership		
Review Yearly Marketing Plans & Take Ownership		

Week 10

Task	Assigned To	Date Completed
Revisit Quarterly Goals Set in Week 4		
10 Week Review Session to Discover Any Pain Points		

Week 11

Task	Assigned To	Date Completed
Revisiting Any Training as a Result of Review Session		
Discovery Session to Add Processes or Admin Responsibilities		

Week 12

Task	Assigned To	Date Completed
Set Team Goals for Next Quarter		
Set Personal Goals for Next Quarter		

CHAPTER 9:

ABOVE AND BEYOND

LEARNING OBJECTIVES

- Prioritize goals and objectives.
- Develop and maintain a budget
- Evaluate performance
- Formulate a professional development budget

ABOVE AND BEYOND

The first eight chapters of *ADMIN: Systematize Your Real Estate Administrative Process* have shown you everything you need to know to succeed and excel as the administrator of your real estate company. As you master wearing each of the four hats in this position, you will begin to look for ways to further hone your skills and advance your professional development.

A good administrative assistant is future-oriented and always looking for ways to go above and beyond in performing their job duties and making the business better. Throughout this book, we've repeatedly stressed the importance of responsibility and holding everyone accountable to their agreed-upon tasks, duties, and activities. Of course, if we don't know where we want to go, it's unlikely that we will ever get there. We can't hold ourselves accountable to something unless we've created a tangible metric or goal to work towards. For this reason, successful real estate companies are consistently setting goals and increasing targets in order to create the future they want to live in.

> *A good administrative assistant is future-oriented and always looking for ways to go above and beyond in performing their job duties and making the business better.*

To help your team to do that, and remain accountable, you will need to:

- Prioritize goals and objectives.
- Develop and maintain a budget.
- Evaluate performances.
- Formulate a professional development budget.

Make sure to include all of these topics on your meeting agenda with your real estate agent. It's possible to include all four at your annual business-planning meeting with your agent or team. You can also discuss goals and objectives at one monthly meeting with your agent, the budget at the next meeting, and so on. Drawing up your recommendations and sharing them in advance will make monthly meetings with your agent even more efficient.

Let's look at each of these areas individually.

The Importance of Setting Goals

A long time ago, two Ivy League universities, Harvard and Yale, discovered something remarkable about the earning power of their graduates. Some of them were paid extremely well, and they reported being enormously satisfied with their lives.

Well, of course they were! Who wouldn't be happy making a considerable amount of money?

Not everyone, as it turns out. While money is necessary to live, true satisfaction in life comes from having *choices* and feeling *significant* in the lives of others. The same study showed that being rewarded with a lot of money was merely a side effect of setting—and reaching—meaningful goals.

Are you curious about the students who were able to reach their goals? So were the universities, and ten years later they followed up with the students.

Not all of the students in the study were highly successful. In fact, 84% of the students reported earning an average wage or feeling somewhat unsuccessful. These students never identified any goals.

In the meantime, while 10% of the students did have goals, they didn't write them down. They felt as though simply visualizing their goals would be enough and, maybe they were right, because those in the 10% category earned three times what those in the 84% category made.

That leaves 6% of the students, and here's where the study gets interesting. This small group of students had two things in common: they wrote down their goals, and they earned 10 times the salaries of their peers in the study.

People who write down their goals are far more likely to achieve them. They will experience greater success and will earn more money. They will also have more satisfaction because they will be leading their lives rather than allowing life to direct them.

You can experience the same level of success if you write down your goals and create milestones that help you work towards them.

WRITTEN GOALS

It's time to get your goals written down.

Ideally, your goals should align with the needs of the business, so assistants may wish to confer with your agent on this. In general, however, make sure your goals include these three parts:

1. An action
2. A measurable outcome
3. A date by which it will be completed

You can then write your goals like this:

Action	Measurable Outcome	Completion Date
Build an SOI database	of 300 contacts	by July 1
Hold an open house	2x annually	no later than November 15
Assist in closing sales	of 43 transactions annually	by December 31

When creating your goals, be vigilant that "dead man" skills don't find their way into your list. These are things that will happen regardless of any extra effort you make, like *smile at people*, *stay positive*, and *be nice*.

These aren't goals: they are actions that even a dead man can do! Writing down superficial goals won't help you move above and beyond in your career or your pursuit of happiness.

Wear a WIG

We've talked a lot about the different hats that real estate administrators wear from day to day. At some point, when setting your goals, you'll also want to wear a WIG. WIG stands for Wildly Important Goals, and you should have at least one WIG on your goals-list and then *make it happen*.

When you do, that kind of success is cause for a celebration. Success breeds more success, and soon you will find yourself coming up with bigger WIGs and achieving them. The feeling is exhilarating, and you'll be proud of what you've been able to do.

Not all of your goals have to be business-oriented. In fact, one goal should be a personal one, whether you want to learn how to carry on a simple conversation in American Sign Language, or your goal is to spend a minimum of 90 minutes at the gym every week. Having—and attaining—personal goals can make you better at your job.

Creating Milestones

Once you have your goals established and written down, it's time to create a plan.

These are your milestones.

Think of your goals as a destination far in the distance, much like a destination on a map. You have to formulate a plan for reaching these goals. You can't merely teleport yourself to them. Instead, you have to make your way step by step.

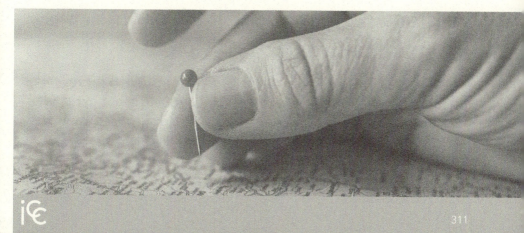

Along the way, there will be obstacles that could prevent you from being successful if you allowed them to get in your way. As you coordinate your journey towards the goal, you will find yourself picking a path. This path may take you across rivers, through forests, and over mountains. As you complete your journey in each region, you will have achieved a milestone.

Milestones are the stepping-stones that lead you to your goal.

According to Stephen Covey (*The 7 Habits of Highly Effective People*), the best way to identify your milestones and map them out is to work backward from your goal. If your goal is to create an SOI database of 300 contacts within three months (which can seem overwhelming), you will break down the steps like this:

GOAL

I will build an SOI database of 300 contacts by July 1.

I.e. July 1: 300 SOI contacts in the database

MILESTONE

I will add 100 SOI contacts to the database every month.

June 30: 100 SOI contacts

May 30: 100 SOI contacts

April 30: 100 SOI contacts

These milestones can be broken down even further, by week and by day.

MILESTONE: *I will add 25 contacts to the SOI database weekly.*

MILESTONE: *I will add 5 SOI contacts daily.*

As you can see, five SOI contacts a day seems much more manageable than the end goal of 300. If you create a habit of adding these contacts gradually, you may be surprised by how much your database grows. Often, by breaking large goals into smaller, manageable milestones, we wind up exceeding the original targets we set for ourselves.

How to Create Your Annual Goals and Business Plan

Successful real estate companies utilize a simple *one-page* business plan to organize *everything* they want to accomplish in a single year.

Often, real estate companies will hold an annual retreat to focus on creating and developing their annual business plan. We've even seen this done biannually where teams hold a second mid-year retreat to assess where they are in reaching their goals and making any needed modifications before finishing out the second half of the year. This can help reenergize and refocus the team. Whether you implement a formal retreat or not, administrative assistants that are committed to going above and beyond are always looking for ways to reinvigorate and motivate their team.

A single-page business plan is easier to refer to than a multi-page document and allows all team-members to follow its action steps to support their compelling scoreboard. Include your business plan in your weekly team meeting as a regular reminder of your goals and to foster accountability as well as encouragement. As each item on the plan is crossed off throughout the year, team members will be assured that the company is growing and improving in direct alignment with your annual goals.

> *Administrative assistants that are committed to going above and beyond are always looking for ways to reinvigorate and motivate their team.*

At ICC, we find that a tidy 1-3-5 format allows leaders to focus on the key activities and tasks that will generate the results they desire.

1:3:5 Format

Determine Your Number 1 WIG

Start by establishing a specific and measurable WIG (Wildly Important Goal) for your company to achieve by next year.

Remember that all goals need to be measurable, so that we can track whether we're ahead or behind at any given point throughout the year. Typically, when creating their goals, real estate companies will use lag measures like total agent count, gross commission income (GCI), total sales volume, or total units sold. These last two are the most common ways to measure goals.

The ambitious among you can establish more than one WIG. However, it is important that each main goal you create has a numeric value associated with it so that it can be broken down into monthly and weekly portions for measuring progress throughout the year. For example, a company that wants to sell 500 properties in a year must close approximately 42 transactions a month, or close to 10 properties per week.

Knowing these numbers makes it easy to determine if you are ahead or behind in the game at all times.

Establish 3 Key Focus-Areas to Reach the Main Goal

For a real estate business plan to be effective, it must be focused.

For each WIG that you create, establish 3 key focus-areas that will need attention over the following year in order to achieve that goal. These focus-areas should represent some of the more daunting tasks that will require a lot of work and input or assistance from others. These are the big tasks that are always looming in the back of your mind that never seem to get done.

Examples might include starting a mentor program, increasing recruiting efforts, hiring a productivity coach, or implementing a CRM system.

PLAN 5 OBJECTIVES FOR EACH KEY FOCUS-AREA

Break down each of your 3 key focus-areas into 5 specific objectives that are in alignment with each focus-area. Each objective should represent a specific action or task that can be completed.

The key to developing effective objectives is to ensure that they effectively correlate to each key focus-area. Otherwise you will just have a scattered to-do list that is unlikely to ever be completed since it is not focused on the accomplishment of your preset objectives.

A sample of what a real estate team's '1:3:5' business plan might look like is shown below. We have also seen teams use a 1:4:6 format or a 1:5:5 format with great success. We encourage you to stretch your imagination when creating your wildly important goals. However, it can ultimately be discouraging and counterproductive if you 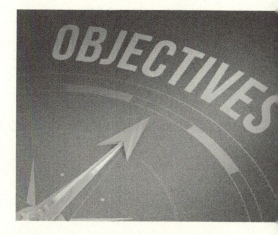 bite off more than you can chew. A 1:3:5 business plan format allows you to be ambitious, but pragmatic, about creating wildly important but humanly attainable goals!

ANNUAL GOAL

$50 Million Annual Sales Volume

3 KEY FOCUS AREAS

1. **Customer Service:** Create the Ultimate Client Experience
2. **Lead Generation:** Track Agent Generation & Conversion Activity
3. **Hire & Recruit:** Attract New Talent to the Team

5 OBJECTIVES FOR EACH FOCUS AREA

1. CUSTOMER SERVICE

1. Admin Assistant to conduct 30, 90, and 120 day follow-up calls to clients after all closings to suggest vendors for improvements & ask for referrals.
2. Produce pre-listing video introducing the team, marketing plan, and services we provide to send to client prior to initial listing appointment.
3. Increase online presence with 4 team websites:
   - Sellers
   - Buyers
   - Neighborhood Farms
   - Blog
4. Enhance/update client database contacts:
   - 33 touches per year
   - Client appreciation event
5. Grow vendor database
   - Contact regularly
   - Vendor appreciation party
   - Create vendor list & web page
   - Refer them systematically

2. LEAD GENERATION

1. Conduct group lead generation every Mon-Fri for 2 hours (9a-11a) for all sales agents. Agents meet at 8:30a for role play and scripts practice beforehand.
2. Sales agents to track lead generation activities (Contact - Appointment - Contract), and submit at end of each week for accountability and to establish conversion ratios.
3. Determine criteria & system to:
   - Distribute inbound leads/calls
   - Make outbound contacts to COI, FSBO, Expireds, Just Listed/Solds and Farms
4. Develop action plans & campaigns to farm 4 neighborhoods.
5. Each month, obtain:
   - 10 new listings;
   - 9 buyer contracts; and
   - 15 closed transactions

3. HIRE & RECRUIT

1. Begin search for an Administrative Lead Coordinator. Interview 4 applicants per month until found. Create job description and establish behavioral profile.
2. Hire an Inside Sales Agent (ISA) - determine compensation schedule, job duties and description, and behavioral profile. Locate ISA training resources or coach.
3. Establish criteria/goals for Buyers Agents to earn Showing Assistants. Establish respective job descriptions and compensation schedules.
4. Develop printed and video presentations to recruit new sales agents.
5. Locate two new sales agents in adjacent geographic locations to expand and service new areas.

WORKING WITHIN A BUDGET

"You can do anything you want, but not everything."

This quotation by productivity-guru, David Allen, is a reminder that we have to focus on what's important to do, rather than trying to do it all.

It's also a reminder that we have to work within a budget. Financial backing won't be available for every dream and initiative, so at every real estate company—whether you're a large operation or a one-man-show—everyone has to work within a budget. Real estate agents (and their administrative employees, as applicable) will determine the budget for the year. Like any goals you set, the budget is a plan, and it should be written down so that you can measure your progress against it.

As we just mentioned, you must be ambitious but pragmatic when creating your annual business plan. Working within a budget helps you to pragmatically prioritize spending, and focus your finances on achieving your wildly important goals.

Added to this, however, is the mundane fact that it doesn't matter what our dreams or goals are if we can't pay our rent or utility bills. In order to prioritize our important goals, we have to budget for our essential expenses first.

As with the time-management strategies that we discussed at the beginning of the book, your essential expenses are like the large rocks in the professor's jar. Smaller initiatives, the pebbles and sand, can be added when the company earns more money. And sometimes, those smaller efforts will prove to be unimportant and give way to other strategies that are more useful and worthy of your time and money.

UNDERSTANDING A REAL ESTATE TEAM PRODUCTION GROWTH BUDGET SCHEDULE

Take a moment to review our sample *Real Estate Team Production Growth Budget Schedule*. In our decades of coaching different real estate teams throughout North America, we have found that, while each of them may look and act and think and sell in very different ways, all of their budgets tend to look very similar. Their success leaves clues that we can now share with you.

REAL ESTATE TEAM

PRODUCTION GROWTH BUDGET SCHEDULE

Total Sales Volume	$8 Million	$13 Million	$18 Million	$25 Million	$40 Million	$60 Million	$80 Million	$100 Million
GCI	$240,000	$390,000	$540,000	$750,000	$1.2 Million	$1.8 Million	$2.4 Million	$3 Million
Units (Divide Sales Vol by Your Avg Home Price)								
OPERATING EXPENSES								
Administrative Salaries (12%)	$28,800	$46,800	$64,800	$90,000	$144,000	$216,000	$288,000	$360,000
Marketing & Lead Generation (10%)	$24,000	$39,000	$54,000	$75,000	$120,000	$180,000	$240,000	$300,000
Training & Education (5%)	$12,000	$19,500	$27,000	$37,500	$60,000	$90,000	$120,000	$150,000
Equipment & Supplies (2%)	$4,800	$7,800	$10,800	$15,000	$24,000	$36,000	$48,000	$60,000
Rent (0.5%)	$1,200	$1,950	$2,700	$3,750	$6,000	$9,000	$12,000	$15,000
Misc. (0.5%) Technology	$1,200	$1,950	$2,700	$3,750	$6,000	$9,000	$12,000	$15,000
Total Operating Expenses (30%)	$72,000	$117,000	$162,000	$225,000	$360,000	$540,000	$720,000	$900,000
Cost of Sales (Deductions from Commissions Checks to pay brokerage + sales agents)	$24,000 (10%)	$58,500 (15%)	$108,000 (20%)	$187,500 (25%)	$360,000 (30%)	$540,000 (30%)	$840,000 (35%)	$1.2 Million (40%)
NET INCOME	$144,000 (60%)	$214,500 (55%)	$270,000 (50%)	$337,500 (45%)	$480,000 (40%)	$720,000 (40%)	$840,000 (35%)	$900,000 (30%)

*All percentages calculated as a percentage of Gross Commission Income (GCI)

Some of you may have experience working with budgets and are familiar with terminology like GCI and Net Income. For those of you who are new administrative assistants, we'll keep things quite simple for now. As you begin to work with your particular company's actual finances, and improve in your role, all of this will become like second-nature to you.

As you can see, your essential *Operating Expenses* will include:

- Salaries
- Marketing & Lead Generation expenses
- Training & Education (professional development)
- Office Rent
- Utilities
- Equipment & Supplies
- Travel (mileage for showing properties/attending events)
- Technology

GCI

Notice that your *Total Operating Expenses* should never exceed 30% of your *Gross Commission Income (GCI)*.

Furthermore, within that 30%, every operating expense item also has a corresponding % amount. For example, your professional development/training & education budget should not exceed 5% of your Gross Commission Income. And, as much as you'd like to work in a super luxurious office, we recommend that your rent cannot exceed 0.5% of the GCI. Administrative salaries account for (a maximum of) 12% of your operating expenses. That's almost *half* of your total operating expenses. Yes, the administrative role is *that* important.

As you can see, *Total Sales Volume* and *Gross Commission Income* increases from left to right across the schedule as sales rise and the company grows and grows. However, your sales volume won't grow by itself. Expansion is a team effort. The more agents you hire for your team, the more revenue you will bring in.

This increases your *Cost of Sales* (commission checks paid out to brokerage and/or sales agents), and your operating expenses will also increase as you continue to expand.

When we deduct cost of sales plus operating expenses from your GCI, we arrive at your *Net Income* or profit—the very bottom row of the budget schedule. The % number in that row is your profit margin. The most successful real estate teams have the lowest margins and the highest net income.

The bigger the business, the smaller the margin. Think of a big, successful business like Microsoft. They may have $100 billion in expenses and $101,000 billion in revenue, so their profit margin is only 1%, but they are making a billion dollars in actual profit. Obviously, Microsoft is not in the business of selling real estate. Each industry is very different and their optimal profit margins will vary accordingly. Our point, however, is that successful, growing businesses always decrease margins over time, *but they also increase total profit.*

INCREASE YOUR INCOME, INCREASE YOUR WORK-LIFE BALANCE

Each uptick in sales volume increases capacity in every area, including potential salary and increased work-life balance. As a company's GCI grows, existing administrative assistants may need to add a part-time, or even full-time, assistant to help run the day-to-day operations of the business. As income increases so should your work-life-balance!

This is one of your goals as a real estate team. The more you grow, the more additional support you can afford to have; and the more additional support you have, the more flexibility you have, and the more room you will have to grow. When you pay your dues and prove your worth, you can slowly begin to give away pieces of your role to the next person and the next person. This frees you up to focus on your strengths and go above and beyond in your professional and personal growth.

While we certainly hope that you solo agents will benefit from our various time-management and operational strategies as you juggle both the sales and administrative sides of your business, eventually you will need to take that leap and hire additional support. It's possible to be quite a successful and competent solo agent, but it's harder to go above and beyond and really increase your income if you aren't willing to invest in your business.

The reason a lot of real estate teams fail to grow is that they are unwilling to spend enough money to grow their team. They do everything themselves, or minimize their administrative staff, because they are focused on keeping expenses low. This is not how real estate businesses grow. Whether it's hiring administrative assistants and additional sales staff, or allocating sufficient money towards marketing and lead-generation activities, you must invest in your business in order to generate more business.

However, the money you invest should always come from your Gross Commission Income. This is why it's crucial that administrative assistants keep a hawk's eye on the company's profit and loss statement to ensure that you are operating in alignment with your budget.

iC

If your excitable lead agent comes to you and says, "I saw this incredible new thing at a conference and I want us to spend money on it," the first thing you should do is to analyze the budget and assess if you can. If you've already spent 10% of your budget on marketing, you will need to focus on increasing your GCI revenue to make room in the budget.

Those hasty and impulsive sales agents might be the 'boss' that is running the team, but administrative assistants need to be calm, collected, and organized when faced with financial demands and requests. The ability to manage a budget and make careful and prudent financial decisions is a characteristic of a top administrative manger or assistant.

CHARACTERISTICS OF TOP ADMINISTRATIVE ASSISTANTS

As we mentioned at the very beginning of this book, we will occasionally cover a topic that pertains specifically to assistant positions. The next section addresses performance evaluation for administrative assistants and how to give and receive feedback.

While not currently relevant to those of you who are solo agents, our sincere hope is that your production growth will soon enable you to hire your first administrative assistant, at which point you will be tasked with giving them feedback and evaluating their performance.

With a view to that point in time, we encourage you to begin thinking about the characteristics of top administrative assistants. After all, if we don't have an "ideal assistant" in mind, then it's difficult to either hire that perfect person or evaluate their eventual performance.

As we mentioned back in chapter 2, the Steadiness-Compliance behavior blend has all of the desired traits and tendencies needed in a top administrative assistant. The best assistants can almost intuit what their agents need next, and they also demonstrate these characteristics:

- ✓ Professional in appearance and demeanor
- ✓ Pleasant and personable but not overly extroverted, emotional or excitable
- ✓ Steady, supportive, and reliable
- ✓ Remains calm and collected during stressful situations
- ✓ Outstanding communication skills (written and verbal)
- ✓ Precise and accurate attention to detail
- ✓ Efficient time management skills
- ✓ High executive functioning (organization) skills
- ✓ Task-oriented and not easily distracted
- ✓ Sense of humor
- ✓ Competence in every area of the business
- ✓ The desire to learn and grow
- ✓ The desire to go above and beyond

With that in mind, let's take a look at evaluating the administrative assistant's performance and giving and receiving feedback.

Giving and Receiving Feedback

Giving and receiving feedback is a key component to a healthy team. Feedback ensures that a dialog takes place between the team's leadership and the team. Feedback helps us know where we stand. Often, assistants on real estate teams will worry that they're underperforming when, in fact, the leadership is extremely happy with their work but have forgotten or failed to provide this necessary feedback.

Too, feedback can provide an opportunity for us to identify areas that we're struggling with or are discouraged about. Though it can be uncomfortable, it's important that teams develop deep communication and allow opportunities for any and all issues to come to the surface.

Informal Feedback

Administrative assistants will receive informal feedback at your regular meetings with your real estate agent and team.

Comments may come in the form of praise, such as "Good job on the Smith package—every document was in order." On the other hand, correction or redirection may come in the form of statements like, "Leave the folder on my chair rather than on my desk."

There should be no surprises when it comes time to your eventual performance evaluation. The ongoing informal communication will have given you insight into how well you've been performing your job. You know how well you've executed every task on your to-do list, and you have data, like those 300 SOI contacts, to show that you're on top of things. As long as you have been performing your role according to the characteristics of a top assistant, there will be nothing to worry about!

Your Evaluation

As you can see, we have provided a copy of our 'Self-Performance Appraisal' form for your use in implementing with your agent, along with any other members of the team.

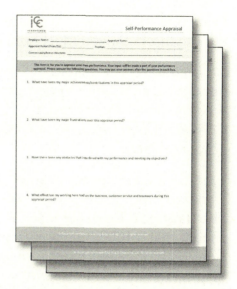

A self-performance appraisal is so called because the employee being evaluated will assess their performance and complete the review form. Once it is completed and provided to the team leader, they can sit down and go over it together. This exercise is typically done twice a year, but it can also be done quarterly, or annually.

When it's time to review your performance, have your data ready. It should all be there in your agenda binders, where you stored a record of everything you've done during the year. An evaluation isn't meant to be punitive. It should be an honest discussion about what's worked, what can be improved on, and how to make that happen. There will be areas in which you have excelled, and other areas you'll want to continue developing.

The most important thing is that you and your agent are giving and receiving candid feedback and maintaining an open and honest dialog with each other. Feedback is simply another way in which we hold ourselves accountable to each other.

The 4 Key Accountability Questions

There's a wise maxim that says an attitude of "I will do it" gets more accomplished than saying "somebody should do something."

You get things done through accountability.

Every member of the real estate team has one vital role to play in the organization: you must hold each other accountable.

Accountability is invaluable. Every team-member knows his or her duties, and they can perform these tasks successfully most of the time. Inconsistent results prevent you from achieving success. Consistent performance, however, comes about as the result of accountability.

Amazon is an excellent example of setting performance standards and holding team members accountable for them. The daily goal for every team in the warehouse is 100%. Teams cannot reach 100% unless every team member reaches the mark. Amazon employees meet regularly to review their metrics and help teammates with accountability.

The team drives performance.

There is no better group to hold you accountable than your team. Every member of the team has to help their teammates meet accountability metrics. However, you may be surprised to hear that you don't have to nag, scold, or threaten in order to hold your team accountable. All you have to do is ask the right questions.

In every weekly team meeting, ask the following 4 Key Accountability Questions:

1. How do you think you did?
2. What got in the way?
3. What do you need to do differently next time?
4. Is there any way we can help?

It is essential to implement accountability questions when reviewing the agent scoreboards and/or contact forms for lead-generation activities completed at weekly team meetings. Oftentimes the administrative manager/assistant leads these meetings and asks these 4 questions every time a team member fails to report their numbers or make their agreed upon number of contacts.

Notice that the first three questions are reflective in nature. Team members look within themselves for the honest answers they need to move forward in meeting accountability metrics. The final question requires a yes/no response. The team member must commit to being accountable for the metric or has to request assistance. Either answer is perfectly acceptable because it will move the team-member to action.

Accountability questions are not a judgment, and they don't solve the problem. Instead, they allow the team member to self-reflect and come up with his or her own solution to the problem rather than provide an excuse or look for blame. At the same time, a top administrative assistant will go above and beyond and seek out ways to support their agents and play a part in being the solution.

If your agent identifies that they didn't meet their goal because they were inundated with phone calls and emails from clients, the agent needs to take responsibility and not use distraction as an excuse; but the assistant also needs to take proactive steps in taking ownership of client communication and ensuring that the agent isn't distracted and interrupted with tasks and duties that the assistant is ultimately responsible for.

If you know you that your team-members will review the metrics you met and ask about the measures you didn't meet, you are more likely to take the actions necessary to meet every task on your list of responsibilities. You are also more likely to support, encourage and celebrate each other as you become more consistent in meeting all of your performance metrics.

The 4 Key Accountability Questions:

- Allow team members to learn from each other's experiences.
- Significantly reduce excuses for performance failure.
- Help individuals find their own solutions and overcome their own objections and excuses.
- Create a successful, growth-oriented team culture.

At every weekly meeting, ask these four questions the same way each time. Before long, your team-members will have memorized the questions, and they can use these inquiries to 'self-coach' before the weekly team meeting.

By consistently using these questions to reflect on performance levels, your team will achieve stellar results. Best of all, they'll be proud to be a part of your real estate group.

 If you would like to delve deeper into strategies for accountability, ICC has an entire course devoted to the subject called, *COACH—Coaching for Business Performance.* The 4 Key Accountability Questions are a fantastic place to begin, but if you want to go above and beyond in developing ways to hold yourself—and your team—accountable, we certainly have many more tools and techniques to help you with that. There is no limit to your growth and professional development.

CONTINUING YOUR PROFESSIONAL DEVELOPMENT

As we begin to wrap up and move towards the end of this book on how to systematize your real estate process, we encourage you to take some time to look back and reflect on everything that you have learned so far.

At the same time, as you go above and beyond in your position, we also encourage you to maintain a future-oriented, growth-mindset, and continually focus on your professional development.

No matter how busy you get in the day-to-day-operations of your business, you—and everyone on your team for that matter, your agent(s) included—must always carve out time in your schedule for professional and personal growth.

The administrative assistant's performance evaluation will suggest continuing professional development opportunities.

Every real estate agent takes continuing education courses to stay abreast of changes in the law and new trends. Assistants should have the opportunity to learn and grow in their position as well.

The professional development opportunities you explore will be based on areas related to the real estate business. Are you expected to speak to groups of people? Joining a Toastmasters Club could help you with public speaking.

You may wish to strengthen your writing skills, learn more about marketing and social media, or study DISC behavioral traits in more depth and detail.

Talk with the real estate agent you work with to see what will help make the business stronger and serve your clients.

NEXT STEPS—LEAD, NOT MANAGE

The best way to grow professionally and serve your team and clients is to think and act like a leader, not a manager.

"But I am a manager," you might say. "Administrative Manager is the most important of my four hats!"

Well, yes, that's true. As the administrative assistant, you are responsible for organizing and managing every aspect of the business, from pre-listing to listing all the way to contract, and from contract to close. You will manage and maintain the company's financial systems and budget, coordinate all purchases, as well as manage the company's social media and a variety of other marketing activities. You will interact with mortgage lenders, escrow/title officers, inspectors, cooperating agents movers, cleaners, stagers, photographers, and insurance agents, just to name a few!

You are an intrinsic part of a large team of people that, together, facilitate the move and purchase or sale of the largest asset most people will typically own.

So, yes, you are technically a manager in terms of tasks and duties, but what *kind* of manager are you going to be as you go above and beyond in your position? We hope you are a manager that learns to lead.

While a typical manager barks orders and manages by position, a leader instills the trust and confidence of their team and leads with influence.

LEADER VS. MANAGER

LEADER	MANAGER
• Leads by influence	• Manages by position
• Develops & coaches	• Drives workers
• Wanted to be succeeded	• Needs to be needed
• Depends on goodwill	• Depends on authority
• Reproduce themselves	• Wants recognition
• Inspires enthusiasm	• Inspires fear
• Focuses on strengths	• Focuses on weaknesses
• Says "We"	• Says "I"
• Invests time in others	• Spends time with others
• Fixes the breakdown	• Blames the breakdown
• Have incredible success	• Has some successes
• Shows how its done	• Knows how its done
• Says "Let's go!"	• Says "Go!"

iC

While a typical manager barks orders and *manages by position*, a leader instills the trust and confidence of their team and *leads with influence*.

As you develop systems and strategies to efficiently manage and optimize operations, you should do so with the mindset and actions of a true leader, gaining the admiration as well as the respect of your team along the way. As your systems prove effective, not only will they see that you are correct and know what you're talking about, they will know that you're on their side and that you have their backs. You're focused on strengths rather than weaknesses. You invest time in others and are rooting for the group's success as well as your own.

That's the difference between being a manager and a leader.

That's how you go above and beyond.

As you embark on your administrative real estate career, you will wear so many different hats, from Administrative Manager to Listing Manager, Transaction Coordinator and Marketing Director. There will be days when you, too, will feel like that poor solo agent who had come to think of herself as a human *matryoskha* doll—a dozen different people inside the same single body.

Whether you're an assistant or a solo agent, we trust that we have given you more than enough strategies, tools, and techniques to manage and cope as you act in each of your capacities. We also trust that inside that single body is an influential and inspiring leader just waiting to emerge!

CHAPTER 9 APPENDIX 9.1

SAMPLE 1:3:5 BUSINESS PLAN

ANNUAL GOAL

$50 Million Annual Sales Volume

3 KEY FOCUS AREAS

1. **Customer Service:** Create the Ultimate Client Experience
2. **Lead Generation:** Track Agent Generation & Conversion Activity
3. **Hire & Recruit:** Attract New Talent to the Team

5 OBJECTIVES FOR EACH FOCUS AREA

1 CUSTOMER SERVICE	2 LEAD GENERATION	3 HIRE & RECRUIT
1. Admin Assistant to conduct 30, 90, and 120 day follow-up calls to clients after all closings to suggest vendors for improvements & ask for referrals.	1. Conduct group lead generation every Mon-Fri for 2 hours (9a-11a) for all sales agents. Agents meet at 8:30a for role play and scripts practice beforehand.	1. Begin search for an Administrative Lead Coordinator. Interview 4 applicants per month until found. Create job description and establish behavioral profile.
2. Produce pre-listing video introducing the team, marketing plan, and services we provide to send to client prior to initial listing appointment.	2. Sales agents to track lead generation activities (Contact - Appointment - Contract), and submit at end of each week for accountability and to establish conversion ratios.	2. Hire an Inside Sales Agent (ISA) - determine compensation schedule, job duties and description, and behavioral profile. Locate ISA training resources or coach.
3. Increase online presence with 4 team websites: • Sellers • Buyers • Neighborhood Farms • Blog	3. Determine criteria & system to: • Distribute inbound leads/calls • Make outbound contacts to COI, FSBO, Expireds, Just Listed/Solds and Farms	3. Establish criteria/goals for Buyers Agents to earn Showing Assistants. Establish respective job descriptions and compensation schedules.
4. Enhance/update client database contacts: • 33 touches per year • Client appreciation event	4. Develop action plans & campaigns to farm 4 neighborhoods.	4. Develop printed and video presentations to recruit new sales agents.
5. Grow vendor database • Contact regularly • Vendor appreciation party • Create vendor list & web page • Refer them systematically	5. Each month, obtain: • 10 new listings; • 9 buyer contracts; and • 15 closed transactions	5. Locate two new sales agents in adjacent geographic locations to expand and service new areas.

REAL ESTATE TEAM

PRODUCTION GROWTH BUDGET SCHEDULE

Total Sales Volume	$8 Million	$13 Million	$18 Million	$25 Million	$40 Million	$60 Million	$80 Million	$100 Million
GCI	$240,000	$390,000	$540,000	$750,000	$1.2 Million	$1.8 Million	$2.4 Million	$3 Million
Units (Divide Sales Vol by Your Avg Home Price)								
OPERATING EXPENSES								
Administrative Salaries (12%)	$28,800	$46,800	$64,800	$90,000	$144,000	$216,000	$288,000	$360,000
Marketing & Lead Generation (10%)	$24,000	$39,000	$54,000	$75,000	$120,000	$180,000	$240,000	$300,000
Training & Education (5%)	$12,000	$19,500	$27,000	$37,500	$60,000	$90,000	$120,000	$150,000
Equipment & Supplies (2%)	$4,800	$7,800	$10,800	$15,000	$24,000	$36,000	$48,000	$60,000
Rent (0.5%)	$1,200	$1,950	$2,700	$3,750	$6,000	$9,000	$12,000	$15,000
Misc. (0.5%) Technology	$1,200	$1,950	$2,700	$3,750	$6,000	$9,000	$12,000	$15,000
Total Operating Expenses (30%)	$72,000	$117,000	$162,000	$225,000	$360,000	$540,000	$720,000	$900,000
Cost of Sales (Deductions from Commissions Checks to pay brokerage + sales agents)	$24,000 (10%)	$58,500 (15%)	$108,000 (20%)	$187,500 (25%)	$360,000 (30%)	$540,000 (30%)	$840,000 (35%)	$1.2 Million (40%)
NET INCOME	$144,000 (60%)	$214,500 (55%)	$270,000 (50%)	$337,500 (45%)	$480,000 (40%)	$720,000 (40%)	$840,000 (35%)	$900,000 (30%)

*All percentages calculated as a percentage of Gross Commission Income (GCI)

Self-Performance Appraisal

Employee Name: _____   Appraiser Name: _____

Appraisal Period (From/To): _____   Position: _____

Current salary/bonus structure: _____

This form is for you to appraise your own performance. Your input will be made a part of your performance appraisal. Please answer the following questions. You may put your answers after the questions in each box.

1. What have been my major achievements/contributions in this appraisal period?

2. What have been my major frustrations over this appraisal period?

3. Have there been any obstacles that interfered with my performance and meeting my objectives?

4. What effect has my working here had on the business, customer service and teamwork during this appraisal period?

Self-Performance Appraisal

5. What new tasks/duties did I take charge of in this appraisal period?

6. How do I feel about my current position in terms of challenge and opportunities to grow and contribute?

7. What was the best training/seminar/conference/coaching session I attended within this appraisal period? What skills did I pick up and implement from the training?

8. Did I meet the goals I set for myself for this appraisal period?

9. What are the areas in which I need the most improvement?

Self-Performance Appraisal

10. What are my short term (next year) career goals?

11. How can the team help me reach my goals?

12. What other topics should be covered in my upcoming appraisal discussion?

LEADER VS. MANAGER

LEADER	MANAGER
• Leads by influence	• Manages by position
• Develops & coaches	• Drives workers
• Wanted to be succeeded	• Needs to be needed
• Depends on goodwill	• Depends on authority
• Reproduce themselves	• Wants recognition
• Inspires enthusiasm	• Inspires fear
• Focuses on strengths	• Focuses on weaknesses
• Says "We"	• Says "I"
• Invests time in others	• Spends time with others
• Fixes the breakdown	• Blames the breakdown
• Have incredible success	• Has some successes
• Shows how its done	• Knows how its done
• Says "Let's go!"	• Says "Go!"

Made in the USA
Monee, IL
12 November 2020

47297209R00204